# Becoming a Student of Teaching

✦

# Becoming a Student
# of Teaching

✦

## Linking Knowledge Production and Practice

### SECOND EDITION

## Robert V. Bullough, Jr. &
## Andrew D. Gitlin

**FOREWORD BY MARILYN COCHRAN-SMITH**

RoutledgeFalmer
New York & London

Published in 2001 by
RoutledgeFalmer
29 West 35th Street
New York, NY 10001

Published in Great Britain by
RoutledgeFalmer
11 New Fetter Lane
London EC4P 4EE

RoutledgeFalmer is an imprint of the Taylor & Francis Group

Printed in the United States of America on acid-free paper
Design and typography: Jack Donner

Library of Congress Cataloging-in-Publication Data
Bullough, Robert V., 1949–
    Becoming a student of teaching : linking knowledge production and practice / by
Robert V. Bullough, Jr., Andrew D. Gitlin.— 2nd ed.
    p. cm. — (Thinking and teaching ; vol. 3)
    Includes bibliographical references (p. ) and index.
    ISBN 0-415-93071-5 (alk. paper) — ISBN 0-415-92843-5 (pbk. : alk. paper)
    1. Teachers—Training of—United States. 2. Education—Study and teaching
(Higher)—United States. 3. Student teaching —United States. 4. Teachers—In-
service training—United States. I. Gitlin, Andrew David. II. Title. III. Series.

LB1715 .D845 2001
370'.71'173—dc21
                                                              00-045948

        10  9   8   7   6   5   4   3   2   1

# Contents

✦

# Foreword

✦

Almost one hundred years ago, John Dewey made a distinction between an apprenticeship model and a laboratory model of learning to teach. The former was more or less learning from experience, learning by trial and error. The latter was a process of sheltered classroom experience, where the prospective teacher could observe and reflect with guidance and support, deliberating and sorting out what he or she experienced without the pressure of keeping order or managing large groups of students. Dewey championed the more gradual approach, cautioning against plunging would-be teachers too early into the real world of schools where they would be forced to focus on details and outward management issues and hence likely to develop habits fixed through "blind experimentation" rather than considered deliberation. He feared the effects of too much practical responsibility too soon in the process of learning to teach:

> The student adjusts his actual methods of teaching, not to the prin-
> ciples which he is acquiring, but to what he sees succeed and fail in
> an empirical way from moment to moment; to what he sees other
> teachers doing who are more experienced and successful in keeping
> order than he is; and to the injunctions and directions given him by
> others. In this way the controlling habits of the teacher finally get
> fixed with comparatively little reference to principles in the psychol-
> ogy, logic, and history of education. . . .
>
> The apprentice may appear to superior advantage the first day, the
> first week, the first month, or even the first year, as compared with
> some other teacher who has a much more vital command of the
> psychology, logic, and ethics of development. But later "progress" may

with such consist only in perfecting and refining skill already possessed. Such persons seem to know how to teach, but they are not *students of teaching.* (Dewey, 1904, emphasis added, pp. 14–15)

Dewey had additional concerns about what he saw happening to teacher education during the early part of the twentieth century with its emerging focus on the science of education. He criticized teacher institutes and journals, on the one hand, for their eagerness to provide model lessons and clear-cut instructions in how to teach, and teachers, on the other hand, for their willingness to accept these without inquiry or criticism. Dewey believed that the "blind search" for "educational gospel" would be impossible if teachers were more intellectually vital and more "adequately moved by their own independent intelligence" (p. 16).

What Dewey was emphasizing in both of the passages quoted above was the importance in the education of prospective teachers of becoming what he called "students of teaching," or those who are prepared to learn from teaching over the course of a lifetime through reflection and on the basis of deep knowledge of the foundations of education. Bob Bullough and Andrew Gitlin's book is aptly titled *Becoming a Student of Teaching: Linking Knowledge Production and Practice*, since it captures some of what is involved in this complex and lifetime process. By using Dewey's words for their title, they invite us to hearken back to Dewey's distinction between apprenticeship and laboratory approaches and to recognize that their book—and their approach to teacher education— is situated squarely and intentionally in opposition to apprenticeships and to training models of teacher education. More than anything else, Bullough and Gitlin demonstrate in vivid and engaging ways what teacher education that is *not* training-based actually looks like and what it means for teacher educators to construct over time the social, organizational, and intellectual contexts within which their students can become students of teaching.

Drawing on rich and multiple examples of students' writing, Bullough and Gitlin reveal how—and sometimes why—prospective teachers change and grow over time. Highlighting what they see as the most important themes in their students' growth, they illustrate how students' initial perspectives and metaphors are transformed, revisited, and/or reinvented through opportunities for collaboration and reflection, questioning (and questioning one's own questions), observation and inquiry, and—perhaps most importantly—a whole lot of writing, rereading, reflecting, and writing again in many different forms and for many different reasons. Bullough and Gitlin comment on why their students' perspectives seem to change, drawing on some of their students' own insights as explanations for growth as well as on their own rich experiences as teacher educators over many years. Herbert Kohl once commented, "As is true of the other creative challenges, the desire to teach and the ability to teach well are not the same thing. With the rarest of exceptions, one has to learn how to become a good teacher just as one has to learn how to become a scientist or an artist" (Kohl, 1984, p. 16). Bullough and Gitlin provide a window into the creative, learning, growing process involved in learning to be a good teacher, a process that equates with the phrase, "becoming a student of teaching."

Bullough and Gitlin's book is unusually readable and engaging, written in straightforward language that is surprisingly free of jargon and grandiose phrasing. They begin by providing readers with background information about how their joint work as teacher educators came to be when changes in programming structures gradually occurred. With simple elegance, they lay out the basic premises on which their work is based, premises that will resonate with the commitments of many teacher educators: that teacher learning is a lifetime process, that the contexts of schooling deserve—and indeed require—critique, that our work as educators is influenced greatly by our own autobiographies and by who we are as teachers, that reflection and inquiry are central to both the immediate decisions and the longer-term choices teachers make, and that teachers need to work in communities to sustain and support the growth and sharing of the knowledge they generate from inquiry and reflection on practice.

Beginning in the second chapter and continuing through chapter ten of the book, Bullough and Gitlin's book shifts effortlessly among three complimentary voices. The first is the voice of Bullough and Gitlin as analysts and educators with many years of experience. This voice locates the discussion of writing assignments and "methodologies" for teacher education within the context of the relevant educational research and in relation to current reforms in the field. A second voice, present in some of the chapters, is that of Bullough and Gitlin as teacher educators engaged in day-to-day work over the period of a year with various cohorts of prospective teachers. This voice, which describes the writing assignments student teachers were asked to complete as they were stated at the time, speaks to students in the second person. This voice reveals an evolving relationship between teacher educator and students. It counsels patience and reflexive thinking, advising would-be teachers to give themselves space and time when they begin to write autobiographically, for example. This voice is clear and supportive, providing helpful hints and ideas; it reappears at the end of the chapters in a section called "extending the conversation." Written directly to prospective teachers, this section suggests questions and challenges in education that the students' work evokes. The third voice is actually many voices—the students of Bullough and Gitlin who speak for themselves through their life stories, their institutional studies, their shadow studies, and their analyses over time of their changing metaphors for teaching. These voices are strong and eloquent, posing questions of practice and willingly offering their own individual journeys as would-be teachers as open texts for the growth and explorations of others. Bullough and Gitlin's first voice returns following the students' examples and is threaded throughout the chapters, pointing out to readers some of the highlights of the writing and some of the themes that emerge, double back, or are recycled.

Bullough and Gitlin's volume has a great deal to tell us about the pedagogy of teacher education. The explicit detail about the methodologies used with prospective teachers for exploring self, exploring school context, and integrating the two will be useful to many teacher educators who are engaged in their own efforts to help prospective teachers become students of teaching. Bullough and Gitlin's thoughtful commentary on each of these methods and on the kinds of learning opportunities they can provide will prompt many teacher educators to rethink some of their own practices and reshape some of their ideas. Teacher educators are invited to think about how these methodologies fit into the structures of their current programs, how they might be used in conjunction with other texts and assignments, and how they might link with other social and intellectual contexts. The Bullough and Gitlin volume also has something to tell us about the changing roles of teacher educators in the academy. Read from a certain perspective, this book provides a case study of the new roles that many of us in teacher education have been working to create over the last two decades—roles that privilege neither practice nor scholarship, but instead blur the boundaries of each. Bullough and Gitlin show what it means to study, thoughtfully reflect on, and write in scholarly (publishable) ways about one's own practice as a teacher educator over the period of many years. This book provides a glimpse of what it means to transform implicit assumptions into explicitly stated premises, examine carefully the learning opportunities created by different invitations to write by examining the data of students' work, and connect theoretically and pragmatically the threads of many individual assignments to the larger issues and discourses of the field.

In *Working Papers, Reflections on Teachers, Schools, and Communities*, Vito Perrone (1989) raises important questions about what we are doing in the teacher education community to help prospective and experienced teachers enlarge their capacity to think, observe children, document and reflect on their experiences, and use writing to clarify and communicate their thoughts. He comments:

> Ultimately, the knowledge that is meaningful, that is the basis for thought and feeling, is that which is personally owned. Second-hand knowledge may be useful, but first-hand knowledge—that which comes from a personal investment, reflection, observation, experience—is what gives an individual power. Teachers and administrators who have developed a personal construct about learning, who own knowledge and are able to articulate that knowledge, can attend to the important issues confronting education because they will be less intimated by external educational models. They will be decision makers rather than captives. (p. 119–120)

In the current era of political fervor over education, and especially the education (or, as some would say, the *miseducation*) of teachers, it seems especially important that we help prospective teachers develop personal knowledge, which they can articulate and use to make decisions that will influence their students' life chances. Just as Dewey suggested that teachers who were more "moved by their own independent intelligence" would be less likely to accept "educational gospel" without inquiry and criticism, Perrone claims that those with personal knowledge that is owned and articulated will not be "captives" of external educational models. It is the ability to question, critique, and act on educational matters that is central to the claims and concerns of both Dewey and Perrone. Fundamentally, the process they are describing is the process involved in *becoming a student of teaching*. It is indeed this process that is described in a compelling, disarming, and thoughtful way by Bob Bullough and Andrew Gitlin, two scholar practitioners with long years of laudable work in the real world of teacher education. I commend their efforts and recommend their book.

—MARILYN COCHRAN-SMITH
Boston College

# Preface

·✦·

*Becoming a Student of Teaching: Linking Knowledge Production and Practice* represents the culmination of many years of work with certification students. Our approach to teacher education has evolved as our understanding of the problems associated with educating teachers has increased. It has also evolved in response to our efforts to forge institutional arrangements and develop instructional approaches consistent with our view of the nature of teaching and the role teachers are to play in a complex and ever changing school environment.

*Becoming a Student of Teaching* presents a challenge to the traditional and dominant view of teacher education as training, which has as its primary concern the mastery of a set of techniques or skills and privileges public theory—theory found in policy documents and educational literature—over private theory—theory grounded in personal experience (see Griffiths & Tann, 1992). Training presents a distorted image of the beginning teacher as passive, isolated, and rightfully dependent on the expertise and experience of others. Teacher educators who espouse this view sometimes think of teaching as a politically and, perhaps, morally neutral act and think of learners as bits of putty to be molded into predetermined shapes.

In contrast to a training view of teacher education, *Becoming a Student of Teaching* emphasizes education. Drawing on the Latin root of education, *educere*, teacher education, in contrast to training, emphasizes the use of methods that lead or draw out, that educe. Thus, we begin from a view that knowledge is socially constructed and humans are actors within dynamic social contests (Wertsch, 1998). We understand that like other learners, the beginning teacher forges personal systems of meaning within the bounds of particular social contexts and acts upon these meanings (see Presidential Task Force, 1993). Given the nature of learning and learners as meaning makers, our challenge as teacher educators is to influence the grounds upon which teachers make decisions (Fenstermacher, 1978).

*Becoming a Student of Teaching* places the beginning teacher and the context of teaching at the center of teacher education. The methodologies described are intended to enable the exploration and reconstruction of context, in particular the school context. We wish to bring to the forefront issues of power that are crucially important to thinking through questions about the teacher's role and the educational purposes and practices that characterize that role. But more than this, the methodologies presented are intended to encourage the commitment to building and extending professional communities where teachers, administrators, along with college and university faculties join together in reciprocal relationships to improve the education offered young people and the quality of life of those who work within schools (see Fenstermacher, 1999). In very broad strokes, this is our orientation, an orientation that centers on the view that teachers produce knowledge and that this knowledge is the key to improving teaching and reforming schooling.

We wish to thank the many certification students who have borne the brunt of our experimentation and given us pointed criticism that has sharpened our thinking. We also wish to thank those who have so generously agreed to allow their work to be published in this volume. This edition of *Becoming a Student of Teaching* is dedicated to our students who have taught us so very much.

## THE CONCEPTUAL GROUNDING FOR *BECOMING A STUDENT OF TEACHING*

*Program Description*

We work with students in our secondary teacher certification programs for an entire academic year and are responsible for their curriculum and general-method courses along with student or practice teaching. Students are organized into cohorts of about twenty-five, which stay together throughout the year. The cohort organization is the foundation upon which we seek to build an incipient professional community, an essential condition for the success of our work and the accomplishment of our aims. Context matters. Early in the term, the students are placed within a few schools and begin to work with teachers and, in time, help select one, sometimes two, who will serve as a cooperating or mentoring teacher. It is within these schools, and with the permission and support of the administration and faculty, that the work described in *Becoming a Student of Teaching* is accomplished. Part way through the program and a few weeks prior to student teaching the certification students plan and teach a "short course," a unit approximately three weeks in length, as a means for identifying strengths and working on weaknesses in anticipation of practice teaching. Practice teaching takes place during the final term and usually runs (depending on the specific program configuration) between ten and sixteen weeks. A few students who participate in a longer program engage in approximately five months of half-time practice teaching. This latter arrangement allows greater opportunities to link theory with practice and for students to study their practice. Finally, along with practice teaching, cohort students are enrolled in a weekly, two-hour seminar that provides a setting for posing questions about practice and theory and for considering alternative courses of action.

## BOOK AND CHAPTER ORGANIZATION

Following the introductory chapter, the book is organized into two sections. Section one, "Preservice Teacher Education," is subdivided into three parts: "Methodologies for Exploring Self," "Methodologies for Exploring School Context," and "Integrating Methodologies," the latter emphasizing the intimate linkage of self and context. Section two, "In-Service Teacher Education," contains one chapter, "Teacher Research Collaborative," and presents an integrating methodology. This particular organization is the result of an extended discussion and compromise. Initially we resisted separating the methodologies this way because, conceptually, self and context must be considered together if teachers are to understand how meanings are constructed and how some meanings gain and maintain legitimacy. However, in the end we opted to organize the chapters around "self" and "school context" for the sake of clarity. Some methodologies emphasize self over context, while others emphasize context over self. In both instances it is important to keep in mind the dialectical and mutually generative relationship of self and context. When using a methodology that emphasizes self, then, it is important to also attend to school context and vice versa. Otherwise the nature of making meaning and knowledge production is badly distorted.

Except for chapter one, the chapters that make up *Becoming a Student of Teaching* are meant to stand alone. We organized and wrote them this way so that the methodologies will still be useful to teacher educators working within diverse programs, and to allow for variations in program emphasis on "self" and "school context."

We have used the word *methodology*—instead of *method, strategy,* or *technique*—intentionally, to distinguish our viewpoint from that of others' who think of teacher education as primarily a form of training. We are not presenting prescriptions to be followed, but rather clusters of diverse approaches on becoming a student of teaching that require adaptation, adjustment, and integration on the part of teacher educators. Integration is essential if the program is to have coherence, a quality typically lacking when training orientations dominate certification programs.

For those of you who are teacher educators, as you read and think about how you might use the various methodologies (which ones, in what ways, and in what order), undoubtedly questions about time constraints will come to mind. Lack of sufficient time in teacher education is a serious problem. As for teachers, so with teacher educators: The battle with the calendar and clock is frustrating, and you may discover that it is not possible to use each of the methodologies or in the manner and with the intensity we suggest. Our view is that depth is to be preferred to breadth.

Each chapter is divided into four parts. The first part introduces the methodology and includes a brief rationale for its use. The second includes samples of student work, which illustrate some aspects of the methodology. This work is included with the permission of the students and is representative of the kind of work we receive or is included because it is especially provocative and possesses unusual potential to stimulate interest and involvement or illustrates a common problem encountered by students when working with the methodologies. Within the third part we consider the student work with an eye toward identifying a few–certainly not all—of the interesting, enlightening, and, in some instances, troubling issues that we believe worthy of the attention of teacher education students. Chapters conclude with a brief section, "Extending the Conversation," written to teacher education students. In this part we invite teacher education students to reflect on issues of importance to educators related to the student work we present. The issues and the questions we pose are intended to provoke thought and challenge opinion. We should mention that not every "conversation" section will follow exactly the same format, but most will. We believe this section is one that you will want to revisit from time to time even after you have settled into your first teaching position. In this section we also present a little background on the methodology and suggest a few sources of public theory that ground it. An extensive Appendix contains "Notes to teacher educators" on each chapter. Preservice teachers ought to know something about the thinking that is behind what they are being asked to do, and so we encourage beginning teachers also to read the Appendix. Our experience convinces us that the methodologies have value for practicing as well as beginning teachers. After all, becoming a student of teaching is a lifetime quest, not an outcome achieved with initial licensure and certification.

*Additional Materials*

We should mention that *Becoming a Student of Teaching* should be used with other texts, ones that place a greater emphasis on the more technical aspects of learning to teach, such as lesson and unit planning and the skills associated with classroom management. These certainly are important topics for study, ones that must be eventually mastered. If an additional text is selected, it is important to help students avoid the seductiveness of the training mentality, where learning to teach is thought of as nothing more than a matter of practicing instructional skills in a classroom. In the quest for technical expertise it is easy to neglect the moral, political, and personal dimensions of teaching and learning to teach, of considering how one thinks about teaching and learning when teaching. *Becoming a Student of Teaching* presents a challenge to a training mentality, but the power of such a view is considerable and not to be underestimated.

The methodologies we describe enable beginning teachers to become, and to understand themselves as, producers and not merely consumers of knowledge. Saying this does not mean, however, that in the quest to become a student of teaching, there is no place for knowledge produced by others. There is and it is an important place. To become a student of teaching requires that texts be compared, ones self-generated with those produced by others, including academics (Bullough & Baughman, 1997, chapters 3 & 4). We will not often specify the exact readings we use with the methodologies; this is a decision teacher educators will want to make for themselves based upon personal and professional values, program structure, and understanding of students. We think it is important, however, that students be provided opportunities to read what others have to say, especially research that has a bearing on their own studies of teaching. Text comparison enriches the study of teaching and elevates it while having the added virtue of introducing the neophyte to the issues and concerns debated in the wider educational community.

### Integrating Methodologies

We need to say a word about the integrating methodologies. Chapters two through ten focus on individual methodologies. The educational value of the methodologies, however, comes when they are linked together and integrated and when means are provided to enable students to examine their development over time and critically. Two methodologies, action research (see chapter eight) and the "personal teaching text" (PTT; see chapter nine), seek to do just this for preservice teacher education; the last chapter, "Collaborative Teacher Research," discusses methodologies for in-service teachers. These "integrating" methodologies bring self and context together. We call these methodologies to attention now because they build on the work done in each of the preceding chapters and require careful advanced planning on the part of teacher educators.

The PTT (Bullough, 1993) is a case record, of sorts, of the beginning teacher's teacher education experience. All written work produced through the methodologies introduced in *Becoming a Student of Teaching* (including action research) is organized by each student into a PTT. We mention this here because a good deal of advanced planning is required for use of this methodology. At predetermined points throughout the year the certification students we work with are required to review and in writing critically analyze their PTTs and their growth as beginning teachers. Although the specific task is presented in chapter nine, at this point it is important to note that like other learners, beginning teachers are often not aware of their development and of the direction they are heading. They tend to be overwhelmed by the here and now, the press of immediate demands. By pausing from time to time to consider what they have been doing and why, and where they are heading, students we work with are encouraged to take charge of their development which is an essential condition for professionalism. Additionally, the PTT has proven to be an important means for enhancing program continuity, a quality often lacking when training dominates teacher education.

ROBERT V. BULLOUGH, JR.
Center for the Improvement of
Teacher Education and Schooling
Brigham Young University

ANDREW D. GITLIN
University of Utah

# ✦ 1 ✦

# Getting Oriented

---

## CONTEXT AND PERSPECTIVES

We have been educators for over twenty-five years: first as teachers, later as teacher educators. We worked together for many years at the University of Utah. Over the years we have sought to challenge traditional approaches to teacher education as training and to develop programs and practices that maximize beginning teachers' control over their own professional development. The secondary teacher education program within which we first worked together was disjointed, fragmented, and confusing. Training was the program's aim: Based on a delivery conception of teaching, emphasis was placed on learning and practicing discrete skills, and programmatically public and private theories were clearly separated. Public theory was privileged over private theory in knowledge production. By "public theory" we mean expert talk—the substance of academic discourse, including concepts, generalizations, models, and ways of making meaning (see Griffiths & Tann, 1992). In contrast, private theory is grounded experientially and is represented by personal, idiosyncratic, biographically embedded, and often implicit assumptions and beliefs by which individuals make life meaningful. These theories, the private ones, are embedded in what Korthagen and Kessels (1999) describe as "gestalts," "holistic perceptions guiding behavior" (p. 9).

Methods courses were disconnected from curriculum courses, and both were separated from practice teaching. Similarly, educational foundations courses, and their concern for the aims of education, were unrelated to methods courses and their emphasis on means. Moreover, students were strangers to one another and dropped into and out of the program at their convenience. Who these people were was of no special consequence to the program or to those who taught within it. Like the students, professors drifted in and out of the courses and felt little connection to the program. Students complained loudly about content duplication and superficiality; about the kind, quality, and quantity of field experiences offered; and perhaps more than anything, about not feeling cared for. No one on the faculty was responsible for the individual student and for seeing that he or she was making reasonable progress toward certification. Student complaints were hard to ignore, especially since they were frequent and loud enough to convince the dean's office that something was amiss and in need of fixing. But what to do about them?

A change in the program would necessitate a change in faculty roles, and under the best of circumstances, this is difficult to achieve even when there is widespread student dissatisfaction. Program fragmentation, after all, plays to professors' desires for autonomy and independence. In response to growing dissatisfaction, the faculty began meeting to explore the situation in order to improve it. Some faculty members understood the problem as simply a matter of providing better integration of methods courses with fieldwork and of improving the quality of student advising; no shift in orientation or change in structure was required. From this viewpoint, all that was needed was for faculty members to share course syllabi and come to some agreement about who would teach which topics and for the student-advising office to shape up and do a better job.

Others had a different view of the problem, a more structural and philosophical view. Separate courses taught by faculty members who rotated through them and felt no deep commitment to them would inevitably give rise to problems of duplication and, perhaps, of superficiality. From this viewpoint, occasional meetings within which syllabi were shared would do little to change the situation and nothing at all to bridge the gulf separating public and private theories about teaching or educational aims from means. Moreover, when both students and faculty members drop into and out of courses, it is unreasonable to expect that caring relationships with students would consistently develop, and caring relationships, some thought, were central to effective advising *and* teaching. Teaching is a relationship, a way of being with and relating to others, and not merely an expression of having mastered a set of content-related delivery skills. And advising is a matter not just of dispensing information in a timely fashion but of building trust, of talking and problem-solving together. Some sort of fundamental change in program structure and orientation was needed.

Eventually, faculty members agreed to experiment with a cohort organization, an attempt to create the "shared ordeal" (Lortie, 1975) that would help students see themselves as part of the teaching profession. Since that time, the early 1980s, the cohort idea has caught on in teacher education (see Wideen, Mayer-Smith, & Moon, 1998). For a full academic year a team of two professors (later this changed to a professor and a teaching associate because of limited resources) would be responsible for planning, teaching, and coordinating a large portion of the certification work of a group of twenty-five students. This included general methods courses and curriculum courses, which met for six hours during the first semester (or two terms), and student teaching, which included a weekly seminar. Moreover, within the cohort organization, professors would do much of the advising that had formerly been done by the advisement office. The courses leading up to practice teaching were to involve significant fieldwork, and to this end the students were to be placed in a school early in the year and continue to work within it throughout the year. Eventually, some of these schools became professional development schools (Holmes Group, 1990), where practicing teachers are specially educated to serve as mentors for student and beginning teachers and study their practice, but this is getting ahead of the story (see Bullough et al., 1997).

We supported this proposal and nudged it along, although we worried about the amount of time and energy that the change would demand of us. Soon, we found ourselves assigned to our first group of students, and with this assignment we faced a daunting problem. Being responsible for such a large portion of a program, and having students for an entire academic year, meant that we would be teaching new courses that required of us the development of new areas of skill and understanding; even when we had previously taught the content, a different approach or organization was needed. As we discovered, our relationships to students would also dramatically change. Despite these fears, however, we recognized that the structure would allow us to experiment with different approaches to teacher education. For instance, for the first time in our careers it became possible, at least in principle, to introduce a theoretical concept, such as the implicit or "hidden curriculum," have students work with the concept in a field site, return to campus for further exploration of the concept, and then, as the students gained experience, return to it later in the year and in different ways. Moreover, it allowed for practice to produce theory and theorizing as students returned to campus with burning questions that arose from their work in the schools. Through this change in program structure we could better link public and private theories and the study of aims and educational means.

## A Shared Perspective on Education

At this point in the story, we need to step back for a moment and share a bit of our biographies. Although attending different graduate schools (Ohio State and Wisconsin), we were both deeply influenced by work being done in critical theory in education, a theory that directed our attention to the relationship between schools and the social priorities and inequalities that characterize capitalism. We thought of public education as an extremely important avenue for furthering social and economic justice, but believed the institution—its organization and traditions—stunted this potential. We understood schools as factories, driven by class interests and infused with the values of a technocracy: control and efficiency, the handmaidens of training. We thought of teachers as oppressed workers, trapped, victims of an oppressive and alienating system. Indeed, much of our early research reflects this view (Bullough, Goldstein, & Holt, 1984; Gitlin, 1983).

Our focus, then, was primarily on institutional critique. We sought to identify the ways in which schooling constrained teachers' actions and student learning, not the ways in which schools could enable their development or the ways in which teachers could shape the institution and create a culture within the classroom and school to achieve their purposes and build desired relationships with students. Not surprisingly, we often found the beginning and practicing teachers who sat in our classes interested but largely disconnected from our analysis of school-ing. Our project, and the public theories we presented, was not their project; being well-trained students, they mastered our discourse to give it back to us but, apparently unaffected, often left us to engage in their lives' work as though they had never been in our classes.

## A Reconsideration

Reenter the cohort: Imagine yourself for a moment in our shoes, being assigned to work with a group of twenty-five preservice teacher education students for an entire academic year, good students who genuinely wanted to become teachers. Now, imagine having as your central professional message that schools are lousy places to work, young people alienated, and the curriculum fundamentally and perhaps fatally flawed! True or not, a year is a long time to endure such fare, and perhaps even a longer time to push it. What the cohort organization did was force us to reconsider our professional agendas, our aims and our theories in relationship to our students' theories and their aim to become teachers and to succeed in the short run in practice teaching and in the long run as teachers. In our work at the university, the question for us was (and still is): How could we develop encounters with teacher education content and theory that would help our students achieve their goals and simultaneously enable us to achieve our aims that they become critically minded educators?

Our dilemma was softened a bit by developments within critical theory and education that led to an attack on correspondence theory (Apple, 1979a). Correspondence theory, representing a rather vulgar, deterministic Marxism, suggested that schooling reproduced social inequality by corresponding with the inequalities of the larger society and, by implication, that persons do as contexts allow them to do; consciousness follows context as day follows night. In this view, human agency was a delusion, a liberal's foolish fantasy. The attack on correspondence theories brought with it a message of hope that rang true to our experience: Persons frequently act in surprising and unpredictable ways. Often they resist institutional pressures to conform, and with their resistance comes the possibility for institutional change and, therefore, hope for school reform. This turn was reflected in our own work as we conducted studies and worked with teachers who, in various ways, exercised their agency and seemed to make school a better place for their students as a result (Bullough &

Gitlin, 1985; Bullough, Gitlin, & Goldstein, 1984). Importantly, we came to recognize that resistance is often grounded in private theory and in powerful beliefs about self as teacher contrary to those that are institutionally preferred. Potentially, then, teacher education could play a part in school transformation, and critical theory could serve as a lens for focusing our work as long as it was seen in relation to the private theories held by students. Biography and history need to be linked (see Mills, 1959).

Our study of the writings of Jürgen Habermas (1971; 1975) also proved important to our development. We found compelling his vigorous criticism of instrumental reason, the kind of reason that reduces human beings to numbers; the universe to a giant, grinding machine, and education to training. But unlike a good many critical theorists, Habermas moved beyond critique. He recognized in the innate ability and desire of humans to relate to one another through language a means for generating a social and political ideal worth striving for: communication without domination. He explored the conditions needed for communication to proceed fruitfully and explicated some of the ways in which communication is distorted, often intentionally for strategic reasons as when we manipulate our friends to get our way and to set aside their own interests. His ideal, albeit utopian, got us thinking about teaching in ways we had never thought of before and sharpened our awareness of the negative influence of the assumptions of training on our students' development as teachers. We recognized that as a relationship teaching always involved unequal distributions of power between teachers and students, but began to explore the ways in which we might minimize domination through conversation and dialogue (see Bullough, 1994; Gitlin, 1990). More broadly, we began to think of learning to teach in terms of engaging our students in the critical and communal study of their own thinking and practice and of linking this study to public theories about institutional power and education.

Working with the cohort groups and getting to know, respect, and enjoy our students also played an important part in nudging along our development. For the most part, they were very able and interesting people—adults—who brought with them a commitment to, as many of them often have said, "make things better." Generally they came to teaching with a lively service ethic; many were called to teach (Stokes, 1997). One could not work with such people and still hold strongly to the view that their actions were merely reproductive of social and economic inequalities, that they were only pawns in a cruel social charade. To incorporate our growing appreciation of the importance of agency in institutional life, we eventually organized our practice within the cohort around the dialectical and dynamic relationship of self and context. We focused on self because of its connection to knowledge production (private theories) and agency. We came to think of our students as moral-political agents about to assume positions of power and authority. We focused on context because critical theory had helped us understand how contexts often direct teacher behavior in ways that run counter to their deepest values and obscure institutionally accepted roles and relationships. Individualism and conservativism result where teachers withdraw into the safety of their own classrooms and classes to find security and a sense of self-worth.

As our thinking evolved, so did our practice; as our practice evolved, so did our thinking about preservice teacher education. We encountered many frustrations. Perhaps the most important frustration came as a result of watching much of our work "wash out" during student teaching and the first year of teaching. It appeared as though, once our students became "real" teachers, they forgot or simply discarded much that we had "taught" (see Bullough, 1989; Bullough, Knowles, & Crow, 1992). We wanted our students to become producers of knowledge and, through the process, students of the practice and politics of schooling. We saw little evidence to suggest that our aims were being met. Survival and the desire to obtain a positive teaching evaluation or to fit into a department consumed many of our students during practice teaching and later during their first year of teaching, just as trainers who emphasize apprenticeships long claimed. Recognizing this problem as partially related to a student teaching format that was a holdover from our program when training was the central aim, we changed student teaching from full to half time teaching so that additional time was available for reflection, for thinking carefully and communally about practice. This helped, but the problem persisted. We came to realize that no matter how hard we worked within preservice teacher education or how many adjustments we made in practice teaching, the problem would continue until preservice teacher education was linked to in-service teacher education and both challenged training assumptions.

A serious limitation of training is that it permits the dropping off of newly certified teachers at the school's doorstep as though the knowledge about teaching that has been poured over their heads makes them a teacher. Our students, we realized, needed ongoing support after certification to continue their exploration of self and context, particularly when the results of this exploration produced tension between institutionally favored roles and relationships and personally valued ones. Thus, our rather limited initial vision of teacher education as a group enterprise defined by cohort membership expanded beyond the confines of preservice teacher education. We found ourselves supporting efforts at "simultaneous renewal," as Goodlad characterizes the challenge, of teacher education and schooling (see Goodlad, 1994). The conclusion cannot be avoided or ignored: Teacher education is never ending, and the creation of a vital community is central not only to educational renewal but also to individual teacher development. Indeed, continuous teacher development and creating the institutional conditions needed to support that development are the essence of educational renewal (Bullough & Baughman, 1997; Gitlin, Bringhurst, Burns, Cooley, Myers, Price, Russell, & Tiess, 1992; Sarason, 1990).

## FIVE CORE ASSUMPTIONS

For the most part, *Becoming a Student of Teaching* presents the results of a kind of informed trial and error approach to teacher education, but this tells only a part of the story. We have not worked within an institutional or intellectual vacuum, and, in our case, we have been fortunate. Within the cohorts we have enjoyed remarkable freedom. Our students have not only tolerated our sometimes crazy ideas but also—through interviews, questionnaires, and other means—have given useful feedback on our work that has greatly assisted our efforts (see Bullough with Stokes, 1994; Bullough, 1997b; Gitlin et al., 1999). Being students of our practice, we have taken this feedback seriously.

Through the years of experimenting and of testing our hunches, along with our reading about and study of teacher education, we have come to a few conclusions about how to make teacher education more educative. We stand by them, although we realize that with time and increased experience adjustments will likely be necessary, as is indicated by the changes we have made from the first to the second edition. They have taken the form of five interrelated assumptions that we believe, when *taken together,* offer an alternative to narrow training conceptions of learning to teach and whose echoes resound on every page of *Becoming a Student of Teaching.* The first assumption is that certification signals only the beginning of teacher education, not its ending. Ultimately, preservice must be joined to ongoing in-service teacher education. The second assumption is that because work contexts both enable and limit human development, they need to be carefully studied and criticized. In this critical engagement with context, the student's own experience of schooling plays a central role. The third assumption is that our conceptions of ourselves as teachers are grounded biographically and experientially. If teacher education is to make a strong, positive difference in development, it must start with biography and find ways to identify, clarify, articulate, and criticize the assumptions—the personal theories and their surrounding gestalts— about teaching, learning, students, and education embedded within it. Public and private theories must converse. The conversation needs to take place in the space between history and biography. The fourth assumption is that reflection, systematic inquiry, is a central and crucial element in making teacher education educational. The aim of reflection is to influence the grounds upon which teachers make decisions, including those made instantaneously in the thick of teaching. The fifth and last proposition has two parts: (1) Given that teachers have a wealth of knowledge about teaching and are central actors in the educational community, it is vital that they be actively involved in furthering one another's development; and (2) recognizing that the context of teaching is often hostile to teachers working with and assisting other teachers, institutional roles and relationships must be created that enable collegiality and community building (see Darling-Hammond, 1997). Altering established patterns of interaction that isolate teachers and minimize their involvement in school decision-making is essential to establishing a powerful and progressive profession. "Full participation" (Pateman, 1970), where individuals and groups have access to the decisions that effect their lives and the power to influence outcomes, ought to be our aim. A brief discussion of the basis for each core assumption follows.

*Certification*

In 1981 Ken Zeichner and Bob Tabachnick published an article that raised a troubling question: "Are the effects of university teacher education washed out by school experience?" At the time, the widely held view was that the university experience represented a liberalizing influence on the thinking of teacher education students that was then crushed by the reality of school practice during student teaching. Teacher education students became increasingly conservative, and to many teacher educators, ourselves included, this was cause for concern. However, as Zeichner and Tabachnick pointed out, it was unlikely that the university experience generally, or teacher education specifically, was ever as liberalizing as many professors assumed or claimed it to be: There may not have been anything to "wash out" in the first place!

If teacher education is to be more influential, a different way of working with students and school faculties must be forged. Teacher educators, teachers, and administrators need to join together collaboratively, not merely cooperatively, and jointly seek to produce conditions within schools that enable reflection on public and private theories about teaching and the aims and means of education. These conditions must become commonplace; shared action should be the norm rather than the exception. Much needs to be done if these two very different institutions and cultures, the schools and universities, are to work productively together, but some schools and universities are committed to the idea and there is reason for measured optimism (see Patterson, Michelli, & Pacheco, 1999).

The challenges are many. Resources are scarce, and becoming more so, and the potential for exploitation of schools is very real, particularly as professors seek sites to conduct their studies and to place students while distancing themselves from the school culture (Goodlad, 1990). Nevertheless, through sharing strengths and resources and openly exploring and accepting institutional and personal differences, there is the potential to develop shared structures and relationships that break the mold of the tried and true and move us in the direction of enabling teachers to become more active participants in the remaking of their educational world. Surely, such a project promises significant benefits to university as well as school-based teacher educators and especially to their students.

Some of you reading these words may be tempted to say, "So what? Who cares if teacher education has little impact? Good subject matter knowledge and some practice teaching are all that it takes to make a good teacher. Good teachers are born, not made." This is a very common perception, and one that we find troubling and not merely because the evidence suggests that teacher education programs do in fact make a positive difference to the quality of teaching (see Darling-Hammond, 2000). It is a view that is widely shared and is not likely to go away, at least in the near future. It troubles us not only because it denies the value of a substantial and growing body of research useful for thinking about and designing encounters with content, what we would call "pedagogical knowledge" (Grimmett & MacKinnon, 1992), but also because it suggests that learning to teach is a simple matter when it is not. Quite to the contrary, excellent teaching may be among the most difficult of human accomplishments. Like any other expressions of excellence, its achievement is enhanced through the study of its practice; and in good measure this is what we conceive teacher education to be. For this reason among others, we have become increasingly involved over the years in the effort to bring schools, colleges, and universities committed to teacher education together to explore ways of creating the conditions needed for beginning teachers to become students of their own thinking and practice, not just student teachers. This is fundamentally important to distinguishing our work from training, and it underscores our contention that the methodologies we present have value even after certification is completed.

*Work Context*

All social contexts, schools included, are defined and given their particular character by the accepted and evolving roles, relationships, and rules that govern interaction. There is no meaning without context, and context shapes what is perceived as valued and valuable. In a myriad of ways, most of which are subtle and generally taken for granted, newcomers to teaching are told what are and are not appropriate actions and utterances and are encouraged and enticed to comply with expectations. School contexts press conformity on the individual, who may respond in any number of ways, including strategic compliance—doing what seems necessary (Lacey, 1977)—and open resistance. Thinking about schools as historical contexts, human creations, within which meaning is made and that value some interests over others, presents a pressing challenge to teachers and teacher educators. Part of the challenge is to provide assistance to beginning teachers so they can examine and perhaps reconstruct institutionally preferred roles in the quest for a place within the school that is ethically defensible, morally and politically responsible, and personally satisfying. Knowing about a context, its history and how it defines what is reasonable and possible, is crucial to successful role negotiation, as it is to changing a role when change is seen as desirable. Another part of learning about context involves enabling the beginning teacher to understand how the local school context is influenced by educational policies and practices at state and national levels. Public theory has an important role to play in meeting this challenge and extending vision.

*Biography*

Despite the assumptions of training, in a manner perhaps unlike that of any other profession, in teaching the medium is the message and the medium is who and what a person is (Goodson, 1992). As a beginning teacher it is in good measure through you—and your values, beliefs, and knowledge of young people and about content and how to teach it—that students will either engage or disengage from learning. Who you are is important in other ways as well. It is in large part through your prior experience and prior socialization that you will make sense of teaching and of your students' backgrounds and abilities, formulate a curriculum, frame problems for study, and ultimately negotiate a teacher role. There is simply no getting around biography.

From our viewpoint, teacher education should start with who the beginning teacher is—or rather, who you imagine yourself to be as a teacher—and then assist you to engage in the active exploration of the private or "implicit theories" (Clark, 1988) you bring to teaching, your gestalts. It is through these biographically embedded assumptions and beliefs, which are generally taken for granted and assumed to be natural and shared, that sense is made of teacher education and, later, the world of teaching. Through them as a beginning teacher you will either screen out, accept, or adjust to what is taught. Confirmation of self is sought first, and this is to be expected. But if you are to become educated as a teacher, you must overcome provincialism. Commonly held assumptions about teaching must be challenged and tested, and much of the testing will take place in classrooms and with children. The challenge to teacher education is to enhance the educational value of the testing. New knowledge must be created. Masquerading as common sense, private theories need to be made explicit, the gestalt supporting one's bias unraveled, so they can be criticized and, when found wanting, reconstructed. Long ago, John Dewey characterized education as a matter of "reconstructing experience," and this is precisely the aim of teacher education: to assist you to confront and, in some ways, reconstruct your thinking. Ultimately, only you can do this. Your teachers can only create conditions that they believe are most likely to facilitate reconstruction. The methodologies presented in *Becoming a Student of Teaching* are intended to help create these conditions.

## Reflection

For the past fifteen years much has been spoken and written about the value of reflection in teacher education both as an aim and a means. The "good teacher," it is said, is a reflective teacher, one who inquires into his or her thinking and practice with an eye toward making improvements. We, too, stand on the side of the angels who champion programs that promote the development of reflective teachers. We also want to encourage teachers to carefully consider the consequences of their actions in the classroom and on others' development. But too often, the calls to get teachers to engage in reflection and to study their practice are only empty slogans and boil down to nothing more than a plea that they "think hard" about what they are doing and why they are doing it. To be sure, there is much to be said for "thinking hard" about something, but how does one think hard, about what, and for what purposes? Moreover, what does one do while teaching to solve a problem, when there is little if any time to stop and think, when reflection takes place in action (Schon, 1987)? The image of teachers as conscious decision makers, who stop and ponder their thoughts and actions, captures only a small slice, at best, of what teachers actually do.

Sometimes when the meaning of reflection is made explicit, one discovers hidden training assumptions. For example, one of the most often articulated reasons for valuing reflection is that it is a means for narrowing the gap between teacher practice and educational theory and research. Prescription is the aim; theory and research provide the models of good practice. The problem with this view is that the self and the private theories beginning teachers hold get lost, as does the way in which teaching knowledge and practice is inevitably and always context specific. Instead, the object is to make practice better by conforming to an external standard of some kind. However, determining what makes practice better and when one or another strategy or method is preferable in what sorts of situations involves a judgment based on contextual and personal factors too easily excluded from the equation. Accordingly, reflection may become merely a training tool, when it ought to be a process of linking means and ends so that self and context can be examined and public and private theories can be brought together in a dynamic and reflexive relationship in action. Reflection should lead to knowledge production and informed action.

Thus, to be reflective means more than just thinking hard about teaching, whether some action is "working" or not or consistent with a preferred teaching model or established institutional practice. In part, to be reflective means that careful attention is given to individual experience and how meaning is made and justified, and to the analysis of the constraining and enabling influence of contexts and how they shape human relations (Bullough & Gitlin, 1989). It also means being actively engaged in the study of one's practice and the intersection of belief, action, and outcome so that in the future wiser decisions can be made and while teaching.

To be reflective involves attending to what is judged a problem, why it is a problem, how it is understood and addressed or evaded. Often, as John Dewey (1910) argued, we do not so much solve problems as get over them, or get around them, by the way we define them. Problem framing goes directly to the issue of what kinds of questions and issues demand attention and what kinds of knowledge are most valuable. In this regard, Liston and Zeichner (1987) offer some help when they assert that teachers ought to inquire into: (1) the pedagogical and curricular means used to attain education aims, (2) the underlying assumptions and consequences of pedagogical action, and (3) the moral implications of pedagogical actions and the structure of schooling. We agree that these are among the issues that should be grappled with. In addition we would add that beginning teachers ought to be involved in ongoing reflection about self and about school context as well. These should be primary considerations, not merely afterthoughts.

One intent of *Becoming a Student of Teaching* is to broaden what counts as a problem and to assist beginning teachers to frame problems in ways that expose the relationship between the technical concerns of teachers and the personal, ethical, and political dimensions of teaching which are so often neglected. With respect to the latter, beginning teachers need to understand that all that they do and say represents their vision of the good life—their social philosophy—and this is inherently political. To be sure, teachers can be reflective about many things, silly and serious; our hope is to encourage beginning teachers not to forget that there is more to becoming a teacher than mastering supposedly proven techniques or the subject matter of the disciplines. Emphatically, they—you—need to become suspicious of the comfort that comes from the common teacher pronouncement, "It works." Many things work, but not everything that "works" is morally, socially, or educationally defensible. Thus, we seek to influence what is seen as a problem as well as how beginning teachers respond to it.

To this end, *Becoming a Student of Teaching* presents some of the processes our students have found useful in their study of teaching and helpful in their development as teachers; they are methodologies of inquiry. Inevitably, their influence is unpredictable and indirect, however. Only trainers would claim otherwise. Put differently, their influence on beginning teacher thinking and development is what you, the beginning teacher, decides it will be. As we have suggested, perhaps the best that teacher educators can hope for is that what they teach *and* how they teach it will influence the grounds upon which decisions are made and assist you to frame problems usefully. It is in this way that teacher education has a bearing on reflection when it takes place in action.

*Educational Community*

Many of the beginning teachers we have worked with over the years have been hesitant to ask for assistance when they have needed it. They do not think of learning as a community affair and responsibility, and why should they? Most teacher education programs are based on an ethic of individualism. Through the cohort we seek to provide for our students a balance between support and challenge. Without support, challenge often leads to defensiveness; with it, confronting private theories and prejudices becomes possible for many but not all. Once our students are hired as first-year teachers, however, they are often left alone by administrators and more experienced teachers to make it on their own. Beginning teachers often discover that teaching is a solitary activity, but it need not be.

Fortunately, because of a growing awareness of the problems faced by beginning teachers and of the importance to the quality of education offered young people of a successful transition for the neophyte into teaching, the tradition of neglect is changing. A sign of change is that, increasingly, beginning teachers can expect to be assigned a mentor teacher. Not surprisingly, it appears as though the aim of mentoring tends to be one of facilitating socialization to the context of teaching, and thus represents an extension of training, but this is not always or necessarily true. Getting oriented to a new context is important, but additional aims (including exploring how the work context shapes relationships and directs meaning making and opens up or closes down opportunity to learn about teaching communally) should be part of mentoring. Mentoring provides the opportunity for beginning teachers to study teaching and their thinking about teaching with others, hopefully with an experienced, generous, and wise teacher, and to make adjustments in the context of teaching based on continual examination of the relation between articulated aims and means. Although the quality of the mentoring offered is often uneven, such programs are inspired by the recognition that becoming a teacher is the responsibility of the entire educational community, including the university, and that the health and vitality of that community is directly dependent upon its ability to attract, induct, and nurture talented neophytes. Rosenholtz nicely captures this view:

> If teaching is collectively viewed as an inherently difficult undertaking, it is both necessary and legitimate to seek and to offer professional assistance. This is exactly what occurs in instructionally successful schools, where, because of strong administrative or faculty leadership, teaching is considered a collective rather than an individual enterprise; requests and offers of assistance among colleagues are frequent; and reasoned intentions, informed choices, and

collective actions set the conditions under which teachers improve instructionally. (1989, p. 430)

The process involved in becoming a teacher is of vital interest to the educational community in part because it is a means by which that community is sustained or reconstructed. But not only the professional community is affected by the outcome. As fragmented as it is, the professional community has a responsibility for building and shaping our collective social being as well; it has broad citizenship obligations. Like it or not, as John Goodlad (1991) phrased it, teachers are "moral stewards" of schooling, and as such have the responsibility to be engaged actively in the "continuous renewal of the schools" for the sake of children, themselves, and our collective well-being. They are charged with creating within schools the kind and quality of life that ought to be lived without them. It was for this reason that Boyd H. Bode argued many years ago that "educational practice which avoids social theory is at best a trivial thing and at worst a serious obstruction to progress" (1937, p. 74).

Communities are strong when there is both diversity and a shared vision (T. Gitlin, 1995). The culture of teaching, however, is one that often encourages teacher isolation and disengagement. These are coping strategies some teachers use to make the work tolerable if not enjoyable. Sikes and her colleagues make a useful distinction between "private" and "public" coping strategies. "Private strategies," they state, "are employed by individual teachers to gain their own ends or cope with whatever is in front of them," whereas public strategies "involve a group of teachers acting together to gain their aims" (1985, pp. 72, 95). One of the most powerful private strategies used by teachers, one that seriously undermines efforts to build community, is simply to close the classroom door and ignore what goes on outside of it. In contrast, teacher education needs to be thought of as an ongoing community affair, one that employs public strategies and brings with it the responsibility to reach *out* to others who share the quest to become effective teachers and to *work with* them and others to strengthen and improve our schools.

These, then, are the five assumptions that underpin the methodologies and analyses presented in *Becoming a Student of Teaching*. We sincerely hope you will critically consider them.

# Section 1

✦

# Preservice Teacher Education

# Methodologies
# for Exploring Self

✦

# ✦ 2 ✦

# Life Writing

## INTRODUCTION

Biography, including years of experience as a student and perhaps in various teaching-related activities, provides a backdrop against which teacher development takes place. From this experience the beginning teacher brings to teacher education a plethora of often unarticulated and unexamined beliefs about schooling, teaching, learning, and the self as teacher that require scrutiny. Life writing is an important means for illuminating and beginning to confront and perhaps alter these beliefs and assumptions. By making them explicit, by uncovering and exploring their biographical origins, one may begin to reconstruct them if reconstruction is deemed necessary. Thus, life writing is a means for shaping one's future as an educator.

To know the past is to know oneself as an individual *and* as a representative of a socio-historical moment in time; each person is a victim, vehicle, and ultimately in some sense a resolution of a culture's dilemmas. We are born into a particular family, holding particular values, within a particular social, economic, religious, and political context that brings with it specific problems and issues and ways of making sense of experience and making it meaningful. Educationally, then, it makes a difference if one is born in an urban setting to a single, unskilled, poor, and unemployed mother or to a large, rural farm family, and these differences are expressed in how the world is made sensible and in how and what one learns. Making the past explicit, finding themes, identifying continuities and discon-

tinuities sharpen and darken the lines around self and, simultaneously, the other. As lines darken, contexts and the values, roles, and
relationships that define them are illuminated. Made explicit, and
then competently articulated, the past as a story of self forms the
basis for powerfully negotiating with new situations, like a first
teaching job, and the roles and subtexts that characterize them.
From this grounding educational judgments can be made and justified, and criticism can be directed toward those elements of a school
context that are seen as uneducative or miseducative. This is so
because to say who one is, is to say what one stands for, what ones
cares for.

To be able to say who one is as teacher and what one stands for,
however, does not mean that what one stands for is "right" or morally
and educationally responsible. Rather, it is part of an ongoing process
of challenging and *perhaps* reconfiguring elements of self. We say
"*perhaps* reconfiguring self" because much of what life writing reveals
is self-confirming, strongly valued as part of self and impervious to
change. The discovery of such commitments, however, does not lessen
the value of life writing. To the contrary, it helps to define more clearly
the nature of the educational project faced by beginning teachers. Life
writing does this, in part, by forcing consideration of what situational
elements or conditions are necessary for maintaining one's teaching
commitments, one's sense of self as a teacher. Of this, more will be said
later, in the section "Extending the Conversation."

Stories are the central means by which life is made sensible
(Gudmundsdottir, 1997); life "is a long process of narrative interpretation" (Syrjala & Estola, 1999, p. 3). Life writing involves composing a story, a plot line, of how we have come to be who we are that
allows externalization of the self. By gaining distance from the self,
we may also gain perspective; we become self-critical and better able
to consider why we do what we do (Fenstermacher, 1997). Thus, as
Syrjala & Estola argue, "While telling a story, we re-assess our own
lives, and while listening to other people tell stories, we acquire
ingredients for our own growth" (1999, p. 2). The stories we compose
are answers to the questions of who we are—"Who is the self that
teaches?" (Palmer, 1998, p. 7)—where we are going, and how we got
where we are. Sharing stories, and teachers do a lot of story telling, is

simultaneously an act of self-discovery and of discovery of the world we inhabit.

Life writing and the sharing of stories bring the realization that there is no single authoritative story line—stories evolve over time and in response to changing conditions and understanding (Elbaz-Luwisch, 1997). One's history, one's conceptions of self-as-teacher, can and do change. Carla, whose story will be presented shortly, nicely captured the point when she wrote: "If you ask me again tomorrow to tell you my life story, I might tell you a whole bunch of other things." After rereading his autobiography and looking backward over the year he spent in our certification program, another of our students observed, in an interview, that his history, his perception of himself, had changed. He had a new history, a new story of self, and he was different as a result: "[Writing] the educational autobiography was really interesting. How my perceptions have changed!" He admitted that his motivation to teach had been essentially negative, a desire to correct evils done to him. Seeing teaching through a teacher's eyes, he said, softened and changed his negative views of his past teachers and school experience, and a different vision of his future role as teacher emerged as a result.

While we author our own stories, these stories are written within social, political, and economic contexts that define what is seen as desirable, proper, and more importantly, possible. Constant scrutiny of one's values and beliefs is called for in relationship to the influence of context, and changes in context, on self and others, including students. Teachers ought to know what theories are driving their actions and be able to defend them.

Life writing will not free you from your history or liberate you from the influence of institutional life, but it is a tool that can enable you to take charge of your history, to assert your ownership of it. It can help you to recognize your place as an actor who shapes the contexts you inhabit and as an author who has before you choices that matter, that make a difference in the quality of schooling offered young people and in your own development as a teacher. As Huberman suggests, "Exploring one's life as a teacher can, and often does, open up alternative ways of reconstruing ways of acting and being in the classroom and, from there, of shaping another career path" (1995, p. 131).

## WRITING AN EDUCATION-RELATED LIFE HISTORY

The following is the life writing assignment we present our students.

> Write an "education-related" life history, a story of how you have come to teaching. Describe how you came to your current decision to become a teacher. Identify important people or "critical incidents" that significantly influenced your decision and your thinking about the aims of education, about the proper role of teachers, and about yourself as teacher. Consider your "experience of school," how school felt, and how you best learned and when you felt most valued, connected, and at peace—or least valued, most disconnected, and most at war with yourself and with school. After writing your story, return to it and where you can connect it to appropriate public theory, literature that illuminates the themes that emerge in your story. Remember, every story we tell is simultaneously personal and social.

A "critical incident" is an event that signals an important change in course, a shift in one's thinking (Measor, 1985). The term "education-related" is meant to be taken very broadly. Do not read "*school*-related," but "*education*-related." Perhaps most of our education takes place outside of schools; and a good many, perhaps most, of the people encountered and the events experienced that are educationally important have little to do with schooling. So think broadly and deeply.

Be patient with yourself. Recapturing the past may take some time. Getting started is often difficult, just as it is often a problem to know when to quit. Quit when you have nothing more you want to say and share. To get started, you might find it useful to make a listing of persons who have influenced you for good or ill, or of critical incidents. Critical incidents might be either positively or negatively loaded emotionally. Some beginning teachers find it useful to start with the present and go backward, marching through names, dates, places, and seeking to recapture memories, feelings, impressions. Once you begin writing, memories will jump into relief and you will find that the storyline you are seeking to create will shift and sometimes dramatically change as a result. A single recalled event may put an entirely different interpretation on your history than the one with which you began. You may discover some painful memories—Mrs. Prince, the cruel, abusive, boy-hating teacher who terrorized one of the authors during first grade—which have such an impact that everything else you write seems an addendum. It is likely you will find that although sometimes painful, writing is also a means to come to terms with hurt and to learn from it.

When writing of the self, there are no right answers. Validity is replaced by authenticity. Does the story feel right? Does it resonate? Does it capture you and your thinking? But if you leave writing feeling uneasy, do not be dismayed. Writing does not end the use of your story. The methodologies that are presented will give you ample additional opportunities to think carefully about yourself as a teacher, and perhaps these will assist you to name your uneasiness. After all, your story is ongoing.

This is our first assignment. At this point it is important for us to mention that we have varied our own emphasis on connecting public and private theories in life writings, and this difference in emphasis is evident in Carla and J.B.'s much-edited stories that follow. This shifting of emphasis is driven by our own struggle to avoid the danger of having private theory overwhelmed by public theory. Emphatically, the story must come first. A complementary second assignment has a different focus, on learning the subject area that you eventually will teach. An example of this type of life writing follows J.B.'s story along with a description of the assignment.

## CARLA: "MY LIFE STORY . . . FOR TODAY"

I am the oldest child of immigrant parents. As such, I always felt different, a little odd. My parents spoke with an accent and did things differently from most people. Sometimes I remember being embarrassed by that fact, other times I enjoyed the uniqueness of my roots. Either way, my roots shaped many of my perceptions as I grew up, but I am only now beginning to see how.

Although I was born in Chicago, we lived in Canada for the first five years of my life. Much of that time was spent with foreign relatives visiting. I loved to listen to them tell me stories of what it was like where they lived. I also delighted in my ability to speak and understand several languages. I realized at a very young age that not everyone spoke a different language in their home or had foreign relatives with whom to speak different languages.

My parents wanted very much to have their children educated in "Amereeca," so they worked extremely hard to gain a visa to move back to the United States. Much of the Latin-European approach to life that I had been accustomed to was gone. Kindergarten was not just the beginning of my education, it was the beginning of my "Americanness."

By the time I was nine years old, my parents were not too sure about the customs and habits of American school children (girls wore shorts under their dresses so the boys wouldn't see their underwear when they climbed on the monkey bars—but why are girls climbing on the monkey bars at school in the first place?) ... My father became a practicing psychiatrist and moved the family to a rich suburb of Chicago. Unfortunately for my parents, these people had even stranger customs than the ones we left [behind].

As time went on, my mother, brother, sisters and I became quite americanized, but my father did everything he could to maintain his traditional ways. This was not a source of conflict in our home. It did, however, serve to illustrate to me how different cultures are and how much culture is part of every aspect of life.

By the time I entered high school two things were very apparent to my parents: their eldest daughter was very independent, and perhaps the money they had saved for her college education would be better spent on an island in the Pacific so she could be Queen. I did not get the island. I did, however, move myself, three days after graduation, to the Florida Keys.... [I did this] to assert my independence. It was ... a wonderful experience. I worked and I paid for everything out of my own pocket (an amazing thing for a rich kid). I loved my independence. I became intoxicated by it, and knew from that experience that I never wanted to give it up. Moreover, I wanted everyone to enjoy the thrill of independence.

I became an activist. If there was a cause, I would be [involved]. I [was] a rebel. Actually, I didn't need a cause, I was just a rebel, outspoken and direct. The causes were all good ones, and they helped me to further shape my view of the world. Most importantly, they showed me that I must make a conscious choice to make [this world] better. If I don't, I consequently make a passive choice to make it worse.

My activism was a little out of place in the conservative [community within which I lived]. But [this] was for me all the more reason to speak out. Somehow, in the midst of all the protesting I went to college. Even more amazingly, I convinced my professors that I was a promising student despite being somewhat of a flake. At the university I worked haphazardly towards a television production degree. My work through the department was well respected and brought me both accolades and job offers (with much needed good pay). I was going a million miles an hour without a destination. Then I met [Rich], my husband. Things like destination began to be important to me.

... I had two children, a girl ... (just turned six), and a boy ... (just turned five). Right before they were born [my husband and I] decided to move his business to our home so we could both spend as much time as possible with our future kids.

Oh, yeah, the college thing. That's pretty much how I felt about it at the time. When my husband and I got married, I was working for a [motion picture company] and making independent documentaries. I was very successful ... but was burning out [and felt unhappy]. College was definitely getting the shortest end of the stick. It all seemed to be a waste of time. I wasn't sure what I wanted, but I knew I was not finding it in school or with the work I was doing. So, I left....

While raising the kids and working on our out-of-the-home business, I became more and more involved with my church. It is important to know that my church is very large, about 1,300 members, and I think about 1,200 of them are kids (okay, a slight exaggeration). Lots of kids and lots of things for kids to do made it easy for me to get involved with the youth ministry. Before I knew it I was running the nursery, and a year later,

I was teaching the seventh-grade confirmation class and running [other education programs]. Then it hit me: "Oh, yeah, this is what I have always wanted to do."

Then all the old tapes began to replay in my mind's ear: Mom: "Honey, you're too smart to be a teacher." Dad: "You can be anything you want, a doctor or a lawyer; don't settle for teaching." Carla: "But I have always wanted to be a teacher." Then my husband, a little fed up with my indecisiveness, said it. The words still echo in my head: "So, do it. Since when do you let other people tell you who or what to be?"

Off to college I went. I was going to be a teacher. "Damn the torpedoes, full steam ahead."

So, here I am, one year to go. I am still independent, but I don't need to be Queen. I am still an activist, but I have softened in my approach. And I am very active in my church. Now I am responsible for [even more of my church's educational programs] . . .

When I become a teacher, the story will not be completed, though. I am and will always be a work in progress: changing, evolving, learning, and growing. . . . I'm not sure if there are any central themes to my life story. Maybe that's because I was a little flaky for so long. I do recognize, however, that I am a product of the experiences, thoughts and emotions of my past, and I am glad of that.

I also know that this life story would be written differently on another day. Different things come to mind at different times. By no means can four or five or one-hundred or even one-million pages of information cover a life even one of only thirty years. So, for this instance in time, the above is my life story (the Reader's Digest version at best). But if you ask me again tomorrow to tell you my life story, I might tell you a whole bunch of other things and skip what I told you here. Maybe that tells you the most about me and my life story.

## FULFILLING THE PROPHECY: J.B.'s STORY

In recalling my life history in school, I soon realized that I had a complex web of experiences that led me to the decision to become a teacher. In addition, I also realized that I had enough material to create a novel; therefore, I limited my experiences to one common theme that I discovered ... (even though there were several other themes I could have pursued). I discovered that I was inspired to become a teacher by some exceptional teachers I had in the past. One common characteristic of all these teachers was that they expected excellence from me, and I generally performed according to their expectations.

Through reflection, I found that these expectations were intricately woven into the fabric of my culture. There were expectations from friends, neighbors, coaches, relatives and teachers which helped to mold who I am today....

I had good and bad teachers. Without criticizing the poor instructors, I want to point out a commonality between the good teachers. The good teachers expected excellence, and my academic performance, for the most part, rose to meet those expectations. From junior high to the present I can recall the names of teachers who pushed me beyond mediocrity.... Their prodding and teaching inspired me to excel in school despite being just an average guy.

During my secondary school experience, I never even dreamed of becoming a teacher, but I have grown to love school and learning.... My father was a truck driver, and he would come home at ten o'clock in the evening and complain about working on the loading docks. The wrinkles on his forehead and his swollen knuckles added credence to his testimony of this awful and backbreaking work. I remember many nights in which my dad would make his way to his favorite chair and warn me to do well in school so I would avoid this terrible labor. The combination of his chilling testimony and the cool air escaping from his worn and tattered clothes left an indelible impression on my mind. I never wanted a job like his. [The unpleasantness of] homework seemed minuscule in comparison to such labor.

My dad always told me how bright I was, and made an effort to make me feel I was someone very special. I was the youngest child and I received plenty of attention from both siblings and parents. My brother and sisters still give me a hard time about being spoiled ... [by my father]. Considering the nurturing I received at home ... I entered the schoolhouse extremely confident. I thought I was the coolest kid in my class.... I loved school. [But] not everything continued so rosily.

During my elementary years, I noticed that there were a few kids who finished their reading or math problems before me, but from what I remember, I was definitely not the slowest in the class.... We moved into a new area [when I was eight] because my dad wanted us to grow up in a [better] neighborhood. This transition was tough; I had to start from scratch and make new friends. The school was much larger and there were many more kids [attending].... No longer did I feel I was the coolest kid in school....

My last year of elementary school I remember my home room teacher issuing us a test. I can still hear her telling us to do our best because if you score high enough, you would be placed in "honors" courses at the junior high. She then told us a little about the advantages of being placed in the honors program. After taking the exam I fully expected to be put in this accelerated group. To my [dismay], the next year I found myself taking classes with the "average" kids. I remember being jealous of my friends who were placed in the honors courses. The accelerated courses were for kids who were referred to as "gifted" and "talented." Around these "gifted" students I felt a sense of inferiority; I was just mediocre. I began to view myself as a plain ordinary student who was not capable of excelling in school.

My eighth grade year I was assigned to be in Mrs. P.'s English class. This truly put fear in my heart because my older siblings had taken her in years previously and they testified of how difficult her class was. Junior high was pretty easy for the most part. If [students] just showed up for class and worked, [they] never had any homework. There were a few exceptions, and Mrs. P. was one of them. She let us know from the first day that she expected high school quality work. This actually meant that we would have to read novels and write essays for homework. I don't think I even knew what an essay was because I remember struggling with some basic ... grammar. [But] I worked hard because she expected it out of me, and consequently I did well in her class and actually learned a lot. In fact, I became one of her favorite students and so she invited me to be her aide the following year.

When I reached high school, I [stayed] in the standard track. I wasn't placed in the honors classes, but my Sophomore English teacher pulled me and some other students aside and counseled us to take the honors course the following year. He assured us that we were well qualified and that the only difference between his class and the honors was the work load. [So] we signed up for Mrs. C.'s honors English course.

For the first few weeks [of Mrs. C.'s class], I was intimidated and questioned if I had the [intellectual] power to compete with these students. After all, they were the same students who had been placed in the "gifted and talented" courses in junior high school. Nevertheless, I stuck with it. Mrs. C. was a tough teacher and she definitely expected us to work hard, but she treated us like we were capable of the quantity and quality of work she expected. I performed well in her class. I was pleased to discover I was doing as well or better than many of the students whom I formerly felt inferior around.

I remember doing a ten page research project in her class on the poetry of Carl Sandberg. I put a lot of research and effort into this paper, but for some reason I was unable to complete the project on time. She instructed me to finish the paper and turn it in in a few days. After reviewing my work, she seemed amazed. She commented that the work was excellent and that it was definitely "A" quality, but that she would have to mark it down a little because it was late.... I will never forget what she said next.... She told me that she wished she would have known earlier the quality of work I was capable of performing.... I thought to myself, "of course it is great work, isn't that what you expected?" Another thought came to mind, "did she expect less of me because I was a jock?" During football season she would scoff at us if we needed to get out early for a road game, and we football players (there were three of us) felt she thought we were less than par academically....

I later realized the powerful influence of [Mrs. C.'s] expectations . . . on my scholastic performance . . . [yet] I have always been mildly haunted by what she said about my last assignment.

I was inspired to become a teacher by teachers who I considered exceptional. . . . I found that each of them expected "a lot" from their students. They would not allow their students to settle for mediocrity. . . . There is a definite correlation between teacher expectations and subsequent student performance. . . . Because I felt teachers like Mrs. P. and Mrs. C. helped me transcend the rut of being merely mediocre, I want to do the same for my students. . . .

I had heard about the [notion] of the self-fulfilling prophecy, but I had never heard it applied to education. . . . I was . . . surprised to find public theory [that] supported my private theory, [that there is a] correlation between teacher expectations and student performance. [I read] a landmark article . . . by Ray Rist [written] thirty years ago entitled, "The self-fulfilling prophecy in ghetto education." He related his study of an urban elementary class beginning kindergarten and continuing through second grade. Tragically, he documents the process of how these young children were tracked according to socioeconomic indicators which ultimately became the benchmark for their future academic experience. . . . Since the Rist article, several other authors have tackled the same topic. . . . [Guttmann, 1988] investigated how teachers' evaluation of their students is affected by knowledge of a student's background. Encouragingly, [this study] found that "teachers' evaluations of the actual performance of a pupil are not affected by their stereotypical expectations regarding the inferior functioning of the children of divorced parents." . . . Through research I found that not only was performance linked to teacher expectations, but to the student and also to the student's parents. . . . It was not until I started reading these articles that I realized what a strong influence my dad's expectations had on my academic performance. . . . Lastly, I did not consider the effect my [own] expectations had upon my academic performance . . . It is not surprising that Haynes and Johnson found that self-expectancy is significantly more influential than the expectations of the teacher upon academic performance (Haynes & Johnson, 1983).... [Formerly] I gave only credence to teacher expectations, now I realize there are other expectations which have a significant influence on the eventual performance of students.

## LEARNING TO WRITE: JOHN CARLISLE'S STORY

As noted, there are multiple approaches to life writing. John Carlisle's story (we use John's name at his request) is a learning history and thus has a very different focus than do Carla and J.B.'s. The assignment follows, then John's story:

### TEACHING SUBJECT PERSONAL LEARNING HISTORY

Over the years we have observed the power of disciplinary cultures in teacher education. Science teacher education students and beginning teachers in the humanities, for example, often think of their work very differently (Shuell, 1992). You probably gravitated toward your academic major because you found it personally engaging and fitting. You likely identify with the major and with those who share your commitment to it. You may have found your major area of study easy to learn, and perhaps you assume others will share your enthusiasm for the subject and will have a similarly positive learning experience as did you as a student. It is important to know, however, that others may not learn quite so easily, and that as a teacher you will need to find or create ways of helping your students to meaningfully engage the content. This assignment takes one of two forms:

Write a teaching subject personal learning history, choosing to respond to items A or B. A. If, as a student, you found the subject you are planning to teach a struggle to learn or your educational experience with the subject in some sense seriously deficient, then write a personal history of your learning the subject. Conclude your paper with lessons that arise from your struggle to learn that have application to teaching. B. If, as a student, you found the subject you are going to teach easy to learn, then write a history of your learning in a subject area that *you found especially difficult or uninteresting or uninspiring as a student*. Assuming that some of your own pupils will feel this way about your subject area, conclude your paper by discussing the implications of this negative learning experience for teaching within your own subject area.

## JOHN'S STORY

My most memorable reading experience occurred when my teacher, Mrs. S. had our class tally the number of pages that students read in their free time. I remember starting *Ivanhoe* after seeing a televised adaptation, but the book was just too boring for me so I shelved it and wrote my report from the movie. Consequently, I had more pages than anyone else at the end of the term, thanks in part to five or six hundred that I didn't read! I've always enjoyed reading on my own, but sometimes I'd resent my teachers' reading assignments. If they wanted me to read, they had better reward me for it. I'd want an opportunity to show what I'd learned. If a teacher didn't discuss the readings in class and there wasn't a test, I wasn't going to read their stuff. I had enough stuff to read on my own. "Because I say so," just didn't cut it. "Because it's good for you," wouldn't work either. I wanted to know they wanted me to read. I wanted to know why. . . .

Since writing is the most important element of my content area, English, I must begin with the research paper that kicked off my academic career. This ninth grade paper was everything that it should have been, at least in terms of traditional writing pedagogy. Mrs. D. required me to select a topic (I selected Poland, a broad one), research the topic, and record ideas on note cards, generate a thesis statement, plot an outline for several paragraphs, hand write a draft for teacher review, revise it for my final draft and arrange the whole thing according to Kate Turabian's rules of academic writing. My greatest obstacle with this paper was my topic. I never whittled it down to a manageable size and ended up with a rambling, general history of Poland. I don't think I said anything [that was] truly mine, but I completed the assignment and passed the class. There was a fifteen page minimum and I filled every one plus a bonus graph and a map.

That is my strongest memory of a high school writing assignment. It must have taken weeks to finish and may have driven Mrs. D. mad, but it initiated me into the "thesis point point point point conclusion" style of academic writing. Strangely, this method didn't resemble any writing I did afterward, although the product of this method became familiar to me [later]. At the time, I thought that I was receiving the stylistic direction I needed to succeed intellectually, but now I realize that she was simply following an established form . . . designed to make each student produce a homogenous written product. It's terrifying. Everything literature enthusiasts praise about writing is absent from this model. Personal voice—nope. Sincere interest by the author—nope again. Consideration for the reader—not really. These old school writing theorists reduced writing to a series of mechanical functions entirely devoid of humanity. . . .

Another writing assignment that I remember was a combined writing assignment/presentation biography. It was a Great Personalities class taught by Mrs. W., a friendly and accommodating teacher. Each student was asked to select a person and write a paper about him or her. We also had to prepare a presentation which conveyed our research to the class. You're wondering who I selected, aren't you? Martin Luther? Martin Luther King Jr.? Margaret Bourke-White? Ralph Lauren? . . . I selected Bruce Wayne. Yup, the Batman . . . I researched the fictional life of my favorite comic book character for a writing assignment. I bought a big Batman poster for the presentation and had a great time telling my class all about the tragic life of Bruce Wayne and how he turned to vigilante justice. I wonder if I'll be as accommodating with my own students [as was Mrs. W.]. Sure, I'm embarrassed about it now, but at the time I really enjoyed myself. I even remember thinking that the girl who wrote about Ralph Lauren was a little tweaked.

Although Mrs. D. required me to select a topic for my paper, she required that it be a topic worthy of a research paper and that I tie it to an appropriate thesis. Mrs. W. must have realized that an easy way to enthuse the class would be to have us get involved with our topics. By giving us ownership of our work, she changed the dynamics of the traditional teacher/student relationship and made us invest part of our lives in a writing assignment. Despite the inclusion of her students in the creation of their projects, her class time was still mainly devoted to direct instruction, reading assignments and traditional homework. . . .

I was learning. . . . I notice that the only papers I can remember are the ones for which I chose the topics. . . . The majority of the English assignments I remember were grammar stuff, book reports, and reading questions. I'm a little nervous about my influence in my students' lives if I can't even remember my own teachers' assignments, but this nervousness inspires me to outperform my own teachers. . . . I've discovered that grammar reviews are just about useless except in preparation for a standardized exam; I've also learned that book reports are easily available on the internet, if not the Cliff's Notes, movies or older siblings; and finally, I learned [from one of my university instructors] how reading questions are pointless exercises designed to consume students' time and to provide teachers with easy, surface-level assignments. So, what's left? . . .

I believe that writing can be taught. I believe writing to be important both inside and outside of the classroom. I believe that writing evolves, that it changes with the author. I believe that grammar will actually improve through authentic writing assignments. I believe that students must recognize their personal voice before they can successfully compose in an academic one, or any other. I believe I am patient enough and self-confident enough to allow students to explore both their writings and their voices. These are relatively new beliefs for me. . . . If I continue to discover and accommodate new educational theories, I'll continue to teach beyond the methods with which I was taught, but if I stop learning and rely on what I know, eventually my childhood experiences with education will dominate my teaching. . . .

I hope I'll turn out class after class of interesting students with useful literacy skills. I'll want them to know the difference between writing for an academic audience and writing for other purposes. I'll want them to communicate effectively.... If my students have the knowledge necessary to continue learning on their own and for their own enjoyment, I'll be a happy, successful, teacher. I believe that the strength of my example as a literate and well-adjusted human will motivate them to learn for themselves.... I'll try to blend different styles of teaching in my classroom. In advocating correct grammar ... I'll use examples of student writing instead of abstract examples.... I'll use journal writing each day.... Since journal writing is never "free" I'll assign carefully chosen topics on which they will base their day's entry. Journals are a fertile ground for paper topics or for expressing ideas which do not receive time during class period.... I want to always be able to answer the question, "Why are we doing this?"

## CONSIDERATIONS

To better understand the influence of biography on becoming a teacher and of how we use life history, we identify themes that cut across the educational life histories. These, along with those identified by the beginning teachers themselves, like J.B.'s concern with teacher expectations or his sense of having lost a competition to join an honors class, are explored in class. A theme we identified was that of being an outsider. This theme is prominent in Carla's writing and, despite their social class differences, is also evident but not fully developed in J.B.'s story of being tested then tracked and of losing then regaining a measure of self-confidence. The theme of being an outsider is a common one cutting across cohorts, and is evident among beginning teachers whose social class and ethnic backgrounds and school experience are different from the majority of students. For this reason it deserves special attention. It is worth noting that men, especially in elementary teacher education programs, often feel they are outsiders as well. Writing at the end of fall term, David, a beginning teacher who as a child spent time in foster care following the unraveling of his family and a student much disliked by teachers, underscores the influence of this theme in the lives of some beginning teachers and the importance of sharing stories: "I thought my personal life history was so abnormal that I would stand out like a sore thumb in class, isolated and unable to relate to the others." Through sharing his story, however, and to his great relief, he discovered connections: "[After sharing life histories], I realized that a lot of students shared experiences, emotions, and reasons for teaching that were similar to mine, and that these reasons were unique and [diverged] from the [expected reasons] for choosing a [teaching] career. I found that [discovery] comforting."

While themes may be shared, many life events and ways of responding to them are personal and unique. Consider: Some beginning teachers have difficulty writing and sharing their stories, but not Carla. "Damn the torpedoes, full steam ahead" nicely captured her approach to the cohort, to teaching, and to life. She took charge. She challenged and sometimes offended, but also reached out and sought to assist others in the cohort, just as she sought during practice teaching to connect with students who were struggling. Illustrating how life history and identity play out in teacher education, Carla's passion and independence lead to some minor conflicts with her cooperating teacher, a mild-mannered and skilled teacher, over how best to work with a student or approach a topic. With a good many students she had difficulty establishing open and productive relationships. Realizing that in good measure the quality of student learning was dependent on the kind and quality of her relationships with them–echoing an aspect of J.B.'s concern—she began to reflect on those relationships: "I tend to be very outgoing and verbal. But this kind of behavior is not welcomed by all students." Carla confronted the contradiction between the much cherished "thrill of independence" that she sought for the students and her need to dominate interaction with them.

Carla, the "Queen," struggled for a time during student teaching. Our observation notes included the following comments, which give a good sense of Carla's teaching practice early in the term: "Carla put rules on the board for [figuring] interest that confused the students because the assignment she wanted them to do required different operations. [She] made errors on the board that the students wrote down without protest as examples to be put in their notes—she didn't catch these until later when I pointed them out to her. She keeps on top of the kids' behavior—students rarely misbehave but a large percentage are not engaged." The feeling in the classroom was oppressive—no "thrill of independence" there. The pupils did not question her errors (although many recognized them) or ask questions about what they were to do, apparently because they did not feel they could or should.

The situation changed, dramatically, as Carla became increasingly unhappy with the quality of her relationship with the students and as we sought to help her address the contradiction evident in her thinking about teaching and how she worked in the classroom. A few weeks and much work later, our notes indicated that a very different classroom ethos had emerged: "Good work! . . . From the last time I visited your class a couple of weeks ago you've made enormous progress. You seem much more relaxed, without losing any control; your skills dealing with the kids are more [diversified] and comfortable."

In contrast to Carla, J.B. connected his story to public theory. In so doing the theme that initially emerged, the importance of teacher expectations to student learning, was broadened and in some ways altered. Not only did his thinking become more complex, but his sense of a teacher's role and responsibilities was altered. Later he came to better understand the often indirect influence of teacher expectations on student expectations for themselves and for learning. When seeking to connect biographically embedded private theories like J.B's with public theory a delicate balance is sought. Had J.B. come to the task of life writing with the theme of teacher expectations already in mind the result would have been an inauthentic story. Fortunately, he did not. Rather, he wrote his story, as was suggested, thought about it, and recognized it as a particular kind of story, a story about the influence of teachers on students. He then recast the story somewhat, wrote a new introduction, and then a conclusion that made some connections with public theory.

As intended, John's story is of a different but related kind to Carla and J.B.'s. He writes about his learning to write; this was his second life writing following his educational life history. Consistent with the assignment, he judged his writing experience as "in some sense seriously deficient" (see above). He described that experience, his "lying," as he called it, about reading Ivanhoe and then writing a report based on the movie and his disappointment in being initiated into a 'thesis point point point point conclusion' style of academic writing." From this experience he extracted what he believed would be a better approach to teaching writing, an approach, he wrote, that would rely on personal voice, author interest, and consideration for the reader. Part of his criticism is grounded in his reading of current research on the teaching of writing, a literature he encountered in his teacher education English methods courses. Rather than cite specific articles or authors, excepting one, he freely draws upon it; public and private theory blended. The public theory he has studied is now his own, part of his view of teaching and learning in English. This is an important development, one where the distinction between public and private theory begins to dissolve and beliefs and public theory unite.

All three of the writers speak authentically. As John would say, they have their own "voices." Each identified plot lines that usefully captured and framed experience, albeit we recognize the stories as incomplete and tentative. Themes emerged that became crucially important in their quest to become teachers, to forge productive teaching identities. As we have discussed at length for Carla, each of the teachers revealed attitudes, values, and beliefs that proved to be sources both of strength and of difficulty in the classroom.

## EXTENDING THE CONVERSATION

The need to mine the past for insight into the present finds a good deal of support in education generally (Kridel, 1998) and in research on teacher development specifically (see Ball & Goodson, 1985; Goodson & Walker, 1991; Hargreaves & Fullan, 1992). The place of life writing in the social sciences dates at least to 1935 and the research of John Dollard (1935) on life history as a research methodology. How best to write a life remains a lively question. There are several different approaches to writing and using life histories or autobiographies that represent differences in purpose. Perhaps the earliest work related to teacher education was done under the direction of Ross Mooney, a pioneer in the field. Mooney's students wrote autobiographies and explored their own development as a lens through which to think about teaching and learning (see Riordan, 1973). In his early work Pinar (1980; 1981) drew upon psychoanalysis and developed a method, "currere," that begins with regression and seeks a healing synthesis of a self caught in socially harmful institutional arrangements, including schooling. Raymond, Butt, and Townsend (1992) encourage practicing teachers to engage in "collaborative autobiography." Teachers write and share their stories as a means for helping them to understand one another's experience, identify "collective concerns," what we have termed general themes, and eventually engage in school-based projects that aim at creating institutional conditions more conducive to teacher development.

For us, as for most of these writers, a great deal hinges on how we conceive of the self. A distinction made a number of years ago by Berger and Luckmann (1966) between primary and secondary socialization is a useful point of departure. They suggested that secondary socialization—the process involved in taking on an identity as a teacher, for instance—takes place against the background of one's primary socialization in the family, which produces a relatively stable conception of self. Secondary socialization, they observe, "must deal with an already formed self and an already internalized world. It cannot construct subjective reality *ex nihilo*" (p. 140). Jennifer Nias' (1989) conception between "core" and "situational" selves represents a similar distinction. Since we are tugged in so many directions and confront so many differing ways of making a life it has become increasingly difficult to achieve a core self, a stable "I" (Gergen, 1991).

Often when one first enters a new situation, like a new teaching job, demands are made that challenge the core self, the central values and ways of making sense of experience which characterize a person as distinct. Sometimes we feel we must to some degree be other than self in order to function in institutionally valued ways. Tension builds. Work feels like an uncomfortable role play. Other times who we are fits nicely with what we are supposed to be and we feel at home. In either case, knowing oneself enables role negotiation from a position of power; one acts, rather than reacts, to contextual demands in ways that enhance one's sense of belonging and of doing what is right even when risk is involved. Institutional resistance and acts of moral courage are both born in self-knowledge.

Tension between what a context demands of us and who we are or want to be raises a range of serious issues for teachers. The context of teaching is changing, and some of what appear to be the most powerful changes have far reaching implications for the quality of teachers' lives in school. Increasingly, across the Western world curricula are being standardized and scores on nationally normed tests are being accepted as proof of either teacher success or failure. The pages of *Education Week*, the national newspaper of education, are replete with articles reporting one or another state or federal initiative designed to improve teacher performance and ensure better test scores. Debate is heated, and opinions varied, but strongly supported by political leaders and educational policy makers the movement toward standardization and testing grows: "About half the states now use tests to make such important decisions as whether students will move on to the next grade or graduate from high school, and which schools qualify for rewards or penalties. . . . Rather than improving student learning, some of the scholars [attending the American Educational Research Association meeting] suggest, high-stakes tests may be narrowing the curriculum, stultifying teaching practices, and driving some teachers and school administrators to cheat" (Viadero, 2000, p. 6). Proof of the value of an emphasis on testing and on sharply focused curricula comes in many forms and from many places: "Long known for the low achievement of its schools and the rampant mismanagement of its business affair, the 12,000-student [East St. Louis] school district has posted some of the most dramatic gains of any system in the state on this year's standardized exams . . . 'I'm proud of our effort and hope this gives our community a lift to continue' . . . the district's superintendent [said]" (Johnston, 2000, p. 7). These trends are profoundly reshaping teacher's work and in so doing changing the nature of student-teacher relationships, perhaps not for the better. Teachers have always faced the question, "Can I be who I am in the classroom?" If the curriculum is narrowing and standardized testing is growing in importance, attending to this question openly and forthrightly will become increasingly important for teachers and raises an important question for those who seek to reform education.

To answer this question, teachers need to know who they are and where they stand; and they need to know something about the kind of institutional arrangements that enhance the quality of a teacher's life in school and how these arrangements may be achieved or strengthened. Clearly the focus on self is central to preservice and in-service teacher education. Who you are as a person—the kinds of experiences you had inside and outside of school, values, beliefs, and aspirations—has a profound influence on what you will or will not learn in teacher education, but perhaps even more importantly, it shapes what you will be as a teacher, what and how you will teach, and how you will respond to the changing context of teaching. So, we ask: What kind of teacher will you be? What kind of life do you wish to live with young people inside of your classroom? When young people think about you as a teacher, what will they say that you stand for? To answer these questions necessarily involves thinking carefully about self and about teaching context.

# ✳ 3 ✳

# Analyzing
# Personal Teaching Metaphors

## INTRODUCTION

One of the most daunting challenges faced by beginning teachers involves negotiating a role within new and unfamiliar contexts. As a student teacher this process is especially complicated because you are, in a sense, just passing through your cooperating teacher's classroom and school. Feeling like a visitor, and vulnerable, some student teachers are sorely tempted—and, in some ways, pressured by established patterns of interaction and expectation—to become imitations of their cooperating teachers. Because they are not their cooperating teachers, however, the best that can be hoped for is to become a comparatively poor imitation of the real thing.

Role negotiation is at the center of professional development. To think of this process as one of passively adapting—even for strategic reasons such as fearing a poor evaluation—to what is believed to be necessary in order to fit into the new context with minimal disruption or distress is to accept artificial limits on that development.

Negotiation is never simply one way. Despite contextual pressures to conform, when negotiating a role the communities one seeks to join are changed in subtle ways, just as the person is changed in some ways. Even as a student teacher, your presence in the classroom alters the context, and will alter the nature of the relations your cooperating teacher has with pupils. Knowing this, some cooperating teachers find it difficult to share a classroom with a student teacher or to, as they say, "give over" the class.

The challenge of negotiating a role is multifaceted. As a beginning teacher, you want to realize your ideals in practice. Yet, you want to fit in. Here's the rub: "Fitting in" may require that ideals be set aside or compromised. Inevitably conflict of varying degrees exists between ideals and what appears to be contextual imperatives to behave in institutionally expected ways, in ways that seem required by pupils, other teachers, and administrators. Facing such conflicts some beginning and experienced teachers engage in one or another coping strategy like "strategic compliance" (Lacey, 1977) such as where there is the appearance of conformity without a change in beliefs. Sometimes ideals are set aside, perhaps painfully, and accommodation takes place; one becomes what the context seems to require. And sometimes teachers resist pressures to conform and work, instead, to alter the context to make it more hospitable to their ideals.

Whichever approach is taken, you need to be acutely aware of the process of negotiation itself if you desire to direct it. Beginning teachers must be not only students of teaching but also students of their own development. As we have argued, to be such a student requires knowledge of self and of context and knowledge gathered in systematic and ongoing ways about the interaction of self and context.

Contexts and the communities that sustain them can be characterized in many ways. One distinguishing feature is found in the metaphors that bind a community and "mark off boundaries and define conditions of membership" (Taylor, 1984, p. 17). For example, in secondary schools "teacher is content expert" is one powerful and institutionally accepted role. This metaphor brings with it compelling images that grow out of one's love of a discipline and experience as a student, particularly as a successful college student. Along with it comes a view of teaching as "telling," and a student role: "empty receptacle in need of filling" (Freire, 1970). To fit into many secondary faculties, to be a "teacher" in these contexts, means buying into these or related metaphors, like "coach" (where the emphasis is on skills rather than content) and "master." Yet, the fit is often found to be uncomfortable. Rachel Marshall, one of our students, recently wrote with passion about this metaphor and of her growing dissatisfaction with it:

> In my first teacher-metaphor, I described myself as a pitcher of liquid.
> My students were other vessels which I would fill with the elixir of

knowledge. The school was a great table where all sorts of vessels would come to fill and be filled. I now intensely dislike that metaphor. For one thing, it puts me in the position of an expert. That is a role for which I am hideously ill suited. The more I learn, the more I realize how much I still have to learn. Hopefully, I will have some knowledge that I can pass on to my students, without seeming like the Grand High Know-It-All. If I didn't, my ambitions of becoming a teacher would be futile indeed ... I am forced to come up with a new [metaphor]. I suppose I'm always hunting for the perfect metaphor, and it keeps changing because my view of myself as a teacher is continually changing. I have almost reconciled myself to the fact that I will probably never find a metaphor that encapsulates all the many things I want to be as a teacher. This time I would like to experiment with a nautical metaphor. As a teacher, I will be the captain of my crew.

Representing embodied experience, metaphors, words that link the known and the unknown, the familiar and the new, that bridge one thing—teaching—to another—improvisational theater or performance (Sarason, 1999), play a significant part in the formation of beginning teacher ideals. This is so because of the fundamental place metaphors hold in human thinking as a means of producing coherence and of making sense of life (Lakoff & Johnson, 1980). Humans are born into metaphorical meaning systems that simultaneously define a culture and are defined by it. Thus, the identification and exploration of metaphors are means for gaining a window into the taken-for-granted assumptions that characterize differing cultural and institutional contexts as well as self.

By their nature metaphors represent a simplification of experience (Dickmeyer, 1989), and their analysis provides a parsimonious means for getting a handle on the interaction of self and context, which is the complex and contradictory process of role negotiation. For beginning teachers who are uncertain of who they want to be as teacher, the identification and analysis of teaching metaphors is a means for thinking about oneself and for beginning to achieve the coherence of thought and perhaps action that is central to negotiating a role, a "situational self," that resonates with one's inner or "core" self (Nias, 1989). Moreover, changes in one's teaching metaphors likely signal changes in conceptions of self as teacher and therefore the focus on metaphors provides a point of reference against which to critically consider the socialization process (Bullough, 1991). As Cortazzi and Jin (1999, p. 153) argue, "metaphors are a bridge towards internalization of concepts and towards changes in the practice of teaching."

## WRITING

The identification and analysis of metaphors may take multiple directions. We note two. One direction focuses on naturally occurring metaphors, metaphors that appear in teacher language. Such metaphors offer a means for exploring the conceptual systems, the beliefs beginning teachers use to make sense of their experience. For example, beginning teachers might be encouraged to explore their use of language to describe students, teaching, and learning (see Cortazzi & Jin, 1999). In this way assumptions embedded in thinking are uncovered. One of our former students, for example, a beginning teacher in a working-class junior high school, found himself speaking about students as "beasts." When he was asked about his usage of this metaphor, he immediately recognized that the term had slipped into his language unnoticed and accurately represented his growing frustration about his relationship with students. Like most teaching metaphors, this one was heavily emotionally laden. He realized his use of the term signaled a serious problem that demanded attention, and began to consider ways of making changes in thought and practice.

A second direction emphasizes the identification of personal teaching metaphors as ideals for practice, ones that inspire and invite conformity. With beginning teacher education students, this approach begins with self but quickly moves to context. This is the approach we take here.

After an introduction to the place of metaphors in thinking, and some of the related research (a portion of which will be shared in the "Extending the Conversation" section of this chapter), the beginning teachers are invited to imagine themselves in the classroom and to think about what it is they are doing, what the students are doing, and how the classroom feels. Then they write:

"Drawing on your life writing, identify a metaphor (or metaphors) that captures the essence of yourself as teacher."

Throughout our year together we periodically invite our students to reconsider the metaphors they generate for teaching, learning, and schooling in the light of their increasing experience as teachers and as students of teaching. This increasing experience includes considerable time spent observing and analyzing teaching both in classes and through videotape as well as planning and conducting a "short course," a unit taught prior to student teaching. A few weeks after the initial writing, they are again asked to think and write about their metaphors in class. A November "update," for example, included the following questions:

1. What is your personal teaching metaphor?
2. Has your metaphor changed? If so, into what? Has it been confirmed?
3. What factors/events/experiences have led to the change or resulted in the confirmation of your metaphor? Do you have a new metaphor?
4. Do you have any concerns about your metaphor?

The results of the updates are shared through discussion. In response to these questions, a lively discussion ensued during this term, as in the past. Those who said their views were changing, like Rachel Marshall quoted above, were encouraged to describe the changes and then to talk about what experiences prompted the change. Thus, we focus on the interaction of self and context. They were in schools at the time and had just finished writing their classroom studies (see chapter six). Based upon their increasing involvement in schools, many concluded that their views of students and of the work of teaching were inaccurate and naive. A few expressed discouragement; they asserted that the students would not allow them to be the kind of teachers they imagined and wanted themselves to be. These students began to see the ways in which self definitions bring with them definitions of other, and how both are influenced by context. In response to this view one of the optimists in the group remarked, "You have to hold on to the belief that you can make a difference." Clearly, a number of students' conceptions of self as teacher had been jolted by increasing experience with students and in schools. How they chose to respond to the challenge was of crucial significance in their development.

Subsequent updates followed about every three or four weeks. One in March asked these questions, and students responded in writing:

1. Has your metaphor changed or been confirmed?
2. What factors/experiences have led to the change or resulted in confirmation?
3. After the short course [during which time they taught a two- to three-week unit prior to student teaching] and looking ahead to practice teaching, how confident are you about your conception of yourself as teacher? Do you have any concerns or worries? If so, what are they? Do you feel as though you are increasing the knowledge and gaining the power necessary to direct your development as a teacher and achieve your metaphor?

Three examples of personal teaching metaphors follow. Each example is drawn from student writing (including metaphor updates and reviews of personal teaching texts) gathered over the course of the year. Once again, these materials are presented with student permission. The first example comes from Mary, who struggled throughout the program under the pressure of needing to work in order to support her small child. You will note that initially Mary was unable to generate a metaphor although she had a general image of what she wanted her class to be like. The second example comes from Terry, a beginning junior high school art teacher. At first Terry thought of herself as a guide, but this view evolved and became increasingly complex as she reflected on her development and teaching ideals. The third example, Martha, presents aspects of "teacher is subject matter expert."

## MARY: BRIDGE BUILDER

**October 8, first writing:**

I don't know how to state it succinctly. I just don't want any of my students to dread my class. I want it to be something they look forward to, a place where they feel comfortable enough to offer their own ideas and opinions.... [Students] should be ... responsible for one another's learning. All my years of schooling have shaped this view. I just sort of intuitively knew that teachers didn't have to embarrass students or put them on the spot to get their point across. I have been fortunate enough to have a couple of teachers who have been successful in creating environments in which the students felt comfortable enough to contribute and to take risks. These teachers de-emphasized incorrect answers and encouraged participation.

**November 14, update:**

When we first wrote about teaching metaphors, I could not come up with one. All I knew was that I wanted to create a non-threatening environment where all students could partici-pate and, hopefully, learn something. Although no single word or phrase can sum up what I want to be, the word "bridge" covers part of it. I want to be able to create a bridge between the content and the lives of the students. I want some aspect of the class to personally touch and engage each student. The idea of teacher as bridge occurred to me after having personal contact with students. Some of them are just so needy, inter-action with the teacher is crucial.

**Writing, December 12, review of personal teaching text:**

I want my students to feel good while they are in my class. Therefore, I vow that I will never embarrass them or put them on the spot, as I have seen quite a few teachers do. An issue which has emerged for me is that of making connections. My teaching metaphor turned out to be the teacher as bridge. I want my class to mean something to each student. I have started thinking about, and have discussed with my cooperating teacher, how to engage different types of students. Some students seem to turn off when they are invited directly into the discussion. This distresses me. But at least now I know some different strategies I can use. The overwhelming concern for me is, of course, discipline. Directing the energy of the seventh graders that I will be teaching during my short course and student teaching will be a huge task. I will have to be on my toes at all times to keep control. And I don't want to come across as too serious or unfriendly (once again, I'm back to the affective aspect of teaching).

Mary taught the short course, a two-week unit in Spanish for junior high school students. Like other students she was asked to identify and analyze a problem that emerged during the short course. Here is part of what Mary wrote (March 3):

> I wasn't in control of the class. But ... I have never been an authoritarian in any area of my life, and I don't want to be one in the classroom. Being an authoritarian goes against my concept of myself as a teacher and doesn't help create the kind of atmosphere that I want. I need to come up with some kind of strategy to bring the class to order that is compatible with my personality.

This said, Mary was not discouraged. She found much that was encouraging about the short course: "I left feeling good. I can do this because I care about the students. I can connect with this age group. Most of the students want to make a connection; they wanted to know me and to know things about me." This experience prompted her to write in an update:

> My metaphor ... has been confirmed. I originally meant it as a bridge between the students and content. But it has been confirmed in a more important way.... Yes, the bridge between content is there but the students seemed to be reaching out for a personal relationship with me. They wanted to make a connection, and so did I.... I am very confident with my conception of myself as teacher because I know that as long as I keep caring I will be just fine.

Shortly after this writing, Mary began practice teaching, which she excitedly anticipated, fully expecting to "knock 'em dead." She taught four Spanish classes, seventh through ninth grade.

### Writing, April 29, update:
My metaphor has been crushed. I have been crushed. Some days I feel like I don't want to teach because everything is so negative. I have to be so negative to keep these kids in line. I never wanted it to be that way. I thought I could create an environ-

ment, full of mutual respect, where everyone could feel free to participate. My metaphor was "teacher is bridge." I wanted to help connect the students with the content and the social aspect of school. I wanted relationships (connections) with the kids, but it's impossible when they don't show me respect. So, I don't know what my metaphor is now. Maybe teacher as supervisor? I have to be so strict about talking in class that my idea of a comfortable atmosphere where everyone can contribute isn't coming about. There are bright spots, however, in this dreary picture. (I hate being a disciplinarian—it goes against my personality.) There are periods when things go well (never entire days) and those are what keep me going. When things are bad, they are really bad; when they are good, they are fantastic.

Following this writing, the cooperating teacher and the two of us who worked with her from the university increased our assistance efforts. We wanted Mary to succeed. Our help took many forms, including ongoing and nearly constant feedback on her teaching, help with planning and curriculum design, and advice on classroom management and on how better to structure the classroom to gain the respect she desired. Mary worked hard to implement those suggestions that made sense to her, and with some good results.

**Writing, May 27, analysis of personal teaching text:**
I can't believe the end is finally here. I didn't think I would ever make it to this point. . . . I survived. I am finally starting to feel more like a teacher than a student. However, I still feel like I am the baby sitter, not the parent. . . . I've discovered my strengths and worked on my weaknesses. I found that I can be authoritative when I have to. I found that I am very patient with the students, and flexible when it comes to methods and lesson presentation in order to reach [kids]. The only disappointment I had this quarter was that I wasn't able to create the type of atmosphere that I would have liked in my classroom. The students wouldn't let me.

At year's end, and in interview, Mary spoke of the changes she went through in her thinking about herself as a teacher. She regretted being forced to give up her initial metaphor, although it endured as an ideal, and wondered if another context would allow her to realize her dream. She doubted it, however:

> I feel like I have to be watching the students, all of them, every second. You have to be able to watch 30 people at once. You have to be doing one thing and out of the corner of your eye be able to tell quickly that somebody is not doing what they are supposed to be doing and tell them so. So, right now, I just feel like a supervisor and disciplinarian. I'm hoping that when it is my own classroom and I have the whole year with the students, I can get that out of the way at the start and they will get routinized, and then I can worry about the bridge part. Maybe that will come later.... Right now, [for me], teacher is disciplinarian or authoritarian or supervisor or something like that.

### TERRY: TEACHER IS GUIDE AND . . .

Initially, Terry, a beginning visual arts teacher, thought of herself as a guide, a "person with some experience and knowledge in an area, yet willing to try new things, unsure of all the answers— one who is still learning and gaining knowledge." She also thought of herself as an "explorer," a guide into uncharted territories. She held this view, she said, because of the "ever changing face of the art world. There is so much happening in the world in the visual media that no one can ever know everything. So, I will never see myself as 'the expert,' because there is an unlimited supply of new information, the rules are always changing, developing, growing. My hope is that I can change along with the world and give new experiences to my students."

> **Writing, November 11, update:**
> I'm beginning to realize that junior high students need set boundaries. They are pushing limits at every chance. They are trying on new and different identities; somehow I must estab-lish the regulations of my classroom. I need to add something to my view of myself [as teacher] that will address this problem. I really hate the image of "policewoman" in the classroom. Yet

I'm not sure what other image could establish the rules [that are needed]. Maybe I need to incorporate some parenting. Parenting—teacher as sometimes parent. An adult that sets goals and limits, rewards a job well done or a valiant effort . . .

**Writing, December 12, review of personal teaching text:**

I am struggling with my teaching metaphor. The first set of images has proven to be idealistic and somewhat naive. To be a guide and explorer, you must have someone following you. The reality of the junior high classroom is that the students are testing roles and rules; in this kind of atmosphere it may be hard to expand their worlds if you are fighting for the right to lead. Yet the second image has faults also. I am not at all sure that I want to parent 200 students a day. . . . I haven't found a metaphor that can describe the kind of teacher I want to be.

After the short course, Terry's images of herself as a teacher gelled into "teacher is artisan" (March 3, metaphor update):

At some point during my short course I reflected on my experience and struggled to find a word or image that combined all the parts of my new experience. My first metaphor now seems ideal and naive, and the second addressed the part of a teacher that must deal with management and discipline problems. Now, I see teaching as a developed set of skills that are used to express knowledge to students. I see myself as an artisan.

**April 29, update, halfway through practice teaching:**

Teacher as artisan seems to still fit, yet it's changed! I find my skills as an artist are not as strong or important as my skills as a teacher most days. There are times when the student as apprentice is overwhelmingly strong. The students need a mentor/parent so much. I am fighting to be a strong influence without dreaming about these kids. I want to see them be successful. Yet I want to be able to turn it off at the end of the day. Some days, that is easier than [in] other days. I still feel that [teaching] is the most right thing I have ever done!

**May 27, review of personal teaching text done at the
conclusion of student teaching:**

I have been struggling with changing my metaphor. As an artisan
you must have apprentices that are interested in your skills. I
find some of my students really do not care about the skills I
have to teach; this makes teaching a more difficult process. Yet,
as an artisan you sometimes parent, guide, and pressure your
apprentices into completing their work. That part of the
metaphor fits very well with who I am in the classroom. I use
everything, anything, to get students involved. I am developing
a sense of who the students in my classes are both as individuals and as a group. This has helped in my planning and helped
me set [reasonable] expectations for finished projects.

## MARTHA: TEACHER IS SUBJECT MATTER EXPERT

Martha—a quiet, very private, and (as she described herself) "very
competitive" beginning high school chemistry teacher and honors
student—initially thought of herself as a "helpmate," one who helps
young people achieve their own goals. It was, however, her love of
chemistry and her desire to share it that was most central to her understanding of herself as teacher.

**Update, March 3, following the short course:**

The times I feel the most successful and good about myself is
when I explain a concept and I see a light go on or when I see
a student do a problem that they couldn't do before. It makes
me feel good about expending the energy to learn my subject
that I know it well enough to teach someone else. The short
course was good for me because I taught a subject that troubled me for a long time, and it still is my shakiest area. I feel
that if I can teach that, I will do fine in other areas.

Martha summarized the changes in her thinking after practice
teaching in her last review of personal teaching text when she wrote:

At the beginning of the year I was the most concerned about
the teaching aspect of being a teacher. I worried that I wouldn't

be able to get a concept across to my students. I have found out that this is almost second nature to me. This is the easy part. Towards the middle of the year I was concerned about classroom management. I had problems, but not any that weren't solvable to some extent. My most pressing concern before I began student teaching was being able to think of myself as the authority in the classroom. I knew that if I was insecure the kids would pick up on that and make my life difficult. I did have some problems with this at the beginning [of practice teaching], but I quickly adjusted, and so did the kids.

It was during the period when she was most concerned with authority that her reliance on the "expert" metaphor was most evident.

**Writing, March 12, review of personal teaching text, following the short course:**

The short course helped me realize that during my three years at the University, I have learned a lot. I know something that I can teach my students.... I believe I know my subject well enough to explain a concept many ways, and I can field questions without much stress at all. This was an extremely important discovery for me to make.... I want to be respected in my classroom as an authority on my subject, and an intelligent, organized individual who cares about the students.... I am nervous that at first my [youth] will be a problem in obtaining respect as the authority figure in the classroom, so I think that I will have to have very clear goals and rules for the class, and I will have to strictly enforce those rules. But I also think that after I have established myself as the person in charge, my youth will help me establish the kind of relationship I want with the students.

## CONSIDERATIONS

Like perhaps most beginning secondary teachers, Mary thought primarily about getting content into students' heads when she thought of teaching and of herself as teacher. She wanted to be a "bridge" across which content and student could meet. There was, however, an emotional dimension to her ideal, one evident in her life writing, that over time emerged clearly and became increasingly important to her self-conception: She wanted to be friendly with students, to avoid embarrassing them as she had been embarrassed as as student, to create a "nonthreatening environment," and to have a "personal relationship" with them. Clearly, this is what she wanted from her own teachers for herself but did not receive and what she hoped to give to students. She feared being singled out for attention by teachers, and she wanted to be cared for. Making emotional "connections" is how she expressed these values; and her metaphor expanded as a result and became increasingly complex.

Practice teaching shocked Mary and shattered her dream, at least for a time. Teaching, she discovered, was more than a matter of making content lively in order to assist students to connect with it, and of caring. Like many beginning teachers, she found the demands of managing large groups of students distressing and struggled with being in charge. Mary had never been in a position of authority before, and it frightened her. The context of teaching seemed hostile.

What Mary discovered was that teachers' concepts of themselves as teachers bring with them definitions of "other," of the students and parent roles in education, that may or may not be reasonable or fitting. She noted that the students wanted to make emotional connections with her, to "know things about me"; but she discovered that too few wanted to cross the bridge and embrace Spanish, and she did not want or know how to compel the crossing. To her dismay, caring about the students did not produce respect or engagement, as she had assumed and hoped it would. In response, she fell back on familiar and unpleasant ways of interacting with students, and she was "strict," an "authoritarian." She did so because this is what she believed the situation demanded, and what the students expected.

Young people are a powerful force in the classroom, and the most significant source of change in thinking about self as teacher. This is so because it is generally to them that beginning teachers look for self-confirmation. Just as teachers seek to influence pupil behavior, pupils influence and shape a teacher's behavior as roles and relationships are negotiated unknowingly. As noted in the introduction, the student teacher's position in this negotiation is complicated and, in some respects, weakened because the classroom into which they enter is not their own. For Mary, as for the other beginning teachers, the classroom environment was ordered by the cooperating teacher to reflect her self-definition; roles had already been negotiated and patterns of interaction set. Thus, Mary was not necessarily engaging in a foolish flight of fantasy when she longed for her own classroom unencumbered by the presence of her cooperating teacher. Perhaps she was right: A change in contexts might enable her to better realize her metaphor. Experienced teachers sometimes comment on how important a change in context has been to their own development. As we have said, some contexts are more hospitable to some metaphors than are others.

Terry gives us a glimpse into a common problem faced by beginning teachers as they negotiate a role. As Terry worked with the students, the importance of content dropped, while she placed increasing value on establishing caring relationships with the students. For some beginning teachers, particularly those who think of themselves as more like the young people they teach than like teachers or those who embrace one or another nurturing metaphor (like "parent" or "mother"), the relationship may take on unexpected dimensions. Teacher and pupil become too close, too emotionally attached. Terry encountered this problem as she found herself trying on a parent role with the students. To be a parent places students in the role of children; and children rightfully demand and usually get a great deal from parents. Children-students expect intimacy, and teachers who set up this expectation and respond to it are likely, just as Terry feared, to worry or even dream about their students and their problems. Terry recognized some of the limitations (some arising because of large class size) of this way of relating to students and yet still found some elements of it compelling.

Other aspects of Terry's struggle to find a metaphor are enlightening. It is with respect to establishing the desired relationship with young people that she thinks about teaching skills. Implicitly she knows that teaching is a relationship. Knowing this, however, only frames the problem in a useful way; it does not solve it. In fact, as she reflects on her relationship, the role of teacher becomes increasingly complex, which we take to be a healthy and positive development, but the problem is to create a learning environment consistent with her aims. Naivete diminishes. As an artisan or master, she knows that some students will not accept the role of apprentice that she seeks to impose upon them.

Comfortable with this self-understanding, and believing that the student role it brings is a desirable one, near the end of practice teaching she is actively engaged in developing skills and identifying resources that will enable her to establish the relationship she desires with the students. Her aim is to adjust the situation to make it more fitting to her conception of teaching, and not to comply as Mary did. These two responses represent very different patterns of role negotiation, with very different educational consequences for young people and for their two teachers.

Like Mary, Martha struggled to be an authority in the classroom. To address her fears, she appealed to the authority of content area expertise. Martha was a chemist, and she played the part very well, white lab coat and all. Her lessons were carefully planned and executed. Student performance went up, somewhat. But ironically, the longer Martha taught the less she enjoyed the role, yet she felt unable to alter it. What bothered her most was that she did not feel, using Mary's language, "connected" to the students. She felt they did not care about her, although she cared about them. "I want the kids to like me, most of them don't. . . . They are kind of resentful and resent how much they have to work." When asked: "How does it make you feel to have the kids not like you?" she replied, "At first it was hard. Now it doesn't bother me so much. I'm a little more used to it. It is not so much that they dislike me, they have no opinion of me as a person, I'm just a teacher." Martha had not anticipated how emotionally demanding teaching can be, nor had she considered her own emotional needs as a teacher and how they might be fulfilled.

Each of the three teachers discovered limitations of various kinds in their teaching ideals and in the contexts within which they student taught. They addressed these limitations differently. Mary set aside her metaphor, believing there was no alternative, and looked forward to the time when she would have her own classroom and feel ownership. She "strategically complied" with the demands of the context. Terry engaged in an ongoing exploration of herself in the classroom, and was sufficiently skilled as a teacher and forceful as a person to adjust the context along the way. Martha settled on a role early and stuck to it even when it became increasingly unpleasant to do so. For Martha, being a chemist was fundamental to her conception of herself not only as a teacher but as a person; it represented a "root" metaphor, connected closely to a cluster of values and beliefs central to her core sense of self and not merely an institutionally valued role. It is little wonder this self-understanding proved resistant to change; she valued it and the context supported it, yet she was miserable. The identification and analysis of metaphors is not likely to result in the change of such foundational conceptions of self, but revealing them may assist beginning teachers in their quest to form more hospitable contexts within which to work.

For each of the beginning teachers increased experience with students and reflection on their metaphors made the role of teacher increasingly complex. Having to confront themselves, each became more sophisticated in their thinking about teaching and learning and about their professional development.

## EXTENDING THE CONVERSATION

Two lines of research are of particular importance to our use of metaphor analysis. The first centers on the place of images in learning and problem-solving and the second on narratives, as suggested in chapter two. Calderhead and Robson (1991) nicely capture the general view underpinning much of the work on images.

> Images have been found to fulfill an important role in chess playing, medical diagnosis, and certain types of problem solving. In order to solve certain problems, it is suggested one has to develop a mental model or image. . . . Generalizing to a teaching situation, one might expect teachers in various problem-solving aspects of their work . . . to draw upon images of lessons, incidents or children to help them interpret and solve teaching problems. In fact, being able to recall images, and to adapt and manipulate these images in reflecting about action in a particular context is possibly an important aspect of the task of teaching. . . . Images, whether representations or reconstructions, provide us with an indicator of teachers' knowledge and enable us to examine the knowledge growth attributable to different training experiences and the relationship between knowledge and observed practice. (p. 3)

These images—rich or poor, elaborated or sparse, vivid or vague—operate as "implicit theories" (Clark, 1988); they represent the "subconscious assumptions on which practice is based" (Johnston, 1992, p. 125). Moreover, they "are not usually consciously articulated without some assistance" (Johnston, 1991, p. 125). They need to be made explicit, and analyzing metaphors helps make them explicit. To articulate images is to tell a story, a self-narrative of the sort told when writing a life (see chapter two; Witherell, 1991). To tell a story is to create a coherence of several meanings, perhaps to impose a pattern (Olney, 1972, p. 326), that allows consistency of interpretation and action. The story, a "myth of self" (Rhodenbaugh, 1992, p. 398), serves as an ideal type, something we long for. Elbaz (1983) noted in her study that this is just how images operate for teachers; they invite, rather than compel, conformity.

Research on the place of story telling in teacher socialization and knowledge development represents a second line of supportive research (Clandinin & Connelly, 2000). By moving to narrative, we have shifted from vision to voice. At first blush this would seem to be a problem until it is realized that we "see" through language; and language creates the world in its own image. Put differently, we see through our metaphors; images are metaphorically embedded (Collins & Green, 1990) and embodied experientially (Lakoff & Johnson, 1980).

As we have suggested, considering metaphors is a helpful means for thinking about self-as-teacher, and it builds upon and extends the value of life writing to self-discovery discussed in the previous chapter. The metaphors we use to make sense of our experience and of who we are as teachers have a profound effect on practice. Classroom management is one of the most serious concerns of beginning teachers. The way in which classrooms are organized represents a teacher's conception of self and of others. Often management problems are understood by teacher education students and teacher educators embedded in a training tradition as primarily a problem of lacking the skills needed to control a classroom. Skills are important to be sure, but there is another, perhaps more fundamental source of difficulty: uncertainty about self, misunderstanding of other, as Martha's struggle suggests. Consider use of the word "control" as the basis for thinking about management. Then think about the personal and instructional implications of thinking about teaching as "management" and as a basis for describing teacher/pupil relationships. Both of these metaphors are grounded in a more foundational metaphor for schooling, school as factory (see Bullough, 1988, Ch. 10). What sources of satisfaction do these metaphors provide teachers and what are their implications for students who soon will be voting citizens in a democracy that is increasingly uncertain of itself? We ask: What are the metaphoric alternatives to this way of thinking that open up and expand educational opportunities for young people? Remember, to teach is to teach oneself, the medium is the message, and the message is who you are. Are you a manager? Are you a policewoman? Or are you something else?

The language we use not only names our experience; it also defines and frames educational issues and problems and how they are understood and addressed. The world is simultaneously opened up and closed in by our language. Labels are used easily as though they offer explanations of student behavior; rather than being seen as metaphors, labels become real: A young person *is* her disabilities ("Attention Deficit Disorder"), *is* his misbehavior ("troublemaker"), *is* his group affiliation ("Gang member"; "Jock"; "burnout") and *is* her track ("gifted" or "vocation bound"). As we have said, the implications of the language you use to make sense of teaching are far reaching not only for the pupils who sit in your classroom but also for your own development and sense of well-being as a teacher. What metaphors dominate your discourse about teaching, learning, and yourself as teacher? Do you believe what you say? Or have you been seduced into a way of thinking that doesn't represent who you think you are and what you value? If so, what possible actions can you take to loosen the hold of these metaphors on your thinking?

# Methodologies for Exploring School Context

## ✦ 4 ✦

# Institutional Study

***

## INTRODUCTION

The school context influences what curriculum is implemented, what relations are established between and among teachers and students, and even the role teachers play in local decision-making. Take tracking, for example. It makes a great deal of difference to your role and relationships with students if you join a faculty that is committed to ability grouping or one committed to discovering ways of working effectively with heterogeneous groups. And yet, despite the importance of context in shaping the quality of classroom life, teacher preparation programs typically look away from the school as a unit of inquiry and instead focus almost exclusively on what happens within the classroom. Conducting institutional studies is a way to open up these contexts and raise a number of critical issues about them and their influence on your teaching and development.

The purpose of studying schools is not to prepare teachers to fit easily into school contexts, an aim that still reflects training assumptions. Rather, the aim is to identify questions and a point of departure for inquiry that will enable you to shape the structures and policies that help form the teacher role. Undoubtedly, you will work in a school context that differs from your current student teaching placement. This does not mean, however, that the knowledge gained in one context has no import for another school context. Not only are there a number of commonalities between schools, but even when contexts radically differ, the knowledge gained about one context can be compared and contrasted with the situation in another. Making comparisons reveals constraints that should be worked on and the "wiggle room" to make desired changes.

It is important to note, at this point, that while context influences how you approach teaching, it does not determine teaching practice. Teachers act on and shape the school context, just as the context influences those who teach. Thus, institutional studies consider not only organizational structures, such as the formal curriculum or the administrative hierarchy, but also the way individuals and groups have shaped the context. To understand this interaction, school structures should be seen in relation to teacher actions and the influence of school culture.

## WRITING

There are three phases in writing an institutional study. Phase One involves problem formation and data gathering; Phase 2, school description, and Phase 3 making interpretations and identifying themes. A description of these phases follows.

### PHASE ONE

*Problem formation and data gathering.* In the first phase of writing an institutional study, you will be asked to conduct informal observations and interviews and review school policies in a general way to see how this information might shape a problem or issue of interest to you. Again, it is important to note that the focus is on context even though relations, roles, and situations will be put into the mix. For example, after doing your informal observations you might find that a central issue concerns the English as a Second Language (ESL) program. Based on this focus, you would try to account for how the institutional context (e.g., administrative structures, class size, selection process, parent attitudes, and even the qualifications of teachers) shapes the nature of this program and ultimately the way teachers interact with ESL students. This focus for an institutional study should produce an understanding of how "structures," attitudes, and relations shape teaching.

Once a problem is identified, you should begin collecting data that address the identified problem. Try to work in teams. Those of you teaching in the same school, for example, can divide up the work. Some of you could do observations while others interview school faculty, for instance.

If interviews are used to collect data, ask leading questions. In addition, confidentiality is essential as is gaining permission from those involved in the study.

## PHASE TWO

*School description.* This phase involves using the data collected to describe the school. If, for example, your observations focus on the types of interactions found in a remedial class as compared to an honors class (i.e., the school tracking system) observation notes could be used to make comparisons of teacher roles, student expectations, and teacher-student relationships in the two settings. The purpose of the descriptive phase is to put into words what you see in the classroom. In doing so, avoid trying to account for all aspects of the school.

Once a draft of the description is written, it should be shared with other beginning teachers. Sharing will help you identify areas that are unclear or perhaps overly judgmental and help you identify themes underlying your description.

## PHASE THREE

*Identifying themes and making interpretations.* The transition from description to a thematic organization signals the third, or interpretive, phase. Themes are reoccurring patterns in the data. For example, if the data indicate that teachers interact more with boys or with girls across classrooms at a particular school, then the issue of gender and teaching may become a theme around which the data are organized. Once identified, the themes are used to locate readings that speak to the issues you have raised. An example may be helpful at this point. If you find that a key theme in the school studied is the influence of tracking on student relationships and learning, then you need to search out readings that focus on this issue. The readings are intended to help you develop an argument, and to see how your interpretations compare with others'. The readings make it possible to start a dialogue between yourself and others who have produced knowledge about teaching. By doing so, you are linking private and public theories. Be cautious: keep in mind that the knowledge you produce comes from a single study and does not provide a foundation for generalizations about schooling. Also, the readings should not be used to turn your institutional study into a typical academic research paper complete with footnotes and bibliography. Instead, the readings and your data should enter into a "conversation" where each informs and scrutinizes the other. Keeping a bit of uncertainty as you enter this "conversation" provides a foundation for a life long quest to become a student of teaching.

Once insights gained from the readings are integrated into your themes, the next step is to make sure that your interpretation considers why the particular school structures (e.g., the tracking sysytem), commitments, or patterns found at the school came into existence. Interpretations of this kind may require you look beyond the school context and consider the broader influence of educational policy. For example, if your focus is tracking, you may want to explore how tracking came into being and how it changed over time.

After a draft of your institutional study is completed we ask you again to share this study with others in your teacher education class. The purpose of sharing these drafts is to locate gaps that make the story difficult to follow, to clarify themes, and further articulate the perspective you bring to the institutional study. Your perspective should be apparent; there is no need to pretend to be neutral, because that is not possible. Instead, it is better to be up front with your views than to pretend yours is an "objective" account of the school. After receiving feedback, a final draft is written and shared with other preservice candidates, teacher educators, and practicing teachers.

Three abbreviated and significantly edited institutional studies follow.

### CENTRAL HEIGHTS HIGH: A CLASH OF CULTURES

The "baby boom" [following] World War II ... [produced] a growth-spurt that forced the [School] District to reconsider its educational [organization]. Home to the three "central city" high schools—the District was forced to open yet another high school to accommodate the record 42,000 plus students flooding the system. Central Heights High School was built as a direct result of this population spurt.

The area surrounding Central Heights is ... fairly [prosperous].... Central Heights has a reputation for being a predominately Caucasian, higher socioeconomic [level] school. It has remained the most highly populated of the district high schools, and has enjoyed the affluence from which it draws its main population. However, this changed. As Salt Lake City began to change and the city population began to decline, the need for South High School was called into question. Because the housing in this [area] is much older and oftentimes more run-down than housing elsewhere, it is often inhabited by young, childless couples, the elderly, and the poor. Young families tend to move to the suburbs ... to buy "starter homes" in what are often considered safer, more appealing areas. [In contrast,] a larger number of [poor] minorities moved into the South High area as the property value and rent decreased.... [These changes threw] ... the entire city into a controversy concerning the question of closing one of the oldest and most beloved schools in the state. Parents, teachers and students alike were concerned that [closing South] would "negatively impact" their [own] school and the education it was providing. On the other hand, the population surrounding South continued to decline.

There was also the concern that leaving [South] open would lend itself to segregation of sorts and that the public perception would be that the district could not stand up to the parents and faculty of the [two more affluent] schools many of whom were against the integration of [South High students]. Thus, administrators and the Board of Education felt they had no option but to close South High despite the protests and controversy that followed. South's population was dispersed throughout the remaining three high schools, and Central Heights High received a little over one-third of the students and became the ESL (English as a Second Language) magnet school, which draws students from throughout the district. Thus, [the] Central Heights minority population was drastically increased (the effects of this increase will be discussed later).

Central Heights High School currently houses approximately 2,100 students in grades 9–12. Of these students 76 percent are Caucasian, 12.5 percent are Hispanic, 1.7 percent are Pacific Islanders, 6.9 percent are Asian, .85 percent are African American, and .33 percent are considered "others." Given the diversity of the population at Central Heights, I was shocked by what seemed to be a nearly all-white student body in honors and "regular" English classes. In four class periods I counted only ten minority students, and when I asked the instructor where the minorities were he told me that "you will rarely find minorities in classes like these." I was afraid to ask why.

From what I had seen and observed in the classrooms and halls, I assumed that Central Heights had no more than 10–12 percent minority students. I was surprised when I discovered the actual figure was 24 percent, and I couldn't help but ask myself just where Central Heights "was keeping" its minorities. The "mystery" was solved, however, when I began observing remedial and basic skills courses, which were literally filled with minority students. It was almost as if Central Heights was attempting to somehow hide its minority students by keeping them in such courses, and the image that came to mind was that of the "bastard child" hidden in the attic of the Victorian mind set. Whether intentional or not, most of Central Heights minority students are in one way or another involved in the remedial, basic skills or ESL programs, and are being tracked into programs that may not necessarily suit their needs and best interests.

According to Jeannie Oakes in her book, *How Schools Structure Inequality* (1985), the decisions that are made concerning a student's placement are often reached "on the basis of counselors' assessment of their language, dress and behavior as well as their (perceived) academic potential." Thus, given the history of Central Heights as being a predominately white, middle-class school, it is natural to assume that the teachers, counselors and administrators make judgments about students and their potential according to what they perceive to be the norm: white, Anglo-Saxon, middle-American students. This also applies to the results of standardized tests, which are often race biased and fail to account for individual differences. Last year at Central Heights an incident occurred that rocked the foundations of this kind of thinking and forced the school to reexamine its policies and attitudes toward minority students. A Hispanic student approached his counselor for a scholarship application and was rejected because he did not, according to the counselor, "look like someone who could win a scholarship." The boy was one of the school's top students and ended up winning over $20,000 in scholarships! The counselor never did give the student the application he requested. When questioned about her actions by outraged parents and their attorney, the counselor repeated her justification, unaware of its prejudicial overtones and the impact of such generalizations. The counselor was eventually forced to resign.

[I observed] very little interaction between minority and majority students, and the various groups tend to stick together.... When asked about race relations at Central Heights High School, students, both minority and majority, came to the same conclusions: students tend to form "cliques" or groups which exclude others who do not fit the criteria for the group. For example, one student that I interviewed told me that he wasn't very sure about the rest of the student body because he "mostly stayed around the jocks—the guys who play sports." This was not unusual, and after I had interviewed several different students I got the impression that the student body at Central Heights is very fragmented and divided. It is almost as if there are several small schools within one, each possessing its own culture, values and goals. You can observe this phenomena in the halls between classes and at lunch—cheerleaders gathered with cheerleaders; "jocks" wrestling on the lawn; "brainers," or academic students, studying in the halls; and minority students gathered together in the parking lot. The district itself has noted this division among students and has attempted to involve students living outside the Central Heights community (mostly minority students transferred from the former boundaries of South High) by chartering "activity buses" to pick students up and take them to school activities such as games, dances and pep rallies. Sadly, the idea failed. Buses returned empty, and it became necessary to discontinue the program for lack of interest.

Whether it was lack of interest that killed the program or a feeling of disassociation, or not "belonging," on the part of the minority students, it is evident that Central Heights has a problem. My interviews revealed that minority students feel separated and distanced from the rest of the school, despite the efforts of the district, the school and the faculty. I cannot help but blame the tracking that is going on in the "attic" of Central Heights as the cause. It is impossible for students to gain respect and understanding for one another when they are being inadvertently separated and segregated. In order to truly mend race relations at Central Heights, administration and faculty must reexamine their curriculum, methods and attitudes to ensure that all of their students are getting the education they deserve. More emphasis should be placed upon integrated, multicultural education rather than upon tracking and structuring the inequalities that exist within the system. Jeannie Oakes contends that tracking systems more than often fail and, in the process, backfire on those who subscribe to them. Perhaps this is what has happened at Central Heights despite good intentions.

Some of the teachers at Central Heights think that there is nothing wrong with "the way things are currently done," [others] feel that there is much to be done at Central Heights. When asked what approaches to teaching style, curriculum and management need to be altered to suit the needs of all students [one teacher] agreed that there needs to be more cooperative learning approaches taken with students and that assessment needs to be more flexible and reflective of the different ways that students learn. Citing portfolios as an example [this teacher] explained that her Asian students hated this method, but her Hispanic students loved the approach and were very successful.

In general, the faculty at Central Heights feels that the integration of South High is an advantage rather than a disadvantage. Most view it as a source of "new blood" and liveliness of new ideas and attitudes that has made them more aware of how and what they teach. Most are optimistic about the future of Central Heights and are concerned with the issues plaguing the school. Increased training, community input, less tracking—all of these are ideas which were mentioned to me as suggestions for improving race relations and the overall situation at Central Heights.

It is now time for all to work together to bring Central Heights up to par by detracking the remedial and basic skills programs through more innovative, creative methods of teaching and assessment—methods that apply to everyone and ensure individual success and, in the process, ensure the success of their school. Also, all students need to feel that they belong at Central Heights, and in an attempt to remedy race-related problems, the school has formed a Diversity Committee this year composed of students and faculty who work together to address issues and concerns throughout the school. Together they decided on a school theme of "Strength Through Diversity," and administrators and faculty alike have taken it very seriously. The students, however, are a different matter. According to the results of my interviews and observations, even more needs to be done to incorporate the entire student body and insure individual recognition and success.

## ESL AT NORTHLAKE JUNIOR HIGH SCHOOL
## (TEAM PROJECT)

### Introduction

We started our institutional study with the intent to look at socioeconomic status and relate that to the broader topic of inclusion. However, as we did our initial research [phase one] we turned more toward studying English as a Second Language (ESL). As our research progressed we discovered the universal feeling that every student has the challenge of belonging to a community. As a result, the school community has the challenge of embracing an inclusive view of education where every student feels that they belong. Through our investigation of inclusion, we have discovered that the most important issue is that every student brings his or her own history into the classroom. It is the responsibility of educators to be aware of these histories and the differences they suggest about students.

### Background

Given that there were no ESL classes at Northlake prior to [two years ago], it is safe to say that some progress has been made at Northlake district. Previously, aides came to the school and tutored ESL students for one period a day. While the tutoring was one-on-one, Mrs M. (ESL instructor at Northlake) says that it had very limited benefits because the tutors did not know the native tongue of the ESL students.

School districts do indeed vary in their levels of support for ESL students. Some schools, however, fall below the minimum level. Dr. R., for example, a former principal at Northlake, notes that the Northlake district was challenged by the office of Civil Rights on the degree to which the district met the laws concerning ESL students.... The 1974 Lau vs. Nichols case established ESL students' rights to receive instruction accommodating for a lack of English with the aim of developing skills in English. The Justice Department's Office of Civil Rights stipulates that students with little or no English need to receive three periods of ESL instruction a day. Further, according to

Lau vs. Nichols these students should not be put in dead-end or low level classes as a solution.

There are not vast numbers of ESL students at Northlake. Perhaps 2 or 3 percent of the student body speak English as a second language. But as stated earlier we feel these students need to be in an inclusive environment. We wanted to find out what the environment was like at Northlake and decided to interview parents, teachers, and ESL students to consider this question.

**Our Data**

We begin with Melanie, a 46 year old college educated mother of three. She identifies herself as middle class. All of her children have attended Northlake and her youngest is currently enrolled there. Melanie is Anglo, and a native English speaker who is married to a Latino man. Melanie feels that inclusion is good:

> because you can see things from different perspectives. I know a lot about what the kids that are learning English are going through because my kids speak both English and Spanish. There is kind of a line between the two cultures [English speakers and Spanish speakers] and I guess two sets of standards. ESL kids that are fresh from another country don't know enough or how to fit in with the other kids so they miss a lot. I'm glad my kids have an American enculturation and speak English—that they are just "normal." There is a lot to be said for just being normal when you are a teenager.... It is good to see and experience diversity.... Being in the school, though, I don't notice much diversity. It seems like bilingual/ bicultural students are not very common.

Melanie felt there was not enough diversity at Northlake. She felt her children were limited by not being exposed to other minority cultures. Her daughter, Claire, agreed with this frustration. She felt she didn't have any peers who were like her and she felt isolated. However, Melanie also felt that students of this age want to conform and are likely to hide their cultural differences. Melanie's views were similar to other parents we interviewed who valued diversity, and wanted more diversity but felt that the "school environment reflected the community environment," which was middle class and White.

Melanie's positive view of speaking both English and Spanish contrasts in some ways with Nikki, a popular student who is active in sports, and comes from a rather poor family. To begin the interview, Nikki notes that she lives with her mom—"my parents are divorced."

> I guess that I would say that I'm Mexican 'cause my mom's from Mexico, but luckily for me I don't look Mexican. I do speak Spanish because my mom speaks it, but I don't like to talk to the other kids in it [Spanish]. . . . I think when people hear you speak Spanish they think you are dumb or something. There are not many kids in the school like me. Like me, I mean Mexican. Since my friends don't think I am Mexican, I don't hand around with Mexican kids.

Nikki's real name is Enriqua, but she uses Nikki because it sounds more American. It is disturbing to see a person go so much out of her way to hide their ethnic identity. It is interesting to hypothesize if Nikki would be so concerned to appear white if the larger population at the school were from her same background. Unlike Nikki, there are other ESL students who cling to their native language and their culture. They do not want to leave the ESL program and are passive in non-ESL classes.

The teachers, for the most part, would like to see more school diversity but felt that the school was divided within, between the honors classes and the other school classes. As Ms. A., an 8th and 9th grade English teacher, put it:

> We have a great deal of socio-economic diversity [at North-lake]—our boundaries take in everything from the golf course to the trailer park across the freeway. If you look at the addresses of most of the kids in the honors classes you will find they live on the hill [the wealthier area]. I have to tell you that I have taught here for about 9 years and it took 5 years before I had my first African-American student.

By reviewing all the interviews, we felt that one important issue related to putting ESL students into a tracked group. These students have individual needs that are not recognized when they are labeled by a program such as ESL. By generalizing the needs of students, in many ways they are being robbed of a fair education. As Nieto (1996) points out:

> The stripping away of the students' native language and culture is usually done for what teachers and schools believe are good reasons. Schools often make a direct link between students' English assimilation and their economic and social mobility ... The influence of this devaluation of native language in the school cannot be dismissed. (p.187)

In Northlake there seems to be a problem with the school trying to implement an ESL program they are unable to handle. Some explanations as to why the ESL program is having problems are: the program is fairly new, the curriculum may need refinement, the non-ESL teachers are not being trained or told how best to help ESL students learn in the classroom, there is a prejudice in terms of acknowledging a proficiency of a foreign language for ESL students, there are not enough ESL teachers. All of these issues need to be addressed if Nikki is to feel it is okay to be Mexican, if Melanie is to feel that ESL kids can be accepted without conforming, and if Ms. A. is to feel that tracks, such as honors, are not to be associated with where one lives.

## GOOD TEACHING AT HILLVIEW HIGH
## (TEAM PROJECT)

The purpose of this institutional study is to examine and critique the attitudes that teachers and students at Hillview High concerning what is good teaching. In examining this topic we pay particular attention to the way school structures and the curriculum influence how teachers teach.

### Background

Hillview High was built in 1964 serving students in grades 10–12. Current enrollment at Hillview is nearing 2000 students, with 99 percent of these students being Caucasian. The socio-economic status of the students is quite high with the median income about $35,000 a year. Hillview has a strong academic focus. Standardized tests run above the state and national average with an Advanced Placement test rate success of 71 percent. The mission of Hillview is to "provide a safe learning environment and to educate all students as they prepare for a productive life in a changing world."

## Data

To help determine what is viewed as good teaching at Hillview, 50 students and 7 teachers filled out a questionnaire that asked: Name three teachers at Hillview you believe are good. What are the characteristics that make these teachers good teachers? What are the characteristics of teachers who in your view are not as good? What advice would you give to novice teachers entering the field?

Nine teachers were consistently named in the questionnaires. Two of these teachers received on average twice the number of nominations as the other seven. One of the common responses was that good teachers cared about students. When talking about the best teachers, most of the students mentioned that these teachers were nice, flexible and understanding and, most importantly, were interested in their lives outside of school. They were able to see things through a high school student's eyes. Unfortunately, previous research suggests that the majority of students do not feel that teachers are caring. As Nodding (1992) writes, it is not surprising that the single greatest complaint of students in these schools is that teachers and administrators don't care. For our purposes it is clear that students at Hillview want teachers to care and feel that those who do are the good teachers.

A second important and common response from the students was that good teachers were interesting, engaging, had a sense of humor, and made the class or subject fun. This result is not surprising. Everyone likes to enjoy the activities that they engage in. Research (Pollak and Freda, 1997) suggests that humor is a way to build rapport and further student interest. Our findings are also consistent with previous studies (McIntosh, 1991) which found that students wanted teachers to be interesting and make the class fun. In hindsight, we should have included additional questions or probed for more detailed information in our study. We want to know, for example, what makes a classroom fun and what is the relation between a sense a humor and the personality of the teachers. As we enter the teaching profession we will investigate these questions informally a bit further.

On the other side of the discussion we also found that students felt teachers who were not that good showed little passion for their subject or content area. They felt limited by teachers who controlled behavior in such narrow ways that laughter never occurred. Students also felt that teachers who were "less good" gave students information, but didn't spend any time informing them why the information was important. The dominant response was that "less good" teachers were boring; students wanted to be excited and enjoy what they were doing and these less good teachers could not engage students in this way.

Turning to teachers, their thoughts about good teaching were more diverse than the students. Some themes that did emerge were the fact that good teachers cared about students, were well prepared and organized, and liked to teach. It was very interesting to see that both teachers and students felt that good teachers were caring. However, what is still not clear to us at this point is what this caring relationship looks like or consists of. In what ways do students perceive that teachers care about them? And perhaps most importantly, what impact does caring have on learning? As teachers we will have to decide what role caring should play in our classrooms and in what ways we will express to our students that we do in fact care about them.

The second goal of the project was to identify and examine the effect that school structures had on teachers' ability to teach at Hillview. Did these factors constrain or enhance their ability to teach? And how do we, as novice teachers, feel these factors will influence our teaching methods?

One of the commonly mentioned structures that hinder teaching, according to teachers at Hillview, was lack of time. Almost every teacher we talked to mentioned that between teaching, paperwork, grading, extracurricular activities, etc., they found they had little time to plan more interesting and engaging activities. They also felt they couldn't cover as much material, or in as much depth as they would like. They could easily spend 12–15 hours a day working on school matters including grading and curriculum work if they were not careful. Overall, teachers expressed disappointment that they couldn't do more for students and still maintain relationships outside of school. It is unclear how to remedy this situation. The two most obvious choices are to lengthen the day or the school year. Both recommendations have limitations but we feel that lengthening the school year might provide more time, if the State didn't require more to be covered and would not have an adverse affect on students or teachers. However, this increase in time would require higher salaries and therefore greater funding from the State. It should be noted that many of the teachers interviewed were those rated as good by students at Hillview.

Another aspect of Hillview that teachers felt influenced their teaching was parent involvement. The administration at Hillview reports a strong degree of parent involvement and support for school policies. The Parent Teacher School Association sponsors lunch meetings each month between administration and parents to "enhance communication, receive parental insights, and to respond to questions and concerns." Further, any parent can access their student's records at any time through the Internet. It is important to note, however, that this type of support requires a high S.E.S. community. The Hillview community had the monetary resources but other communities would not have the money needed to access the Internet. Another "structure" that may facilitate parents' involvement in their children's education is that if a student misses a day of school, a phone call is automatically made that night to the parents. If kids aren't in school they cannot learn. Therefore, the school wants to find out quickly if there is a reason why the child missed school. As a teacher, this high degree of parental involvement is likely to make our jobs easier by enabling us to focus on teaching instead of outside issues. Parents can find out how their child is doing and the administration solicits help. This leads to better communication and fewer headaches for teachers.

In conclusion, teachers and students thought good teachers care about them, are passionate about their work, make learning a fun, engaging activity, and are organized and well prepared. The major structure that limited teachers was the lack of time. The major factor that helped their teaching was parental support. We will continue to think about what these good teaching characteristics mean in practice, at the same time we try to figure out the issue of time and how to gain parental support.

## CONSIDERATIONS

To better understand the limits and strengths of institutional studies, it is helpful to revisit the abbreviated examples presented in the proceeding section. One of the obvious strengths of the institutional studies is that they brought to the fore issues that went beyond the bounds of an individual classroom. The Central Heights and Northlake studies focused on how students of color are either included or marginalized within the school community. The Hillview study, on the other hand, went beyond a classroom focus by looking at what is considered to be good teaching in this high school and considered structures that shape teaching. These institutional studies suggest the importance of looking at issues of inclusion and exclusion, the school community, tracking, parental involvement, and even the lack of time teachers have to prepare and teach. If teachers are to continue to develop and improve the quality of education offered to all students, their gaze must include not only the classroom but also the larger institutional context that shapes so many of their decisions and practices. These novice teachers identified fundamentally important issues that can and should be revisited as they continue to develop as teachers.

It is important to note that these institutional studies didn't simply focus on the limitations of schools. While a focus on what can't be done serves the function of showing the significant bounds within which teachers work, if taken to the extreme this focus paints a distorted picture that leads teachers away from teaching. In contrast to a focus on what can't be done, the three institutional studies were able to point to instances of "wiggle room," spaces where teachers could make a difference in the nature of the education offered to students.

The institutional study done at Central Heights, for example, noted the existence of a Diversity Committee that addressed the marginalization of students of color; many of the teachers at Northlake, on the other hand, found value in student diversity; and the Hillview study showed that parent involvement can support and encourage "good teaching." In each study, the authors didn't limit their analysis to fitting into the current school context, nor did they lock themselves into following the school's approach to change. Instead, they pointed to constraints, such as tracking, lack of diversity, and limited time to teach, while also identifying possibilities for the future, including detracking and the expansion of the school year to allow for more teaching time. In making these arguments, the authors of these studies moved easily from their data to the research literature. The views of these novice teachers were heard, while they also considered the long history of academic research that addressed similar issues to those identified in the institutional studies.

With these strengths in mind, the studies described also point to areas that need more thought and examination. In all the studies there seemed to be more emphasis placed on interviews, or the identification of events, than observations. This is not surprising. Observations tend to be very time consuming and often are so wide ranging that themes do not immediately jump out. Nevertheless, without observations, the foundation for the institutional studies, the descriptive account, often lacks the detail and specificity needed to set the stage for the analysis and arguments that follow.

Another limitation of these institutional studies is that they informed the reader what teachers or students felt, but only occasionally used their words to make the case. Without the exact quotes from teachers, it is more difficult for the reader to understand the interpretative claims (Phases Two and Three) made by the authors of these studies. Furthermore, while these institutional studies did provide a brief glance into why particular structures came into existence (the Central Heights study probably made the best attempt in this regard), too often the structures identified simply seemed to appear at the school. To address this limitation, it may be helpful to spend some time on the historical factors that have influenced what you see when you look at the institution of schooling. For example, in the Northlake school it would be very important to know how the ESL program came

into existence. Was there teacher resistance? Did the district mandate such a program? Was the principal at the time of the implementation of the program enthused and knowledgeable about the program? These questions might provide helpful insights into why particular structures came into existence. Finally, each study struggled with the idea of presenting an authoritative voice while also acknowledging that the knowledge produced comes from a single case study. The final institutional study, on "good teaching," presented a possible way to address this dilemma. In this study the authors identified what more they could have done (e.g., the lack of investigation of what caring meant in practice) in doing their institutional study. By doing so, they acknowledged the limits of their methodology while also providing a good deal of support for their claims about "good teaching." A degree of uncertainty should enter into your writing to allow for future questions and inquiry. When this is the case the institutional study becomes a continuous process of examination and knowledge production.

## EXTENDING THE CONVERSATION

The idea for institutional studies is rooted in certain segments of the sociological tradition. Before American sociology gained some notoriety, sociology was dominated by surveys and quantitative methods (Metz, 2000). With the emergence of the University of Chicago as a major player in the sociological field in the 1920s, however, sociology took a turn toward qualitative methods and an understanding of the way individuals make sense of a situation and the way this "sense" is colored by the context in which they live and/or work. This move by sociologists focused attention on context and the way an individual's understanding is highly interpretive and socially shaped. Institutional studies, as we conceive of them, are based on many of the same principles—there is a constant moving back and forth between educational participants' understanding of issues and how this understanding is shaped by both school structures and the culture of schooling. In the institutional study on "good teaching," for example, the focus was on both how educational actors interpreted good teaching and the institutional factors, such as "time" and parental involvement, that helped shape that understanding. While we want to be very clear that the examples presented previously do not represent the systematic rigor of the work coming out of the Chicago School of Sociology, they do reflect many of the same assumptions. Specifically, both approaches to inquiry avoid viewing schools as formal institutions, but rather as small communities where school structures (e.g., tracking) and culture (e.g., school culture) interact on a continuous basis (Waller, 1932). By looking at schools in this way, these approaches to inquiry are able to "open the black box" of schooling and peer inside to better understand how context and educational actors, help form what we eventually see as schooling.

Understanding the roots of institutional studies is one way to extend the conversation on this methodology. Another way is to look closely at the issues raised by the studies presented. In the section that follows we focus on two issues raised by the institutional studies that we find provocative and deserving of careful attention.

*Integration and Segregation*

All the institutional studies in one way or another raised issues about integration and segregation of students. On the surface, this issue appears easily resolved— we want more integrated schools where differences in race, class, gender, sexual orientation, etc. do not keep these student groups apart. The author of the Central Heights study, for example, argues for an integrative approach to schooling and recommends a form of detracking that would allow greater connections across student differences, specifically differences in race. While there are many strong arguments for integration, not the least of which is that separation of student groups often leads to the reinforcement of inequalities between those groups (Orfield, 1996; Kozol, 1991), there is clearly another side to this issue.

bell hooks, a prominent black feminist writer, in the introduction to her book *Teaching to Transgress* (1994), recalls her early experiences in a Southern segregated school. Her recollection is that having a segregated school allowed her teachers to cover required subject matter and teach African-American students about how prejudice toward African-American culture limited opportunities for this cultural group and what might be done to challenge these limitations. This focus was only possible, in her view, because the student population was entirely African-American. When hooks transferred to an integrated school, the "political" aspect of her education disappeared, and the emphasis was solely on subject matter mastery. According to hooks something was lost when she went to an integrated school.

Questions about integration have also been raised in discussions about the importance of coeducational schools. While coeducational schools are clearly the norm, several influential researchers (Tyack and Hansot, 1990; Lasser, 1987) have consistently argued that single gender schools hold tremendous advantages for young female students. Their argument is that in coeducational schools the normative assumptions about boys and girls place girls and young women in a position of trying to achieve a positive identity on "male" terms. Coeducational schools, in their view, encourage girls and young women to feel good about themselves by pleasing boys and young men. In contrast, single gender schools provide girls and young women space to think about themselves outside of a "male framework." Further, these authors suggest that in single gender schools girls are less likely to be subject to the verbal and physical violence that men often use to gain advantages over women.

Our purpose in bringing up the other side of the integration issue is not to convince you one way or the other, but rather to encourage you to consider how you will deal with differences between groups of students. Are there times when it might be appropriate to segregate groups of students in your class, or is an integration approach always the way to go? Under what circumstances would you argue for a separation? And if you did argue for segregation, how would you assess the results of this teaching approach? As you reflect on your own institutional studies, considering these questions might encourage future institutional study projects and help you further develop your educational positions on this important issue.

*Tracking*

Each of the institutional studies also touches on student tracking. In some ways tracking brings us back to the issue of segregation and integration. Tracking not only keeps groups apart, but intentionally separates them based on a consideration of the students' abilities, talents, and skills. As is true of integration and segregation, examining tracking may be more complex than it first appears. The Central Heights study, for example, suggested that tracking kept minority students "hidden" in the basement; the Northlake study, on the other hand, argued that tracking, in the form of an ESL program; kept second language students separated from the majority of Anglo students and acted to limit their educational opportunities. These arguments about tracking are powerful, and there is little doubt that tracking can lead to situations where particular groups of students get a dummied down curriculum which limits educational opportunities. However, there is another side to the tracking story. One scholar taking up that other side is Nell Noddings (1992). Noddings passionately argues that all students should not be expected to participate in the standard liberal arts curriculum (i.e., math, science, social studies, and language arts). If a student wants to concentrate in science, and be "tracked" in such a way where science is the primary emphasis of the curriculum than that would be acceptable for Noddings. Conversely, if a student's focus is on auto shop, she sees no reason why s/he should not be tracked according to this interest. Tom Loveless (1999) also supports tracking, although his argument is based less on acknowledging the importance of interest in setting the "track" the student enters. He suggests that tracking simply doesn't have the negative implications asserted by popular theorists such as Jennie Oaks (1985).

Several important questions related to this issue come to mind: What is the criteria used to track students? Given a certain criterion such as "intelligence," is the test used to measure this criterion accurate? If standardized tests are used, for example, are you going to accept these results? If so why, and if not, why not? If teacher recommendations are to be used, or even student interest, are these helpful ways to track students, and what are the limitations of these approaches? Are the student tracks rigid or flexible—can students move in and out or is the "line" between tracks a solid one? Finally, what does the approach to tracking hope to accomplish, and how could you collect data to see what consequences tracking has for students? Considering these questions now, before the intensity of teaching makes such consideration difficult, is likely to further your ability to act on and remake educational institutions in a way you find to be justifiable.

## ✳ 5 ✳

# Shadow Study

---

## INTRODUCTION

Shadow Studies enable you to better understand how students construe classroom and school life, how they have internalized, reshaped, or rejected institutional norms. The degree to which students have internalized, or failed to internalize, institutional norms has a profound influence on what they learn in school and on what teachers are able to do with their own autonomy, their "wiggle room." Without question, students are powerful socializing agents, whose expectations of teachers and classroom behavior constrain and shape teacher thought and action (see Bullough, Knowles, & Crow, 1992). As teachers struggle to find a place within the classroom and school, they do so in relationship to their pupils and the roles they have forged. Knowledge, then, of how students make sense of their experience in school is crucially important to successful teacher role negotiation, particularly since the quality of the relationship with students and student performance form the backdrop against which teachers, especially beginning teachers, judge their performance in the classroom.

Beginning teachers often generalize from their own experience as pupils to others' learning experience. While it is inevitable that when making sense of the behavior of young people you will draw on your own past experience as a student and perhaps as a parent, this experience needs to be recognized for what it is: partial and limited. But there is no substitute for spending time and talking with young people, particularly when their backgrounds differ significantly from your own, as they likely will.

## WRITING

The following are the guidelines we give to our students on how to conduct a Shadow Study.

> The purpose of the Shadow Study is to begin to understand how students experience and make sense of their lifes in schools. With the help of your cooperating teacher, identify a student and obtain permission to follow him/her for an entire school day. Pick a student to "shadow" whom you find interesting, and who comes from a background different from your own. Make certain he/she understands what you are doing and why. Take notes that will help you recall significant events or comments. Do your best to get to know the student and to understand his or her feelings about school and about teachers. There is much that you might attend to: How does the student spend his/her time? What seems most important to the student during the day? What topics and issues demand attention? What events are found upsetting or irritating? What kind and quality of relationship does he/she have with other students and with teachers? How important are teachers to students? Does the student have any power? Whatever focus you take, conclude your paper by describing what, in your view, school is like for the student—what kind of experience is school?—and what part teachers play in shaping that experience.

The Shadow Studies are discussed in class. It is during this discussion, and drawing on the life histories, that comparisons are made between experiences—beginning teacher and shadowed pupil—and attention given to the diversity of ways of making a life in schools. At this point a problem should be noted: A good many of our students have difficulty identifying a pupil to shadow. They feel uncomfortable and awkward; they are outsiders. One beginning teacher wrote: "I approached the study with mixed emotions. [One side of me] couldn't wait to get into the world of a high school student. [But] ... knowing I would be [with] high school kids and seeing an intimate part of their world caused me [to feel] uncomfortable. ... I felt out of place." The temptation is to shadow a little brother or sister or the child of a friend. Neither is acceptable. Being uncomfortable is to be expected, even hoped for. Nevertheless, it is not always possible to gain the permission of a student who is most challenging and interesting, and sometimes compromises must be made, as we will shortly see.

Three abbreviated and edited Shadow Studies follow. Veronica's study is the first. Veronica did not get to choose her student. Despite this, Veronica's study proved to be a source of rich insights into school life and how a young woman made that life tolerable. Tangi's is the second study. Jamal is an outgoing African-American student who showed Tangi a side of life within South High School that was enjoyable and quite different from her own experience in high school. Mick's is the third study. Mick chose a friend's son to "shadow" thinking the day would be comfortably spent. He was wrong.

## VERONICA'S STUDY

The student I shadowed is Janie C. Janie is a sophomore at South High. I met Janie through her seventh-period English teacher, who offered her seventh-period class extra credit points for participating in the Shadow Study. Two people from the class volunteered. I chose Janie mainly because [my cooperating teacher] indicated that she needed the extra credit to make up for some absences. [My cooperating teacher] characterized Janie as a "good kid" who seems to be enthusiastic about school and life in general; except when she is absent, she generally completes her assignments on time and doesn't cause problems in class. I first contacted Janie by phone and found her to be very personable and outgoing. She seemed to be at ease with me immediately. I explained the nature of my assignment, and we arranged to meet before school on the day of the Shadow Study. After several conversations with Janie and my observations at school the day of the Shadow Study, I decided that I would like the first part of this write-up to focus as much as possible on the student's perspective of school.

Consequently, in an effort to achieve accuracy and authenticity, Janie and I have collaborated on this portion of the write-up, and it is written from the point of view of the student.

### A Day at South High (Student's Perspective)

*Well, I'm here a little early because I have to meet this lady who's going to follow me around at school all day today. She goes to the university or something, and this is some kind of an assignment she has to do, kind of to get an idea of what life is like for a high school student, I guess. I don't really mind doing this with her; it might be kind of fun, and besides, I really need the extra credit in English. I'm supposed to meet her over by the [school mascot]. There she is. "Hi, I'm Janie. You must be Mrs. H. Well, my first class is drama. It's right here in the auditorium. Let's go in."*

*"Look at that. There's coke spilled all over the floor.... I wonder if they're going to turn the house lights on in here or if we're going to have class in the dark. Our regular teacher is pregnant and won't be back for at least at month or two, so we have a sub in this class. Yeah, the stage crew is always in here when we are. You get used to the noise after a while. Besides, everybody in this class just talks most of the time, anyway, especially since we have had this substitute teacher." She's reading something from a paper about a story or something we're supposed to do on Monday. That's the next time we have this class. How come she didn't say anything about this [assignment] before? I don't really understand [it]. I guess she wants us to retell a story. She's reading to us from some children's storybook, but I really cannot hear her too well (the stage crew does seem especially loud today); and with the lights off in here I definitely cannot see the pictures. Oh well, she said that was an example of the kind of story not to use, so I guess it doesn't matter if I couldn't hear it. I wonder what kind of story I can get. Okay, I get it: we're not supposed to read the story; we're supposed to retell it in our own words. I understand that part. But what are these criteria and activity sheets she keeps talking about? I wonder if I could transfer to stage crew? They seem to be having a lot more fun. Why does she keep reading these stories? They are really boring! Okay, we have the rest of the period—that's about 50 minutes—to work on our*

stories for the next time. The only problem is, I don't have a story to work on. "What, Ms. T. [the teacher]?" "No, we don't have a story yet. I guess I'll go to the library later and try to find one." Oh, everybody seems to be leaving. I didn't hear the bell ring. It's not supposed to ring for about five more minutes. I guess we can leave if we want to, but I better not, since I have this lady following me around today. We'll leave when the bell rings.

The next class is upstairs—third period—Life Skills (school days are divided into odd and even, with periods running 80 minutes each). We're going to meet in the classroom to watch Channel One and then go to the computer room. "Yeah, I [Mrs. H. (Veronica)] already know how to use the computer. I took word processing in the ninth grade." "What? Yeah, this should be pretty easy for me." Channel One is pretty boring today, as usual—more stuff on the presidential election. "Yeah, the class next door always comes in here for Channel One. They don't have a TV in there. There aren't enough seats for everyone, so we usually just stand around while it's on. Sure, it's hard to hear, but we don't really have to listen to it anyway, so it's no big deal." Now it's time for the announcements; oops—as usual, we cannot hear them. Well, Mrs. J. says we can just go on down to the computer room then. Oh, I forgot my assignment. Oh good, she says we can finish it today in computer. "Let's go to the computer room—it's this way." The computer teacher isn't there, and Mrs. J. doesn't know anything about WordPerfect. That's okay. I know how to work this. She said we should help each other. What are we supposed to be doing again? Oh, okay. Write something about technology and how it affects our lives. "How do you spell technology? Never mind, I'll use the Spell Checker." Oh, that lady who's with me, Mrs. H., knows WordPerfect. Mrs. J. asked her if she can help some of the other kids until the computer teacher gets here. Okay, I'm done. "Do you have a copy of the assignment that's due today?" Okay, this is pretty easy. I'll just fill this out and turn it in, and I can talk with Sharon and Tess until the bell rings.

"Okay, let's go. Next class is history—it's just down this hall and around the corner. I have to stop at my locker, but it's right on the way." Oh, here's Mr. P. He always yells "Quiet!" when he comes into the room, then he calls the roll and passes back our homework. He *seems to be acting nice today—probably because Mrs. H. is here. Those girls better be careful passing those notes, because if they get caught, he'll probably explode. Oh, I thought we were just going to watch the last part of the movie today, but I guess he's going to talk for a while first. Boy, I hate these notes he puts up on the overhead. His writing is hard to read, and he never leaves it up there long enough to copy it all down.* "What? No—I mean I don't know. I wasn't really listening. I was trying to copy down all the notes." *Now he's saying something about page 55 in the book:* "If you want to look at page 55 in the book." *I don't want to look at page 55; I just want to finish copying these notes and then watch the movie. This is actually a pretty good movie we've been watching—The Last Emperor. It's about some guy from Japan or China or something. Oh, there's the bell. I guess we'll see the last part of it next time. I have to hand in my extra credit notes before we leave.*

"Okay, we only get 30 minutes for lunch. No, I never go to the cafeteria. I usually just run over to the [convenience store] and buy something to eat. Want to come? Okay, let's go." *Well, we better be heading back—the bell's going to ring in about three minutes.* "Yeah, lunch goes by pretty fast; we don't have too much time to eat or anything."

"This class is a pretty good one. English isn't my favorite subject, but Mrs. B. usually makes it pretty interesting. We have been reading I Heard the Owl Call My Name. Have you read it? Yeah, it's pretty good." *Looks like we're going to start with free writing today. I'm glad we're going to talk about some ideas we can write on. I can never think of anything to write. Oh, yeah, that's a good idea. I can write about the two characters in Chapter One and why they have a hard time understanding each other. Okay, time's up. That wasn't so bad. I actually had enough things to write about for the whole ten minutes. We're going to have a test on the first seven chapters on Monday. Now we're working with a partner to make up some questions for the test, only the questions can only start with the words on the board. This is kind of hard.* "Mrs. B., what about 'Who is Jim?'" "No, 'who is' isn't on the board." "Well, I guess I can reword it to start with 'who did.'" *Let's see, who did Mark first meet when he arrived?* "Is this okay, Mrs. B.?" "We're done. Now we can work on this cross-word puzzle for the rest of the period. If I can get this all done now,*

*I won't have to do it at home. There—almost done. Oh, there's the bell.* "What? Oh, sure. No problem. Anytime. It was fun hanging around with you today. Nice meeting you, too. Bye."

## A DAY AT SOUTH (MY VIEW)

Janie corroborated that the "stream of consciousness" presentation above was fairly typical of most of her days in school.... I have to admit to some disappointment at what seemed to me to be the tedious and lackluster nature of Janie's day....

The experience Janie had in her first-period drama class was appalling to me. Drama is an elective, so presumably most of these kids are in this class because they are interested in the subject. However, the outrageous conditions under which the class was expected to be conducted (stage crew shouting, banging things around, turning the lights on and off) and the substitute teacher's apparent lack of preparation and engagement with the kids seemed to produce an overwhelming sense of apathy among the students. Most of them barely paid attention to her during the entire class period; those who did, like Janie, found a way to use the time somewhat productively but not to fulfill the assignment that was given them. It seems completely ridiculous to me that a teacher would give students 50 minutes of class time to complete an assignment when none of them had any advance notice to bring materials with them to do so. The assignment was to retell a story, but not one of the students had a story with them to work on. Several students asked if they could go to the library to find a story, but they were not allowed to leave. The teacher read three children's books to the class as examples of stories that would not be good candidates for retelling—there was no modeling of what a good retelling looks like. It is not surprising to me that none of the students worked on the assignment during the class period. I feel the time could have and probably should have been used for teacher-guided and structured practice; as it was, 50 minutes of potential instructional time was virtually wasted. One student was reading a book; Janie's group was practicing for an after school musical production; most of the students were just talking. The group nearest to me were discussing their favorite types of alcohol and mixers. *No one appeared to be working on the assignment,* although the teacher did eventually walk around the room and ask the students, "Do you have a story to do?" Each group apparently put her off with some vague remarks about working on it later, which she appeared to accept before moving on to the next group.

The next class was a little better. This class, "Life Skills," is a new class designed to teach students personal skills, thinking skills, technology literacy, career exploration, and communication skills. Today was apparently technology literacy day. Although the Channel One time was essentially [a waste], time in the computer room did seem to give some students who were heretofore "computer illiterate" at least a nodding acquaintance with WordPerfect. As mentioned above, however, the computer teacher's absence when the class arrived posed a problem for the regular teacher, who knew nothing about the WordPerfect program. Since I am fairly knowledgeable with WordPerfect, I was immediately drafted to help the students get started. If I had not been there, I assume those students not familiar with the program would simply have waited the 15 or 20 minutes it took for the computer teacher to arrive, or tried to figure it out on their own with help from one of their fellow students. At least these students were engaged in doing something, not just sitting, although most of them finished well before the end of the period and spent the rest of the time talking with one another.

Janie's next class, fifth-period history, was also an eye-opener for me. I guess I really have been out of high school too long, because I was somewhat stunned by the teacher's manner with students. He began the class by shouting at them and continued to treat them in a rude and condescending manner. I was even more surprised when Janie confided that she felt he was "being nice" today because I was there. My immediate thought was, "If this is nice, I'd hate to see him when he's being rude." After roll call, the teacher launched into a lecture on the history of civilization in China. During his lecture, he turned out the lights and posted some handwritten notes on the overhead projector. He moved up and down the aisles in the class-room while he lectured, but the attention of nearly every student seemed to be directed toward copying down the notes on the overhead. This behavior was reinforced by the teacher, who would pause at intermittent points in the lecture and demand, "Haven't you guys finished writing this stuff down yet? I'm ready to move on; you're going to have to learn to move faster." The content information being presented was really quite interesting, but the manner of presentation had me "zoning out." Following the lecture, the class watched a part of the film *The Last Emperor* until the end of the period. Perhaps some background information on the film had been given in a previous class period, although if it was, Janie couldn't remember much of it. None was given the day I was there.

After history, we had our frenetic lunch period. We barely had enough time to run across the street [to] buy a sandwich and drink, wolf it down, and run back to Janie's locker and then to her last class. It was, however, the most active part of our day. It seems a shame that some portion of the time that was wasted in this morning's classes couldn't somehow be added onto the lunch period to enable the students to take ten deep breaths before returning to class.

Janie's last class was the highlight of the day for me. I admit I am biased because English is my area of expertise, but I also sincerely felt that Mrs. B. made a genuine attempt to employ various activities to help students with different teaching styles to find a way to relate to the novel they were reading. She took the time to brainstorm with the class to make sure everyone had an idea before requiring them to complete a ten-minute free writing exercise. The students came up with some great ideas dealing with their reading, and I was shocked to realize that this was the first class all day in which I had observed any kind of meaningful class discussion. Most of the kids were writ-ing during the free-write time. The partner activity composing test questions also seemed to engage most of the students, and the teacher moved around the room a lot monitoring the groups, helping them with their questions, and trying very hard to engage reluctant participants. Since this was the last class period of the day, I think it would have been very easy for many of these students to give in to fatigue and eschew the class activities, but it appeared to me that most of the students were involved and interested. . . .

Based on experiences during this day, I have come to the conclusion that the teacher's role is crucial in shaping the student's experience. It seems to me a "bad" teacher can cause a student to have a bad day at school; it also seems to me that too many bad days in a row could kill any desire the student may have had to succeed in school. If I had to give the four teachers I observed a grade for the day, I would have to rank them as follows: first period—F, third period—C, fifth period—D, seventh period—A. I realize that allowances ought to be made for the fact that first period was taught by a substitute. It is entirely possible, and perhaps even probable, that the regular drama teacher is much more effective and dynamic. It is also possible that the four classes I attended on this day were not a representative sample of the teaching being done in the school; in fact, I sincerely hope that they were not. However, the mere fact that one student had to spend one day in a place supposedly dedicated to learning and growth with relatively little in the way of intellectual stimulation until the last class of the day seems to me to border on the tragic.

If my observations of Janie's day at school can be considered in any way typical, educators have a long way to go to fulfill the public trust and to provide students with the kind of nurturing and enriching environment to which I believe they are entitled.

## TANGI'S STUDY

For Jamal, school is, among other things, a large gathering of available and cute women. As we walked through the crowded halls at South High School, Jamal was waving, admiring, talking, and sighing at numerous girls. He explained to me after his first class (English) that we needed to make a run to his car for some Advil for M'Lisa, his old girlfriend—not to be confused with his new girlfriend, Meg. "See," he explained to me as we walked to his car, "I dated M'Lisa for about 10 months and then she made me mad and so I broke up with her, but now we might . . . you know?" "Get back together?" I said. "Yeah." Then I asked him, "Well, what is that?" pointing to the ring hanging from the necklace he was wearing. "Well, this chain my dad gave me and this is Meg's ring, but don't tell M'Lisa that because she thinks it's my sister's ring." "Oh," I said. He smiles, proud of his carefully executed plan.

Jamal took me on a tour of the school during second class; it was a slow day. During the tour, he would stop at the door of a classroom, "Wait, she's cute" and make a gesture with his head: "Come here." A girl would appear at the door, and as he walked away he would say, "You've been mean to me this year." She would say, "No, I haven't," and he would say, "Yes, you don't even talk to me anymore." She would follow until the false accusations were revoked. Another line he used was, "I've got a secret for you." Again, he successfully captured the girl's attention.

[Despite all of this sex play], it's not that school isn't important to Jamal; [it is]. At one time he expressed concern because he forgot to hand in chapters 7 and 8 for his business math class. But he doesn't know where his book is. In fact, he doesn't know where any of his books are because he has forgotten his locker number and his books and various assignments are scattered between several different girls' lockers—and he cannot remember who has what.

He also expressed concern about failing his biology class, but talked as though it was an inevitable fact. He cannot find his book and just missed another class. He saw his biology teacher in the hall and said, "I need to talk to you. Are you in your classroom after school 'cause I came to see you and you weren't there." "Jamal, I'm always in my classroom after school. Where are you?"

He also told me about his anxiety to take the ACT test. He said, "I need to get at least a 16 so I can go to the University and play football." But he said that he doesn't want a football scholarship because he doesn't want football as a career. He doesn't know what he wants to do, exactly, which is why he says that he doesn't want to leave high school.

"All I know," he said, "is I want to make lots of money." Right now he works at a drive-in theater sometimes until three o'clock in the morning. On Saturdays he sometimes works 14 hours. He needs the money to make his car payments and repairs.... And (I'm assuming) he needs the extra cash to entertain his many female friends. He and his buddies [have] already picked out the tuxedos they're wearing to the Prom— black with pink satin collar and pink cummerbund.

Jamal is an enjoyable kid; he is witty, smart, and considerate. The teachers I spoke to about him said he's a good student "when he comes to class." He made everyone laugh in first period with his quick wit as he defended himself and his friends as they were being tried as witches and warlocks. However, his love of socializing is what interferes with him getting to class. I asked him what he does when he sluffs: "Hang out, go to breakfast, usually." He cuts class after lunch because, he said, "I just get caught up and then it's just too late to go [to class]."

Jamal has great relationships with adults. We spoke to many of his teachers and adult friends while walking around the school. He says the principal is quiet, but he really likes his counselor, whom he introduced to me. About the counselor, he said: "He's cool and he's going to help me get my time down for football." He says he likes all of his teachers; he couldn't pick a favorite. It was obvious to me that for teachers, Jamal is a hard student to get upset with [in part] because he is so honest. Most of his teachers joked with him about not coming to class, but in the end they praised him as a "good kid" and a "pretty good student."

As you can see from my study, Jamal is definitely the shaper of his own world in and out of the classroom. He doesn't hide the fact that he sluffs to his teachers (though he might say, "Mr. S., it wasn't my fault"), and he is perfectly honest about missing his books and assignments. All during the day he was very upfront with me about his life inside and outside of school. He said that he was in one fight at the beginning of the year because someone told him this guy was going to "flatten him" at a party. Jamal said, "I just went up to discuss it with him and he said a few things I didn't appreciate and I punched him." He hasn't had any problems since then. I respected his honesty with me.

Jamal [has lots of confidence], especially with the ladies and adults in the school. He is friendly to everyone; he doesn't seem to limit his friendships to one group of students. He was especially considerate about introducing me to everyone, including his buddies. When he said to me, "I'm going to take you to breakfast," a girl behind him said, "She's here to watch you in school." He said, "Hey, she's following *me* around" (pointing to his chest), "and I'll show her what I do."

As it turns out, he just took me on a visit of the neighborhood in his car—where his grandma lives, where he went to junior high school, to the gas station—and finally he dropped off his mom's Visa bill. If Jamal feels like going to class, he does. And if he doesn't, he can tour the classrooms to visit the ladies, maybe go to breakfast with [his buddies], Kent and Jason; and if he gets caught [sluffing], most likely he can smooth-talk his way out of a sticky situation. That's the way he likes it.

## MICK'S STUDY

This may be the most unique Shadow Study you receive. It turned out to be a jolting experience. I knew from the start who I was going to shadow.... Ed's the son of a family I have known well for several years. That is the central reason I asked him, because I believed it would be a comfortable situation for both of us.

Since I'd been working in Hood Junior High School as a volleyball coach, and Ed is on the team, I see him on a daily basis. I have constant interaction with him and his father.... So we set up the time last week for the two of us to get together before school and spend the day doing this assignment.

I should have realized that something had happened in Ed's life. He lives [in a lower socioeconomic area of the city] but attends Hood [which is in a better-off neighborhood], because of poor performance and citizenship in his old school. He is an excellent athlete, and his grades have improved dramatically since [transferring]. I am still unaware of his problems in his "old community," but as for the new situation, my eyes were opened....

On Thursday, when we had originally agreed to meet, I was ditched by Ed. He neither showed up nor called the school. When I saw him that afternoon at volleyball practice, I asked him where he was. He told me he had forgotten, and was just running late that morning. I set up a time [to meet] the next day. I got a list of ... his classes.... [The next morning] I went to the principal's office to double check the room numbers Ed had given me. To my surprise, [the principal] said he was in with the vice principal and I "could do the shadow study on him right out the door." I was informed that he and a friend had been caught smoking marijuana at the bus stop that morning, and since he was already on a waiver to attend school, he was immediately expelled.... I felt like my world was out of skew. Here was a boy that I have known for several years. A young man I saw everyday as an athlete ... being kicked out of school for using drugs. Dozens of thoughts and emotions struck me simultaneously. What would his parents say? What would I say to Ed? How was I going to explain to the team that their captain was caught doing this?

The principal told me I could join the meeting with the boy and vice principal. I declined. I felt I had no business going in there. [I waited outside. The door opened.] Ed looked horrible. He saw me, then our eyes met. His glance went directly to the floor. He stumbled over a couple of chairs as he made his way to the door of the office, and I caught his attention and simply asked him if he was alright. He only shrugged his shoulders and solemnly [walked] to his locker to collect his things.

I went into the vice principal's office and asked to speak to her. She knew who I was and was in no way reluctant to speak with me concerning the matter. She handed me the report that had been filled out [on Ed]. [She told me that] Ed was so stoned that he could not even remember his address or phone number. He had scratched it out two or three times, and eventually had to look it up in the phone book. She said he had freely admitted his guilt and would never be accepted back into that school again.

I was devastated. Why didn't I know more about what was going on in his life? How could I have not noticed [that something wasn't right]? Then I began to think back over many practices when Ed didn't seem like himself, or times when he moved as if in slow motion. Were these other occasions when he was using? I also remembered him on these occasions using foul language and doing other things that seemed out of character.... I wept that night. If I ... only have students for a few months, how can I make a difference in their lives? ... I felt like a failure.... How does a student who is ... popular, successful, and [apparently] happy deceive us so that we [teachers] can't help.... I thought I knew this young man. I felt as though I had some power. Now ... I believe he had all the power....

## CONSIDERATIONS

Veronica's study immediately stands out. She does not think of Janie as an "object" to be studied, but as a co-participant within a culture whose insights were valuable and deserving of respect. They share the context and, in varying ways and degrees, the struggle to make sense of it meaningfully. Although Veronica is a beginning teacher and Janie one of her future students, Veronica has not yet broadened her conception of self to include teacher images. They are both students, and this proves to be an important bond.

Veronica seeks to preserve Janie's voice within a context that consistently appears little interested in her or what she has to say. To Veronica, the day was almost unbearably tedious, but to Janie it is simply the way school is. She does not expect anything to be different: School is boring, and teachers are disinterested in students. Within this context, Janie has learned how to take advantage of the opportunities that come along during and between classes to engage her friends which makes school life relatively enjoyable. Janie expands the wiggle room given to her by her teachers. Unfortunately, the origin of this wiggle room, at least as Veronica sees it, is that Janie's teachers—except her English teacher—do not care about pupil learning. Janie really doesn't complain, however. For Janie, school seems to mean enduring long periods of relative boredom in order to interact with friends whenever possible.

Veronica was appalled by the condescending manner of Janie's history teacher and wondered, openly, why so little learning took place during the day. This is not the way it is supposed to be, and she begins to think critically about the teacher's role and responsibilities: "It seems to me a 'bad' teacher can cause a student to have a bad day at school; it also seems to me that too many bad days in a row could kill any desire the student may have had to succeed in school." Things were better, Veronica thinks, when she was in high school. Janie's teachers, Veronica concludes, betrayed a public trust: "Educators have a long way to go to fulfill the public trust and to provide students with the kind of nurturing and enriching environment to which I believe they are entitled."

The picture Veronica presents of Janie is of a young person who drifts through school, doing minimal work, only what she needs to do to get by. Like most of her teachers, Janie is little interested in learning. She is interested in avoiding trouble, however; she knows where the boundaries are to her passive student role. In most ways she is a "good" student, one who does what she is told and causes no trouble; she deserves better from her teachers. The teachers, Veronica thinks, have failed Janie.

Jamal skillfully manipulates the school context; likely he would be labeled a "resister" (Willis, 1977). He understands the institution and its norms and uses this understanding to resist unpleasant aspects of institutional life and make his life as enjoyable as possible. He maximizes his interaction with friends and minimizes institutional control through his disarming honesty and winning smile. Teachers enjoy Jamal's personality and give him a large degree of slack; school rules soften in the light of Jamal's grin. But there is a dark side to this playful relationship: Jamal is not encouraged to study. Unlike Janie, Jamal makes no pretenses. For him the value of school is strictly social, and yet he worries about his future. Although Jamal fails to see a connection between attending class and test performance, the upcoming test for admission to the university looms large and there is no manipulating the norms that govern college admission. Apparently, no one has taught him that there is a connection. He wants to play football but claims to not "want a football scholarship because he doesn't want to make football as a career." We get the feeling that Jamal is a confused boy who puts off making some very important but inevitable decisions as long as he can. In the meantime, he plays, and plays hard, and teachers seem unconcerned, perhaps because they do not believe there is anything they can do to help.

Unintentionally, Ed breaks Mick's heart. Mick thought he had a close and open relationship with Ed, the volleyball captain, and that by shadowing him he would have an easy day. What he discovered was that Ed had a private life that excluded adults, a life lived outside the norms of school. Shocked, Mick wonders what he could have done to help Ed and, perhaps feeling a little guilty, recounts missed signs that something was wrong. In despair, Mick wonders what a teacher can do to help young people when they spend so little time together, an hour or so a day for a few months.

To Mick, Ed was a successful "jock," a good and popular student. While in some ways true, this conclusion blinded him to times when Ed behaved in uncharacteristic ways, like during practice when his reflexes seemed slow. Mick lost sight of the person under the label. But it was too late. Ed was expelled from school for what was deemed unacceptable behavior even for a popular athlete.

Each study illustrates aspects of how young people find a niche in school and build a life. They also underscore how important relationships with friends and teachers are to the quality of that life and how school norms shape interaction. For a good many young people, like Janie and Jamal, the value of schooling is intimately tied to the quality of their social lives. Veronica, Tangi, and Mick thought it should be otherwise. Perhaps it was different when they were in school, but it is likely that they have simply forgotten. We do not know. This said, Jamal and probably Janie see school in some ways connected to their future and do what is necessary to make their way economically and perhaps socially, but they generally stay within the institutionally acceptable bounds of the student role even though Jamal pushes those boundaries outward. Recall, Jamal is a good student "*when* he comes to class."

Teachers are centrally responsible for providing an engaging academic climate, but too few of these students' teachers did. Some schools are characterized by a culture and norms that allow little education to take place (Kozol, 1991). Publicly, of course, this would be denied, but privately norms operate that actually discourage learning and encourage minimal performance from both teachers and students. Facing such a culture, where learning is of little value, students find other ways to be occupied as they put in their time—and they must put in their time! Janie's English teacher resists these pressures, and students learn as a result. But not all teachers share this teacher's vision, and the students suffer. Some teachers—and these views would emerge in interviews with them—have given up on their pupils, believing they either cannot or will not learn.

## EXTENDING THE CONVERSATION

Studying children's lives has been part of teacher education for perhaps a century or more beginning with what was called the "child study movement" (Hall, 1907). The study of adolescent lives, however, is more recent, dating from the 1930s and the growing concern for the dramatic effects of economic dislocation on young people and their families (see Rainey, 1937). Writing in 1940, John DeBoer, a professor of teacher education at the Chicago Teachers College, argued that "a comprehensive study of the learner is central to an acceptable program of teacher eduation for the secondary level fully as much as for the elementary-school level" (1940, p. 267). More recently, case studies of young people have found their way into teacher education:

> The case study can focus on a classroom or school situation or on a particular student. When students are the objects of inquiry, the case study can help teachers learn to apply knowledge of development, learning, motivation, and behavior to specific children as they function in their family, school, and community contexts. (Darling-Hammond, 2000, p. 532)

Case studies are more elaborate and involved than the Shadow Study, although they are closely related (see Yin, 1989).

Unlike most of the other methodologies presented in *Becoming a Student of Teaching*, the value of Shadow Studies is not directly supported by research, although their value is attested to in interviews and questionnaires given to our students as they exit the program. They may best be thought of as representing elements of ethnographic research which aim to uncover the meaning of a context to participants. The theoretical support of the Shadow Study, however, is considerable. As Riseborough notes, students are "critical reality definers" (1985, p. 262) for teachers, and as we have said, beginning teachers, in particular, look to students for confirmation of their self definitions, of who they are in the classroom. It is crucially important that beginning teachers know something about how pupils make the context they share with teachers meaningful because together they must make their way within the institution. Moreover, such knowledge is a means for ameliorating the "narrow, pessimistic perspective on pupils" that beginning teachers frequently develop (Diamond, 1991, p. 35). Rather than being seen as enemies, students come to be seen as persons who share a context with teachers and who, like teachers, are trying to forge a meaningful life within a set of sometimes rather tight-fitting institutional norms.

This said, as Veronica reminds us, teachers enjoy a superordinate position and have a surprising amount of power by which norms within and without the classroom can be reconstituted. Teachers have a moral obligation to exercise this power with, and on behalf of, their pupils' learning and for the purpose of improving their own work environment.

These three studies point to a set of issues that are very troubling. Although we would like to believe differently, drug and alcohol usage in American secondary schools is a serious problem. Ed had serious problems. Janie's friends openly discussed in their drama class their favorite alcoholic drinks. Nationwide, the affects of alcohol and drug abuse on young people and their families are devastating, and teachers inevitably are at the front lines of the battle because the vast majority of them care deeply about children and their learning. Poverty, abuse, crime, and, of course, poor school performance go hand in hand with alcohol and drug usage (for consistently updated statistics see the web site of the Child Welfare League of America). Consider, what is your responsibility to help a young person like Ed? What would you do to help him?

There is another set of issues that emerge from these three studies that center on gender differences. For several years girls have been outperforming boys in school, but little attention has been given to the plight of boys (National Center, 2000). Janie will certainly graduate from high school and enter college. She will probably graduate from college as well. Currently, nearly 60 percent of all baccalaureate degrees are awarded to women, and the majority of master's degrees. If

Ed continues on the road he is traveling, he will likely not complete high school. Jamal will graduate from high school, but his academic skills are seriously underdeveloped and the odds are against him succeeding academically in college. Janie makes the best of school, even though the schooling she is offered (with the exception of her English class) is generally not high quality. The two boys are disengaged from learning or in Ed's case disengaging from school.

Given your experience as a student, how would you explain these different levels of performance? What might be done within classrooms and within schools to maximize the likelihood that both boys and girls will do well in school?

# ✶ 6 ✶

# Classroom Studies

---

## INTRODUCTION

Through spending time in your cooperating teacher's classes, you will know that classes differ in subtle and not so subtle ways. These differences, however, can make it difficult to see that there are patterns of interaction that define normative behavior. It is these patterns that concern us in this chapter.

Walking into a classroom for the first time may feel a bit like walking onto an empty stage, but this stage is never empty. Teacher and student relationships are already defined by the context of schooling: the habitual and accepted ways of interacting and of working that characterize institutional life. Life in the classroom is bounded by institutional priorities and the structures that sustain and maintain them. Boundaries produce cultural continuities, patterns of understanding and interaction that function as norms governing practice. Yet, as beginning teachers quickly discover, even within the same school context, classrooms differ. How is this possible?

The norms that govern schooling help define school culture and shape teacher and student relationships, but they are not monolithic. They do not form a tightly woven cloth. Each generation of beginning teachers must be inducted into the culture, but induction is never fully successful; the fit is never perfect. There is always some tension—sometimes a great deal of tension—within established norms and ways of interacting and between these norms and the beliefs and values of individual participants within the culture. Thus, norms powerfully shape but ultimately do not determine teacher or student practice, for that matter.

As constructed patterns of meaning and action—historical creations—norms require identification and scrutiny. Understanding them enables beginning teachers to see why teaching and schooling are as they are, how they are contextually shaped, and to begin to consider the ways in which norms both enable and constrain meaning and action. When norms are accepted as right and proper, such understanding enables the negotiation of a desirable teaching role. Similarly, when they are found wanting, such knowledge is crucial to identifying space within which alternative ways of thinking and acting can be tested in relative security. Without this knowledge, and of how students and teachers normatively within it, the pressure of norms and the structures that maintain them likely leads to teacher disengagement and passivity. Exploring wiggle room, in contrast, plays to teachers' sense of agency and strengthens the belief that people can and do make a difference.

There are many ways of gaining knowledge of the norms that shape school and classroom life and of locating wiggle room. One way is through studying classrooms as cultural creations. Culture is commonly thought of as the customs, practices, and traditions that characterize, distinguish, and give stability to a group. More generally, it is "the knowledge people use to generate and interpret behavior" (Spradley & McCurdy, 1972, p. 8); it is knowledge of shared norms or rules. Our focus is the culture of the school and of the classroom studied by one who seeks to become a participant. Being an "insider"—or more accurately, one who seeks to become an insider—presents some difficulty. Sometimes it is difficult to be critical, and sometimes criticism comes too easily, as when seeking confirmation of a viewpoint. Both dangers can be tempered if data are gathered systematically, and if they are attended to carefully and allowed to "speak."

When you study schools and the classrooms within which you will practice teach, you will begin to see how context shapes and constrains practice and how students and teachers deflect, redirect, and resist pressures to conform. In this way, you will have the opportunity to consider the ways in which you too can adjust the context to better realize your aims. Reflection on context can lead to action. Moreover, by studying culture through interviews and observations, you will develop a set of methods which will prove useful for examining new settings when you formally enter the profession as a first year teacher.

Having spent many years in school as students, school and class-room norms may be invisible to you, or, when recognized, you may assume them to be natural rather than constructed. When norms are assumed to be natural, simply part of life within classrooms, the ways in which norms constrain and shape interaction and understanding are ignored. Socialization is assumed to be passive, a matter of fitting in rather than of negotiating a place within the context. The implications of such views of socialization are far-reaching; one catches a glimpse of the shadow of training. When fitting in is the driving ambition of begin-ning teachers and when teacher educators think of their job as assuring a quick and tight fit, the wider professional community is impoverished, albeit slightly. The accumulative effect, however, can be devastating. Communities and the causes they champion remain vital only when socialization is, and is understood as, a dynamic process of reform and renewal, where seeking membership involves testing boundaries and exploring and challenging accepted ways of thinking and acting.

## TEACHER INTERVIEW

Both interviews and observations are essential tools for studying class-room culture. Prior to conducting the classroom study, we require our students to formally interview their cooperating teacher. Just as the Shadow Study focused on how pupils construe classroom and school life, it is fundamentally important to carefully consider how teachers make sense of their experience as teachers. Knowledge of this kind is central to understanding how classroom norms are constructed and operate. Aside from providing essential knowledge about the teaching context and how it is made sensible, the interview has the potential added bene-fit of strengthening your relationship with your cooperating teacher.

Arranged in advance, the interview begins with questions that seek background information about the teacher, which often proves to be knowledge essential for comprehending how meaning is made. How long has he/she taught? Where did he/she study? What factors influ-enced his/her decision to become a teacher? The aim is to begin to understand the teacher's actions in relationship to life history and values. Questions then follow that seek to reveal the teacher's understanding of his/her role, ideal and real. Questions like these are asked: What do you find most and least satisfying about teaching and why? How do you spend the majority of your time? Would you spend your time differently if you could? Why or why not? Describe your relationship with students, other teachers, administrators, and parents. What are the major institutional and personal factors that shape these relationships? How much influence do you have with these groups and how much power do they have to shape your life in school? The answers to these questions often prove very revealing. How teachers understand their responsibilities and what they think about students, for example, profoundly influence what they do in the classroom. Decisions about what and what not to teach and how to approach a lesson are grounded in just such understandings.

The interviews are written up and then shared in class. Commonalities inevitably emerge as a result of the similarity of teachers' work across settings where, for instance, teacher isolation remains a factor of life (see Bullough, 1987; Gitlin, 1987). But important differences are also identified that reveal differences in teachers' personalities and the work contexts that enable satisfying and interesting teaching roles to be negotiated. Sources of teacher power are also revealed, indicating in various ways that teachers take advantage of wiggle room. The discussion is informed by readings on the nature of teachers' work in schools, including studies of sources of teacher job satisfaction and dissatisfaction. The crucial point is that you start exploring how your cooperating makes teaching sensible, perhaps enjoyable. The classroom study follows the teacher interview and builds on it.

## WRITING: THE CLASSROOM STUDY

The following is the assignment we present to our students, drawing on insights from ethnography.

> Ethnography, simply stated, is the "work of describing a particular culture" (Spradley, 1980, p. 3). The challenge is to grasp how those within the culture understand it, how they make sense of their experience. Identify a class that you will be student teaching and that you find interesting or challenging. Your task is to gather data—through observations, informal

and formal interviews, and whatever other ingenious means you can come up with—that will enable you to describe how the classroom environment is understood and recreated by the teacher and students. What are the *formal* and *informal rules,* the *norms,* that give order to the classroom? In what ways are they enabling and limiting of meaning? What roles do the students and the teacher play and what is the relationship of these roles to one another? How do the students and the teacher experience the classroom? What are the key words, metaphors, ideas, and concepts that they use to give meaning to the classroom and to structure their experience? Try to get *underneath* surface appearances by asking not only What do I see these people doing? but, *What do these people see themselves as doing?*

Begin your paper by describing the context and the players: the school, the classroom, the teacher, the students, the subject area and level. What kind of school is it? What kind of kids?

As you observe, look for *patterns* of behavior and of language. Look for events that disrupt the patterns, which often reveal otherwise hidden norms (for example, what happens when a student acts contrary to classroom routine?). Listen for comments—pay attention to the language used—that reveal the meaning of events. Again, the aim is to get on the *inside* of the culture of the classroom, to become knowledgeable about it, so that you may eventually become an effective agent within it.

The assignment is given and questions quickly follow. Inevitably a student will ask, "How much time should we spend observing?" A second question follows on the heels of the first: "Is it acceptable to spend one entire day in a classroom, instead of observing one or two classes over an extended period of time?" To the first question we respond with a question: "Having already spent quite a bit of time in the classroom observing, how much time do you think it will take to complete the assignment?" This question provides an occasion for further exploring the task. It is quickly realized that what is being required is extremely complicated, and a good deal of time will be needed if useful insights are to be produced. Generally speaking, our students, at least those who produce interesting studies, spend several consecutive days with a single class—sometimes two—observing and talking with the teacher and students. To assist them we typically have canceled two or three of our classes with the understanding that the time will be spent in the schools. We explore the second question in light of the challenge before them. "Is it possible," we ask, "to get depth of understanding in one or two days of observation, even when several class periods are observed?" They realize it is not possible.

After the classroom studies are written, conclusions are shared and comparisons of the results made. At this time it is not unusual to have a few students complain that the writing task was too vague, that we should have told them specifically what to look for. Other students counter that if we stated specifically what to look for, then what would be seen would be what we wanted them to see, and this also has draw-backs. Generally speaking, our experience has been that it is best to resist the temptation to be prescriptive. The feeling of being adrift for a time can be productive of many interesting and lively insights that might otherwise not emerge if one enters a cultural context expecting to identify examples illustrative of conclusions reached by others from studies of different contexts. Concerning the latter point, it is worth noting that some of our students have produced studies that challenge research conclusions—public theory—presented to them in one or another class reading. We celebrate such moments, seeing them as occasions to confirm a central value underlying the propositions presented in chapter one: Teachers are producers of legitimate knowledge.

A final point: A good many of our students need reminding that their first task is *descriptive*, while the second is *interpretative*. In your writing you need to not only describe the context and what is going on within it but also to attempt to understand the meaning of events to pupils and teachers. If you spend comparatively little time in the classroom looking, listening, and asking or jump from class to class likely you will find it very difficult to move beyond description, as we shall shortly see.

Three edited and abbreviated classroom studies follow. The first is representative of studies that present generally interesting descriptions that are of importance to the writer but fail to move beyond description in part because too little time was spent observing. The second (written by Mark Pendleton, whose name is used at his request) and third studies present efforts to understand the meaning of events, one through production of a single, unifying concept (the "social contract") and the other through a flood of insights of lesser generality that center on the students' power to shape classroom culture.

## LOTS GOING ON: NICOLE'S STUDY

Grant High School is an old school located [in a working-class neighborhood]. Most high schools in the city have the same curriculum, and similar extracurricular events and activities. However, national standardized test scores are generally lower for west side schools, [like Grant], than they are for schools on the more affluent east side.... To add to the seemingly lower [quality of] education available from Grant, a teacher informed me that an option was given to students which allowed them to choose to attend one of the four other schools.... Therefore, the students left at Grant are the bottom of the barrel and are not too involved in school.

Despite these circumstances, Grant High School's scores on national tests have risen dramatically in the past year. A large part of this is due to the school's participation in a [vocational education] program called Passport, which is an effort to restructure the educational system [by linking the schools with local business]. The principal is very enthusiastic ... and supports many of the teachers' ideas which promise to improve ... education.

The school is set up on a block system which means the students have eight classes. They go to four extremely long periods each day. They go to the even periods one day, and the odd periods the next. Although this gives the students an extra day to do their homework, they also have more time to forget what they have learned before they attend that class again.

The mathematics classrooms are located in a building behind the main school. This building does not seem to be territorially divided by the students, since no particular group of students hangs out in the halls or around the building. Therefore, all students may feel comfortable to use this building....

The math department has its own faculty room in this building. This room unites the math teachers, as they are able to retire here during lunch and discuss students, lesson plans, or any problems they may have. However, each teacher has a unique teaching style. . . .

As you enter [my cooperating teacher's room], the students' desks are arranged in neat rows to your right. The students have assigned seats according to the alphabetical order of their last name. The teacher's desk is directly in front of you, facing the students' desks. Windows line the wall beyond the teacher's desk. Lists of the students' grades hang on the wall opposite the windows. There are few decorations in this classroom.

[My cooperating teacher] has been teaching for a long time and is looking forward to retirement. His teaching style is the traditional arrangement of lecturing and then letting the students work on homework in class. His years of experience allow him to know how to handle his students.

He knows what to . . . expect from the students. When discussing grades, he said that you cannot expect all the students to be an expert on the subject when they leave the class. The students who come most of the time and learn something deserve to pass; those students who learn more should get the better grades. . . . Each day a student accrues points for coming to class on time, bringing [his or her] book, taking a daily quiz, and turning in [his or her] homework. The daily points are then averaged and the grades are posted on the wall so the students can see where they stand.

The class period begins by going over the homework. Students are encouraged to ask the teacher to work problems from the homework which they have questions about. He calls on students to participate in working the problems. After the students cease to ask questions about the homework, he has them take a short quiz. Then new information is covered by doing the even-number problems from each section of the homework. And the students are allowed to work on their homework for the rest of the class period.

The students are shown how to do the homework before the test is given, so that they can work on their homework after they finish the test.

The relaxed atmosphere in the classroom comes from the informal rules which exist. Food and drinks are allowed in the classroom. Students are allowed to get up and sharpen pencils or throw garbage away at any time. The T.A. passes out homework while the teacher begins answering questions about homework. The students pass a stapler around the room to staple their homework pages together. And the students are allowed to talk while doing homework, and during quizzes and tests. The teacher emphasizes, however, that simply copying answers does not promote learning and is therefore considered to be cheating.

I observed an algebra 1–2 class. There were a few students from different student groups. There was a cowboy, a greaser, and a few minority students. About half of the class seemed to be quiet students who were doing what they had to do to get a good grade. And there were a few students who seemed not to care about what was going on.

One day was a big test day. It was amazing to me that there wasn't a lot of cheating going on because the teacher actually left the room during part of the test. A few students chatted about events, but in about five minutes most were busy working. One boy offered to pay another boy to do the test for him. The other boy replied, "I'll do it, but I can't guarantee the answers will be correct." That was the end of that discussion. Another boy, who had not been paying attention in class, obviously did not know how to do much of the test and was looking around to see if he could see someone else's answers. After seeing that the students around him were guarding their answers, he began doing what he could on his own.

During the test the teacher posted a new sheet of grades on the wall. Some students came up during the test to see how their grade was doing. Others waited until after the test. I thought it was interesting that some students, who had a lot of the answers during lecture time, did not come up to see their grades. They just began working on their homework after they completed the test . . .

The next time I visited, the class seemed extremely subdued.

It may have been the stormy weather, or the end of a term and beginning of a new term, which caused them to be so sleepy. But whatever it was, there was little interaction between the students. In fact, the teacher taught almost the whole 85 minutes because he felt the kids would get more out of the time that way. He said the kids were so sleepy that many of them would have just put the books away after he stopped talking.

I also observed a geometry class three times. The students in this class were generally more aware of the rules of good student behavior. They knew when it was appropriate to behave in different ways. It was definitely the harder class to observe. When it was test time, they settled right down to take the test. When it was homework time they either did homework or quietly talked among themselves.

There seemed to be a couple of groups of students who liked to talk in this class. The main group ... surrounded a cheerleader. After the test this group did act up a little and began trying to throw a paper ball into the garbage can until the teacher put a stop to it.

Through talking to a few students, other people, and through my own retrospection [sic], I have come to sense that the major feeling of the students is that school is important. At least the diploma is important to get a better-paying job, but the students fail to see how math relates to their lives and their futures.

I feel I can fit into the teacher's classes. I hope I can continue the comfortable atmosphere of learning ... without losing control. . . .

## MAKING A CONTRACT: MARK'S STUDY

Mrs. G.'s eighth-grade English class is located in a side hallway of ... Ridges Junior High School. The walls of the classroom are painted white and there are windows on two sides; but they only provide views of other parts of the building. The building itself is old—they say around one-hundred years. The hallways look old and tired.

Ridges Junior High School lies situated on the top of the ...

Valley and directly below the widening mouth of [Sandstone] Canyon. The abruptness of the mountains behind the school is startling. The ... neighborhoods that feed Ridges are well-off, though there must be some exceptions. Mrs. G.'s English class is a calm, homogeneous collection of students. Mrs. G. is a calm woman of around forty who loves what she does. I think the students catch on to that.

The first time I talked to Mrs. G. she asked me if the English department at the university teaches classes on how to teach writing. I told her I had not taken one yet. When we arrived at her classroom, she showed me a few books written by teachers who had generated good reading and writing programs in their classrooms. *In the middle* (Nancie Atwell's book) is the only title I remember. She asked me again what I knew about the writing process, and I just answered around her question. I could tell that she was excited about writing—and excited about getting the students to write. I think Mrs. G. looks at teaching as a craft, or as a nurturing exercise. She involves the students in exercises that nurture the skills she wants to see. She uses interesting assignments—I was involved in them; I enjoyed doing them with the class and learning something in the process.

Mrs. G. begins every class with a ten-minute reading time. The students bring their own books to class. She told me that if she did this at a different school, she would have to supply the books because the kids would not have any books at home to bring. Even at Ridges it took a while for the students to bring their own books. When I was there everyone had a book and everyone read quietly for ten minutes. They talk about their books. She introduces new books. They seem almost as excited about it as she is.

One of the days I sat in her class we came together in groups of four and read each other's books. In order to participate I picked *Lost Horizon* off her shelf and passed it on to the next person in our group. We had about five minutes to read from each of the four books. Two of the books were high school books about high school situations. Mine was a classic and the other one, brought by a boy, was a gruesome modern thriller. I did not read much of the thriller, and the other two were almost interesting. If I were Mrs. G. I would have a hard time being non-judgmental about the books being brought to class. Yet she accepts almost all the books her students bring. She just wants them to bring books.

For me the time passes quickly in Mrs. G.'s class. I smile often at the things she has the students do, and I smile at the things the students actually do. The students amaze me. They have a lot of energy; but I cannot remember seeing or hearing any one of them really speak out and react against something Mrs. G. was doing. This could be the way eighth-graders are, but I really did not see any disruptive behavior. They read and wrote and listened when they were supposed to. . . .

I think Mrs. G. sees herself as someone who is slowly and softly immersing her students in reading and writing. I also think she is aware of her success. She knows when the students are really enjoying what she is doing with them. I think the students see themselves as going along with what Mrs. G. wants. For them, enjoyment comes and goes. Talking and inter-acting with one another is what they naturally do. They do that in between and during exercises. Some other classes I have seen have a very thin border between the hallway and the class-room. Others have too much of a border, and the silence is tense. Mrs. G.'s class is neither tense nor wild. Of course the students try to get out of assignments; they lie and cheat—if that is what they normally do. But this is harder to do in her classroom because most of the assignments come in the form of reading logs, journals and book reports. A lot of people think of English as a lot of busy work. I did not see much busy-work—work for the sake of being occupied—in Mrs. G.'s class-room. What I did see is the kind of quiet learning that comes from a gentle exposure to language and literature.

There are other things in Mrs. G.'s classroom that make it more [typical]. Clothing, physical appearance, names and name calling—society speaks everywhere. Ridges is a Channel One school, so they watch it every day. Mrs. G. does not like it, but she does not oppose it. There must be a million minute things that add life to Mrs. G.'s classes. I feel like I need to name all of them, while I only know a few of them. I do not feel baptized into the culture. [I was given] a name, and I think that is the first step to conversion.... In Mrs. G.'s class I was introduced as Mr. Pendleton—an observer from the university. My relationship [with the students] was instantly formalized. I realized that the "Mr." tag is necessary, but I was disappointed. [I wanted something less formal].

As I watched Mrs. G.'s class, and a few others, I realized that there was a social contract being carried out by two consenting sides. I feel that the first thing necessary to making a contract is the identification of the two sides: "I am this; you are that." After the two sides are identified and made distinct, then agreements can be made. Both sides make promises. Both sides forfeit certain rights so that both sides can gain other, more important, rights. Both sides acquire roles that are mutually beneficial. The substance of the acquired roles is a combination of the initial identifications and of the subsequent release and gain of rights or privileges. The day-by-day implementation of the social contract provides a basis for the continual process of [coming to know] one another. I have tried to get to the bottom of this "classroom [study]" stuff, and this is what I have come up with....

I think what [I have read about student culture] applies directly to the social contract, although in a general sense. All kinds of teachers and all the kinds of students, in all the behavior they exhibit, always and inevitably participate in the social contract of American public education. The questions in this situation are: What is at stake? What is being lost or gained? What is really going on—what are we agreeing to? ... There does not seem to be any escape from the sides and the roles that the contract demands or encourages. Once someone enters the domain ... they will fall into a slot—there is no other possibility. The only way to nullify the contract is to enter into another one.... Ironically, ... the social contract is less structured yet more complex [than at first it appears]. Boundaries of the sides blur; the roles can blend into each other.... Maybe the blending occurs when everyday life overrules the institution for a while. All the people in the classroom slip out of their roles because for a moment they are knowing and being known [differently]. Yet still, in an instant, if either a teacher or a student jumps back into a rigid role—by either making a demand or by resisting one—then the spell can be broken. I wonder now which is the fulfilling of the social contract—being social by filling a role and exchanging rights, or being social by finally giving up the roles and the rights and seeing eye to eye. . . .

A social contract is the foundation of Mrs. G.'s eighth grade English class. All the in-class reading, all the exercises in writing, and even Channel One—there is a contract behind them all (especially Channel One, which is naturally a lucrative one). Once I entered the classroom and I was called Mr. Pendleton, I knew I had joined a side. My "Mark" was given up to acquire a "Mr." I really did not have a choice—the contract [operating in this setting] demands that I be a mister. Seeing eye to eye is probably best left for the devout—university students and their professors. Knowing and being known takes a long time. . . . Mrs. G. has accomplished a lot in the space and time she has been given. She and her class understand one another. She wants them to love reading, and they bring their own books to school.

## STUDENT POWER: LAURA'S STUDY

The classroom I observed is at Taft Junior High School, a relatively new school. I would not consider this school to be a "big bucks" junior high, but it is clean and has some technical devices such as a small computer lab (about 20 terminals) and a TV in every classroom. The houses around the school look clean and small to medium in size. This makes me think that the school is in a working- or middle-class neighborhood. . . . According to the teacher, the student body consists mainly of Caucasian students; several Tongan, African American, and Hispanic students; and some Asian and Native American students.

The classroom I observed is located on the outskirts of the

school building. There is only one other classroom in the hallway, and the hallway is far from the main office, cafeteria, and library. Because the classroom is far from these heavily trafficked areas of the school, I did not see a lot of students or other teachers walking past the door. The hall was quiet so the students (about 20–25 in each period) and teacher could focus their energy on what happened inside the classroom rather than be tempted to find out what was happening out in the hall. All of the students I observed are ninth graders who represent a range of academic skills and possess varying degrees of desire to be in school.... The English class I observed emphasized literature because the English department is organized so that writing and literature are taught separately and the students take a semester of each every year.

The teacher, Mr. H., has been teaching junior high English for the past seven years. Through observing his classroom and talking with him, I [learned quite a bit not only about how he teaches but also what he values as a teacher]. One of his main concerns is good discipline. In his disclosure statement (written at the start of the year to inform parents of teacher expectations) given to each student when they entered his class, he defines good discipline: "Good discipline is the pleasant atmosphere where a teacher's relationship with a class has encouraged every student's self-control and participation." From what I saw, good discipline is that which produces [student passivity]. The students show self-control when they sit in their seats, do the assignments, and respond when the teacher asks them a question. I came to this conclusion because I heard a lot of comments such as "Open your book and read the story" and "Answer this question in your journal," which were directed at individual students who were staring at the wall or playing with their pens.... The few students who did not do their assignments were quiet and did not attract the teacher's attention.

The teacher's desire for control is also reflected in the seating arrangements. Rather than a traditional setup with the students' desks facing the teacher's desk at the front of the room, the desks are on each side of the room facing each other with a large aisle down the middle. When I asked him why he had chosen this arrangement, he replied that with this arrangement he can be close to the students and see what they are doing because no one is in the back of the room. Instead of the rows being five to six desks long, the rows are only three to four seats long. If he is close to the students, then he can monitor their activities. This seating arrangement also gives him the opportunity to approach each desk quickly. . . .

Another one of Mr. H.'s main [concerns is to see] that each student participates and receives individual attention. He told me that when the students are participating in class discussions, he feels they are receiving individual attention. So, when he would lecture or have student discussions he would randomly call on students to respond to questions. He mentioned that when he calls on students, he is particularly concerned about getting the silent student to participate. He is aware that some students hate this procedure, but he feels all students should be comfortably saying the answers as well as writing the answers.

Although Mr. H.'s formal intention is to give all students individual attention, the informal rule is that boys receive more attention than girls. When he would call on students randomly, he called on a boy about 75 percent of the time. . . . I was surprised to see Mr. H. point out that the term "heroes" can be either boys or girls, since most definitions and textbooks leave out the term "heroine." It seems to me that the formal rule is to give equal attention to both boys and girls, but his actions [conveyed something else]: boys receive more attention and opportunities to talk in class than girls.

Mr. H.'s philosophy that students receive individual attention when they are called on to participate in class created a different learning environment in each of the three periods I observed. This is because different kinds of students influenced the atmosphere in each class. . . . In first period the students did not participate in class very often. At first I thought that the lack of participation was due to the early hour and that the students were simply tired. But this hypothesis was refuted when I came to first period one day and found sixth period. The change was due to a schedule rearrangement for an assembly. Even though it was the same time of day, these students answered the questions and half of the students showed the desire to participate by raising their hands. In first period, some students discovered that they could beat Mr. H.'s system by responding to questions with a shoulder shrug or by saying "I dunno." They found out that eventually Mr. H. would tell them the answer. One day in particular it seemed as if the students had all made an agreement to remain silent. The teacher sensed their attitude and said, "Sometimes I get the feeling that you just don't want to answer me." Even though the students say they do not know the answer, Mr. H. told me that there are about four students who know all the answers on assignments and tests. When these students are called on in class, they will say they don't know because that is the expectation in that period.... Even though the teacher feels participation is essential, the students in first period have decided not to respond to the teacher. The contradiction of teacher and student expectations has created a dead feeling in the classroom because there is no connection made between the teacher and students.

However, this is not the case in second and third period. The majority of the students in these two periods respond when they are called on. In first period I could not determine which students in particular had established the attitude of the class, but in second period I felt the class atmosphere was determined by a group of three or four girls. These girls appeared to feel comfortable talking with Mr. H. and discussing literature in front of the class, and they did their assignments when asked. Because of their willingness to participate other students followed along....

Although third period also participated in class discussion and answered questions, this class was not controlled by one small group of students. Instead, three or four groups of students created the atmosphere in the class while those students who did not belong to a group sat quietly, listened to the groups talk, and participated when Mr. H. called on them. I sensed a little competition between the different groups to dominate the conversation and control the classroom. Because of this competition, third period was noisier than the other two periods....

Through listening and observing ... I was able to discover some of the key concepts and attitudes which [shaped] the learning atmosphere in each class.... I was able to [gain insight into] some [aspects] of the roles the teacher and students played by listening to repeated phrases. One phrase Mr. H. used often when talking both to students and with me is "with me." He told a couple of students to "stick with me and you'll get better grades." Sometimes when a student was not paying attention, he would look at him/her and question, "Are you with me?" These types of phrases imply that the teacher is the source of important information in the classroom. When the students are with the teacher, then they are learning because the teacher has the knowledge. They need the teacher's guidance to discover knowledge. If the teacher plays the role of the source of information, then the students can tap into that information only when they recognize the teacher is the source.

One of the most common phrases used by students in all of the classes is "What are we supposed to do?" The phrase indicated that the students see their role as one in which they are people who must meet requirements and conform to expectations. Since the teacher records grades and gives assignments, then the students' role is to fulfill the teacher's requirements. It is important to note that the students say "we" rather than "I" even though the speaker really wants to know what he/she is supposed to do. This illustrates that the students see their role collectively. A student is not a single person, but one who is part of a student body.

To me Mr. H. frequently made remarks such as "You must always be the teacher or they'll take you to the cleaners" and "Keep the teacher-student distance or else they'll take you to the cleaners." This metaphor, "they'll take you to the cleaners," suggests that both the students and the teacher have the ability and power to control the classroom, but the teacher's power is superior to the students', since the students gain control only when the teacher relinquishes power. This metaphor also suggests that once the teacher's superiority has been cleaned away, then it is too late; the teacher cannot regain authority from students. . . .

I also discovered some informal rules of the classroom when Mr. H. relaxed slightly on control. . . . This happened every day at the end of second period when the TV turned on so the students could watch Channel One, a nationally produced news show anchored by teenagers. The students generally got out of their seats and walked around or sat on their desks and talked with each other. Since this type of activity is just the opposite of that which he expected while lecturing, I concluded that the informal rule states that if Mr. H. is not the main source of information, then good discipline is not essential. . . .

Another time that his discipline stance relaxed was when he was dealing with certain types of individuals. One of the girls who is influential in shaping the attitude in second period was often out of her seat to look out the window or talk with a student across the room. In the same class there is a boy who is out of his seat just as often and for the same reasons. However, when the teacher gave out grades and citizenship marks, the boy, who received the lower grade of the two, was scolded for being out of his seat constantly. The teacher only made comments about a missed quiz to the girl student. . . . Students with good grades are given . . . privileges because they are "good students." The fact that Mr. H. relaxes somewhat on his good discipline stance when dealing with "good students" illustrates [an] informal rule.

Throughout my observations it seemed to me that Mr. H. continued to organize his classroom in a similar *manner* for *each* period, but the students *in each* class reacted to *his* rules and expectations in different *ways and, thus,* created different learning environments. . . .

## CONSIDERATIONS

Nicole's study includes some interesting descriptions of the context within which she will eventually practice teach, but little interpretation. There are moments when she raises a question or uncovers an issue, but she does not push herself to get to the meaning of events. For example, she was amazed there was so little cheating during test days despite ample opportunities; the teacher even left the room. Rather than take this occasion as an opportunity to locate and explore cultural boundaries—norms—she let the observation pass perhaps because she lacked sufficient time to pursue the question or because she did not recognize it as an issue worth exploring. Nicole comments that the geometry class "was harder to observe" than the algebra class. This is a point that will be considered later. Here we should note only that on the surface, well-routinized classes and well-behaving students seem to offer to novice teachers little that is deemed worthy of attention; the landscape appears smooth, and nothing reaches out and grabs attention. Good teaching is often invisible.

Mark's insight, that a contract had been negotiated between the teacher and students, offers one of several potential points from which to view and get a handle on an otherwise placid and too familiar classroom scene. Like Nicole when she observed the geometry classes, Mark is surprised that the eighth-graders he observed were so well-behaved. Apparently he had expected otherwise. Unlike Nicole, he wonders why this is so and he speculates about possible reasons. As he considers these reasons, it strikes him that Mrs. G. and the students have negotiated a particular kind of relationship that benefits both parties. He explored some aspects of the "contract," particularly observing that by working with Mrs. G. he would be expected to maintain it; the contract came with the territory. He would be Mr. Pendleton, not Mark, as he comments, because "the contract demands that I be a mister." He begins to uncover some of the ways in which culture constrains practice. Yet, he also notes—and in noting softens what otherwise seems an overly deterministic interpretation—that it is possible in the classroom to slip out of a role, with the result that teacher and pupils come to know one another differently, as people who are not only, and certainly more than, the roles they inhabit.

Mark identified a set of questions that promises to be useful in the future as he considers the nature of the contract he will negotiate with his students when practice teaching: "What is at stake? What is being lost or gained [through the contract]?" What is being agreed to? Although Mark offers relatively little supporting evidence that would enable the reader to understand the source of his insight, it is clear that the concept of "social contract" has enabled him to think richly about his future relationship with students. His implicit ideal of being able to see "eye to eye" with students appears tempered by his increased understanding of the contextual demands placed on teachers.

Laura is struck by how class norms seem to differ despite her cooperating teacher holding to a consistent set of expectations. It is the power of young people to shape classroom norms and influence teacher behavior that proves most striking to her. She observed that some students and student groupings were extremely influential and that the kind and quality of relationship that existed among student groupings had a profound impact on the type of learning environment that existed and on the culture of the classroom. In one class Laura concluded that competition among groups was the central factor in making it noisy. This insight could prove important once she begins working with that class in practice teaching.

The power of students to shape the classroom culture was not the only important insight that emerged for Laura and that helped her to make sense of classroom events. Wisely, she did not take her cooperating teacher's description of what he was doing as necessarily accurate. Instead, she checked his claims, not to criticize them, but to come to her own understanding of the norms operating within the classroom. What she discovered was contradictory. She observed, for instance, that despite the cooperating teacher's expressed desire to involve all students, he played favorites: Boys received more attention than girls. Although Laura did not seek reasons for why this was so—perhaps as research suggests the boys were more disruptive than the girls—it was an important insight that may well influence her own classroom practice. Additionally, she checked to see what definitions of "good discipline" were played out in practice. Was good discipline what her cooperating teacher claimed it to be: the pleasant learning atmosphere that encourages student self-control and participation? As she explored this question, she concluded that student passivity and conformity masqueraded as self-control. Clearly, Laura was beginning to think about how she would handle discipline and management problems and to consider the implications of those decisions on student roles. She listened carefully to what the teacher had to say that might reveal the boundaries of his understanding of the teaching role. Several phrases stuck out, each prompting the conclusion that for her cooperating teacher, controlling information and dispensing it was the essence of teaching. To gain knowledge, students necessarily went through the teacher. Moreover, she asserts that the students became a "we," a faceless collective, devoid of individuality. Students who accepted their place received benefits; those who did not were punished.

The power of Mark's study comes from a single idea that enables him to think about his practice in new and interesting ways. Laura's study has similar virtues, but her insights are more eclectic and diverse. She poses many different questions of the context before her and tests a variety of interpretations—hypotheses—seeking ones that better explain what she sees. There is a tentativeness even when making bold claims about her conclusions that suggests hers is an ongoing and unfinished quest for understanding. One gets the feeling that better interpretations, ones more useful for thinking about and making sense of the teaching context, will be forthcoming with additional experience. It is this attitude, perhaps more than any other quality, that makes Laura's study worthy of careful consideration.

## EXTENDING THE CONVERSATION

There has been an explosion of interest in the study of school culture the past few years. The picture that has emerged is quite different from the one presented even twenty years ago, when researchers commonly assumed a uniform culture, particularly of teaching. This view is now untenable (Feiman-Nemser & Floden, 1986). School cultures differ, just as subgroups of teachers within the same school differ—for example, the teachers in the science department compared to those in the English department (see Grossman & Stodolsky, 1994; Shuell, 1992). Despite this research finding, the tacit nature of cultural norms and their function as rules by which everyday life is made sensible and meaningful make it nearly impossible to imagine that practice might be organized differently (see Sarason, 1990; 1996). For beginning teachers this problem is especially acute not only because of their relatively low institutional status and high vulnerability, expressed in the desire to fit in, but because they are too familiar with the culture. "Like anthropologists studying their own culture, they are apt to miss the underlying cultural knowledge organizing practice because it has become so familiar to them that it is, in fact, invisible" (Florio-Ruane, 1989, p. 164).

Classroom studies of various kinds have found a place both within campus-based teacher education courses and in field experiences (see Gitlin & Teitelbaum, 1983; Zeichner & Liston, 1987) as a means for encouraging reflection and knowledge production. Through studies of this kind, norms can be made visible. However, most of the work supporting its use is anecdotal. For example, after describing their own classroom practice, Teitelbaum and Britzman remark: "While we have no longitudinal empirical evidence to support us, we contend that our use of . . . ethnography with education students has been successful in promoting the goals of reflective teacher education" (1991, p. 179). We echo their words: The classroom study has encouraged our students to explore culture and begin to build a knowledge base about school life; they develop observational and interpretative skills that have long-term value; and they debate about how life in schools is structured and how it might be transformed.

Mark and Laura's studies illustrate how inquiry can lead to making the familiar unfamiliar, strange. School and classroom life are, as these beginning teachers discovered, fraught with contradictions. The source of these contradictions is "the fact that teaching and learning have multiple and conflicting meanings that shift within our lived lives, with the theories produced and encountered, with the deep convictions and desires brought to and created in education, with the practices we negotiate, and with the identities we construct" (Britzman, 1991, p. 10). The discovery of contradiction is fundamentally important. With the discovery comes the increased possibility for confronting one's own limitations as well as the ways in which institutions both enable and limit human action. Such knowledge makes alternative practices possible, even for student teachers. This said, a caution is in order: "The fact is, to place student teachers in compulsory school settings and to expect them to act as if they have entered a neutral zone where they can single-handedly fashion it into places [sic] of learning sets them up for . . . self-blame" (Britzman, 1991, p. 221).

Consider just a few of the many contradictions of teaching that are played out in the classroom: American schools are generally thought of as having a major responsibility for encouraging democratic citizenship values, yet young people usually have remarkably little influence over the decisions that most effect the quality of their school experience. Teachers often hear the rhetoric that teaching is a profession, but they have little say over their schedule, who will be enrolled in their classes, or what standards will be used to assess the quality of their teaching. Teachers are expected to facilitate high levels of student performance, the values of meritocracy, but simultaneously are to embrace the values of equality—they are to sort but not sort students, grade but not grade them. Teachers are told they should treat boys and girls identically, equally, but equity requires something else. In class boys are more likely to act out, more likely to be behind in their school work and in their academic performance particularly in reading and the language arts, and are more likely to have learning disabilities and to require remedial help (see Hoff-Sommers, 2000). Teachers are accountable for student learning, but ultimately the students are the ones who chose whether or not to learn (thus the emphasis on external motivation in teacher education and in teacher in-service meetings). Teachers are expected to care deeply about their students as people, yet they must not care too much, for caring too much will exhaust them, cause a loss of perspective and potentially result in misunderstanding of teacher motive on the part of students and parents alike. These and many other contradictions are ever-present. Knowing about them helps explain some teacher actions, perhaps some of the actions of Mr. H., for example, in Laura's study.

Effective teachers learn to live with high levels of ambiguity. To steer a course through contradiction requires that a teacher engage in a complicated balancing act among interests and teaching demands. A strong sense of self, knowledge of where you stand ethically, and clarity of purpose are among the teacher qualities necessary to skilled balancing, the sort of balancing that keeps student learning front and center, and not control or self-preservation, both of which can produce a classroom environment that is uncomfortable for students and less than fully productive of learning. Using Mark Pendleton's concept from this chapter, in such a class the "contract" negotiated would involve an unholy trade-off.

Typically teacher education focuses its attention on possibilities. Coping with and managing the contradictions of teaching requires a different kind of focus, a recognition of limitations. Reconsider the contradictions we have noted above in the light of these questions, the answer to which will profoundly influence your classroom: How might you involve your students in the decisions that effect their learning without abdicating your responsibilities for the classroom? Similarly, how might you gain access to the decision-making process that effects the quality of your life in school? How can you encourage very able students to stretch themselves while simultaneously rewarding the performance and effort of less able students? Will you be able to defend a decision to give an exceptionally able student a lower grade than a less able student, who works very hard? Will you try to treat all students the same even when to do so is to make certain that some students will not receive the help they need to learn? If not, on what educational grounds will you treat young people differently? Given all the demands of teaching you likely will be tempted to shut your door and keep to yourself. But if you care about your own learning and that of your colleagues you will need to seek opportunities for professional interaction. Where will you go for this interaction, and what do you expect to give to others and get from it? When you discover students who are not interested in your subject, what is your responsibility to get them interested and how will you go about fulfilling this responsibility? Are there limits to what you can do? How will you express to your students that you care; how much will you get into their lives and how much will you let them into yours?

The contradictions of teaching are opportunities to learn. Wrestling with them can be and is invigorating, part of what makes teaching so very interesting.

# ✴ 7 ✴

# Textbook/Curriculum Analysis

The curriculum in a large percentage of American classrooms is the textbook. One estimate is that 75 percent of a student's classroom time and 90 percent of homework time is spent with textbook materials (Keith, 1981). Preservice teachers such as yourself are often highly critical of experienced teachers' heavy reliance on textbooks. Ironically, once in charge of your own classroom, you are likely to find yourselves similarly dependent. It is very important that you consider how textbooks and curriculum guides should be used with students and for what purposes.

There is an intimate but generally ignored relationship between curriculum, textbooks, and the role of teachers (see Apple, 1979b; Apple, 1986; Zumwalt, 1989). Buried in textbooks and curriculum guides are preferred teacher roles, ways of working with young people, definitions of the disciplines, and even beliefs about the social world. Choosing to use a particular textbook or curriculum is, therefore, inherently a political act. No wonder heated battles have been waged across America over textbook and curriculum adoption.

Recently, the establishment of state and national curriculum standards has moved to the forefront of discussions about education reform. Curriculum battles have intensified. Clashes have taken place not only over content but also over how curriculum standards are to be used and how student performance is to be demonstrated. There are signs of what is being called a "standards backlash," as some parents, civil rights activists, and educators have become increasingly concerned about the effect on students of tying high school graduation and promotion to scores on standardized achievement tests (Hoff, 1999; Olsen, 2000). Yet, nearly all the states have either created curricular standards or shortly will have them.

Content wars have been especially heated in history. Release of the national history standards drew attacks from a variety of perspectives (T. Gitlin, 1995), right and left. Too multiculturalist, some critics charged; in the name of political correctness trivial events were given a prominent place and not enough space was given to Western history. One unhappy reviewer wrote: "In failing to concentrate on the ugly underside of non-white history, the NHS has been depicted as a 'radical' document out to subvert traditional American values in favor of third-world cultures. Actually, in several respects, the NHS is quaintly conservative in a religious sense, which . . . can only guarantee that 'history from below' will keep people below. . . . The NHS reads more like a prison house of group categories than an analysis of freedom based on natural right and power as individual growth and self-development" (Diggins, 1996, p. 503, 519). Other critics thought too much Western history was included. The authors (Nash, Crabtree, & Dunn, 1998) fought back, arguing they had produced an "inclusive" history of America and inaccurately labeled their detractors representatives of the "far right." Even the United States Senate got involved, condemning the standards on a 99–1 vote. What all the debaters understood was that the "recorded history of a nation shapes the identity of the nation" (Morris, 1998, p. 2). Now as in the past a great deal is at stake when deciding what knowledge is of most worth.

The challenge for you and all teachers is to become a critical consumer and producer of curricula and to learn to approach textbooks and curriculum guides with a skeptical eye, one sensitive to the assumptions about teaching, learning, knowledge, and the nature of social life that are embedded within them. Some of these assumptions are hidden, and it requires a bit of detective work to reveal them. For example, the way a curriculum is organized—its "curricular form" (Apple, 1982)—tells a great deal about what the developers most valued. Frequently, curricula follow a technical form, where knowledge is broken up into discrete "bits" that are supposed to add up to something, like the ability to read or write, for example. To facilitate measurement, educational objectives are stated in behavioral terms, as skills to be mastered (see Mager, 1962). Such a curriculum form has the effect of prescribing teacher behavior and of elevating isolated bits of information to the status of knowledge (Bullough, Holt, & Goldstein, 1984). Yet such an organization promises higher student achievement test scores, which increasingly are the currency of educational reform and teacher and school success.

Teachers stand at the middle of all curriculum debates, juggling interests and seeking as best as they can to do what is right for young people. Ultimately, what gets taught is their decision, and a weighty decision it is. When deciding to adopt or adapt one or another curriculum or text, it's important to carefully consider educational aims and the relationship of aims and means. The potential influence of a particular curriculum on the types of relationships you will have with your students needs to be considered. Issues of bias, hidden prejudices, are important as well. To be sure, like other teachers you will adjust and adapt the materials given to you to make them more compatible with your understanding of teaching, your students' abilities and interests, and even your assumptions about education (see McCutcheon, 1982). Our hope is that these adjustments and adaptations will be mindfully made and educationally justified.

To become increasingly critical consumers of curricula, our students conduct a textbook or curriculum analysis. The questions presented are only suggestive: A good analysis does not necessarily address all these questions, and a good analysis may come from other questions. Thus, our questions only provide a point of departure.

Before turning to the actual writing, we should mention that prior to introducing the analysis we explore with our students four central curriculum concepts that are essential for focusing curriculum criticism: the *explicit curriculum*, the *hidden* or *implicit curriculum*, *null curriculum*, and the *curriculum in use* or *implemented curriculum*. The explicit curriculum is what the public is told young people will be taught. The explicit curriculum is contained in curriculum guides and textbooks. The hidden curriculum is "the tacit teaching to students of norms, values, and dispositions that goes on simply by their living in and coping with the institutional expectations and routines of schools day in and day out for a number of years" (Apple, 1979b, p. 14). These are not all negative learnings; the "implicit curriculum of the school can teach a host of intellectual and social virtues" (Eisner, 1985, p. 95). The null curriculum is "what the schools do not teach," what is missing (Eisner, 1985, p. 97). The curriculum in use, or implemented curriculum, is what actually gets taught.

Both the hidden and null curriculum get at issues of bias and implicitly raise questions about inclusion and exclusion. What belongs in the biology, art, or health curriculum? Are there good reasons for excluding sex education from the health curriculum or should it be included? If included, whose values should inform the selection, organization, presentation, and study of the content?—the teacher's? One or another special interest group's? The writers of the state competency examination? Should a unit on Native Americans be taught? How much emphasis should be placed on the study of slavery in America? These are issues of interpretation and emphasis. Addressing issues of this kind is not only essential to becoming a critical consumer of curricula developed by others but is crucial to assuring that your own curriculum work is educationally defensible. It forces us to directly attend to the politics of curriculum development and to the right of young people to encounter powerful and productive systems of knowledge that represent the best that is known and in ways likely to connect with and enrich their experience and backgrounds.

Recognizing that there is a difference between the explicit curriculum and the curriculum in use is important for two closely interrelated reasons. First, this distinction underscores the central place teachers have in remaking the explicit curriculum so that it better reflects their educational values, students' needs, and school and district priorities. This is one of the sources of teachers' wiggle room discussed earlier. Remember: It is only at the teacher's bidding that the explicit curriculum enters the classroom door. Second, it also underscores that teaching, as we have argued in Becoming a Student of Teaching, is a moral and political enterprise, one that places a tremendous responsibility on the teacher. To meet this obligation requires that when teachers use textbooks and curriculum guides, they consume them critically. It is toward this aim that the textbook analysis is addressed.

WRITING

The following is the textbook or curriculum analysis assignment we present to our students.

Obtain a copy of the textbook or curriculum guide used by your cooperating teacher or one that is commonly used in a local school. When analyzing the textbook consider the following questions: (1) Who wrote the text or guide? What part did teachers play in its production? (2) Is a rationale or statement of philosophy included? If so, is it academically, intellectually, and ethically defensible? Do you find it personally compelling? Explain and support your conclusion. (3) Are goals and objectives included? Are the goals worthy ones? Are some goals you deem worthy missing? Are some goals and objectives included that ought not be there? Why not? Explain and support your conclusion. (4) How is the text or guide organized (e.g., thematically, topically, chronologically, logically [an expert view of the discipline], psychologically [based on a conception of how people learn], or ... )? Is the organization a sensible one? Is it intellectually defensible and consistent with how children learn? Does it facilitate teaching and learning? Why or why not? (5) Is the content adequate? Is it intellectually and socially defensible? Do you see signs of a hidden or null curriculum? If so, how so? (6) What are students supposed to be doing when they engage the content? What kind of student role is encouraged by the textbook or guide? (7) What is the teacher supposed to be doing when using the text? Is there a preferred teacher role? (8) Is provision made for evaluation? What kind of information is sought through evaluation and what is to be done with the information? Are some kinds of activities or types of knowledge excluded from consideration, others emphasized? If so, what are these? Is the evaluation linked to the goals/objectives/philosophy? If so, what kind of connection is made? (9) Is the text or guide usable, teachable? For textbooks only: (10) Is the text written at a level that makes it easily accessible for students? Is the writing engaging? Note: In your write-up, use evidence—quotes—to support your conclusions.

Two edited analyses follow. The first is of a junior high school mathematics textbook and is written by Irene Tomsic, who requested that her name be used. Irene demonstrates some of the power of using the concepts of hidden and null curricula as analytic tools. The second, written by Adam, is of *English, Yes!*, an ESL textbook.

## IRENE: TEACHERS ARE STUPID BUT . . . IT'S AN IMPROVEMENT

Review of *Mathematics—Applications and Connections*. About the authors: The text is jointly written by twelve people. The authors are a fairly diverse group, comprising six females and six males, of which one was black and one Hispanic. Of the twelve, eleven were teachers; six were junior high school teachers and five were from the university level. One was a consultant. Approximately fifty other consultants were listed. Interestingly, one of the junior high school teachers had experience teaching in Ethiopia with the Peace Corps.

### Rationale and Statement of Philosophy

The primary [purpose], according to the authors, is to answer two questions for students: "Why do I have to study this?" and "When are we ever going to use it?" It is the belief of the authors, based upon their research and the research of others, that students don't see math as having much to do with their everyday lives, and that they see little connection between math and other subjects studied.

I agree with this philosophy; I remember thinking the same thing when I was a student. I also hear this sentiment from students today. I think the reasons why a subject is being taught should be clearly conveyed to students. If they can be convinced of the need, their interest and participation should increase.

### Stated Goals and Objectives

The development of the ability to solve problems is the overriding theme of [the text]. In order to meet this goal, there are sections in each chapter on problem-solving strategies, problem-solving hints, applications, connections with other math concepts, critical thinking exercises, decision-making lessons, and "make up a problem" sections. Other objectives include (1) incorporating technology into the classroom (calculator and computer lessons are included); (2) providing a multicultural perspective on math; (3) meeting individual needs; ... (4) meeting NCTM (National Council of Teachers of Mathematics) standards....

I believe that utilizing this text would provide the opportunity to meet the stated goals. I was particularly impressed by the fact that problem-solving strategies were discussed throughout [the text].... Heavy emphasis is placed on analyzing information and deciding exactly what is being asked. From there, differing strategies and different techniques for solving problems are reviewed. For example, eight different ways to estimate solutions are covered. Students are also encouraged to use estimation techniques to see if their solutions to other problems seem realistic. Open-ended questions as well as problems which lack adequate information are included. I think this would encourage information analysis and critical thinking skills.

The problems are related to the lives of students, and generally involve real-life situations. They generally relate to teen life. I think more emphasis could be placed on situations and professions where math is used after graduation so that students could envision future use.

I find it beneficial that NCTM information is spread [throughout] the text. This could help reduce the need to disrupt the normal curriculum [to prepare for standardized tests].

### Overall Text Organization

The chapters are organized topically and logically.... The order in which topics are presented should be considered, but at this point, I don't think I have the experience necessary to [judge it].

## Chapter Organization

Each chapter is organized in the following way:

1. Chapter introduction, consisting of a two-page scenario that is intended to motivate or arouse interest in the topic that follows.

2. Objective statement [which] states what the ... section seeks to accomplish. I really liked this feature, and felt it was well done. I think it is valuable to give students an overview of where you are heading ... before embarking.

3. Body of the lesson, explaining the concept. Concepts were explained in simple, concise terms.

4. Examples. Often, only one or two examples were provided. More examples would be helpful.

5. Checking for understanding. This section provides an in class review of the concept that has just been explained. In this section, students were generally required to explain a concept in their own words, without using symbols. I think this is a great idea. It helps students clarify ideas, and assists the instructor to evaluate understanding.

6. Exercises. Adequate, but more would have been [helpful].

7. Journal entry. Here students [are] to explain their feelings and thoughts about the topic. I suspect that you could get some real entertaining responses from junior high students in this section! Instead of explaining their [students'] feelings, [the authors would provide] a written explanation of the concepts covered.

8. Mid-chapter review.

9. Summary of chapter contents. I thought this was a great feature, and one that I've never encountered in a textbook. Good closure tool.

10. Chapter exam. Exams did test exactly what had been covered.

11. Vocabulary words listed in margins.

## Adequacy of the Content

As far as I am qualified to judge, I felt that the topics covered were [consistent] with the stated requirements. The teacher's text indicates which topics, problems, and exercises are included in the NCTM standards. It is the authors' claim that all topics are covered.

The text also included other [useful] topics.... In general, the text touches lightly on subjects such as algebra, geometry, statistics ... that will be encountered in future courses. I see this as useful [in that it prepares them for what is to come]....

To improve upon the text, I would recommend providing more examples following each lesson body. I don't believe there were enough practice problems provided. I think that math ability is developed by practicing and working a greater number of problems than what [the book provides].

## Socially Acceptable

It is the goal of the authors to provide a text that includes people of all races. They attempt to meet this goal in several ways. First, students and adults of all races are pictured in the text. Another technique is a section entitled "Cultural Kalei-doscope," where people of various races and their accomplishments are highlighted. Also available are optional booklets emphasizing multiracial accomplishments.... I was encouraged [by this]. Pictorially, the people shown in the text were a good mixture of people and students from all races. They did a good job here. On the other hand, the "Cultural Kaleidoscope" section could have been better.... For example, one person highlighted in the Kaleidoscope is Cesar Chavez. His contribution to the betterment of the working conditions of migrant farm workers is to be praised. Granted, Mr. Chavez's accomplishments were truly noble, but just what does this have to do with mathematics? I think the authors should have highlighted people of various cultures and races who made contributions to the field of mathematics. They missed an opportunity to show how our knowledge of math has been put together piece by piece by people from all over the globe. Of the six Kaleidoscopes in the book, only one was directly related to math contributions....

The null curriculum [showed up] with gender [issues]. To be socially acceptable by my standards, I feel that it is vital that we stop portraying women as cooks, gardeners, seamstresses, and secretaries, and men as carpenters, business owners, realtors, plumbers, and sports jocks. In reviewing the word problems, the authors generally [presented] situations where people were in sexist roles.

[I noted signs of a] hidden curriculum in [the authors'] portrayal of American life. The authors seem to project the daily lives of Americans as being focused around excessive materialism, dieting, and sports. Many of the word problems focus on females shopping, males competing in sports, and both sexes dieting. They seem to embrace the idea that it's divine to be thin, affluent, and leisurely. On the positive side, there were a fair amount of examples involving community projects, such as fund-raisers.

### Student Role

It is the goal of the authors to provide a student-centered text. A lot of effort is focused on making the text interesting to students. Through increased interest, the students are seen as active explorers of math topics. Working cooperatively in groups is included. [Various] tools [are used] to meet this goal: "Teen scene" provides little trivia factoids meant to capture the student's interests. I felt the "teen scene" section was there for the teen's entertainment only. Once again, there was too little connection to math. For example, one "teen scene" explains that [when] the "first two-piece swimsuit was seen at the beach, it was named for the shock it caused. Bikini is the name of an island in the Pacific Ocean where the hydrogen bomb was first tested." This is nice, but I'm not so sure it would be of interest to pre-teens, and I'm confident it has no relationship to math. It seems to me that the authors could come up with better examples . . . related to math. For example, explain the correlation between the number of hours a teen spends watching television, and school performance!

[A second tool to capture student interest involves] the use of blocks titled "When am I ever going to use this?" These show the ways various professions utilize math principles. These tidbits were very informative and provided concrete examples of math applications.... As an example, the way photojournalists use math to estimate distances and calculate F-stops was explained. "Save Planet Earth" is [another attempt to gain student interest]. This section [presents] environmental issues and explains how students can make a difference. I think students would find this section interesting. They were well chosen, ... and I agree with the intent of teaching social responsibility. However, I wonder if it wouldn't be more appropriate if these topics were discussed in a civics or science textbook rather than in a math book....

**Teacher's Role**

The way teachers are viewed is an example of a hidden [value]. If I were to give [the authors'] view of teachers as a metaphor, I'd say they see the "teacher as a robot." The role of the teacher is to follow their step-by-step program, and all will be accomplished.... The information given in the margins of the teacher's manual gave me the first clue that these authors believe that teachers are stupid. For example, there are directions for "checking for understanding." Included in many of these blocks is the statement that "you should work through these exercises with your students and then monitor their work." Do they really believe that we wouldn't figure this out on our own without their instructions? Another example of "helpful" items found in the margin is the "error analysis" blocks. In the section that teaches inequalities, our error analysis tells us to "watch for students who use the symbols $>$ and $<$ incorrectly"!

The second reason I didn't care for their view of teachers is that this text attempts to fulfill our every need. There are twenty optional packages available which cover everything from lesson plans to transparencies. I got the impression that we were being handed a complete set of instructions on how to proceed. Obviously, these packets spell added sales and revenue, but I felt they were lacking in quality, and were written at a very elementary level (I had access to four of the twenty).

**Evaluation**

Overall, I was impressed with the evaluation process because it offered a variety of ways to assess understanding.... [But] too often the problems [used for evaluation] were stated in the exact same manner as the examples. Varying the way questions are posed should prevent students from developing the habit of plugging numbers into formulas without knowing what they are really doing. In the answer section at the back of the book, almost all solutions were given, instead of the traditional odd or even problems only. On the positive side, this could provide students with more feedback but would hamper the teacher's efforts in using part of the problems for homework.

**Activities**

Twenty activity pamphlets are available to complement the text. These included pamphlets covering topics [from] various cultures [to] technology.... These booklets were rather sparse, and seemed more of a frill than useful materials. Group activities as well as cooperative learning sections are found throughout the text, which I thought would be helpful....

**Writing**

The book is written in a manner that is intended to tweak the interest and curiosity of the student. The level of writing seems appropriate for junior-high-age kids.

**Overall Impression**

... It seems that a lot of thought and effort went into the preparation [of this text].... I see [it] as a sign of progress [in math textbook writing].

## ADAM: IN NEED OF ADJUSTMENT

Realistically, I would look for a text from an author that can claim to have some experience with the theories and practice of second language learning. Not that I need an expert to tell me what to do, but I see my use of a text as a collaboration between myself as teacher and the author as aid to my teaching. With the huge influx of second language learners in schools today, I have reservations concerning every Tom, Dick, and Harry stepping forward and claiming to be an expert. I tend to think that some of these people are not motivated so much by a desire to provide quality materials as they are by the opportunity to make a profit in one of the largest niches in the textbook market. It appears that Burton Goodman [author of *English, Yes!*] has relied on his own education and experience only in creating this text. No other teachers or other professionals appear to have been consulted in this text's creation.

**Rational and Statement of Philosophy**

What is interesting is that there is no rationale or statement of philosophy provided in this text. That may be that this is a student's edition, yet I would think that such an important statement would be helpful to even the student. If there is no rationale or philosophy statement at all, the reasoning behind this lack is something to speculate on. By looking at the tasks that are given in the text, the philosophy seems to emphasize an audiolingual approach to learning through top-down drills of discrete grammatical points (fill in the blank, change the sentence into a question, complete the sentence with the correct present tense form of the verb, 'to be,' etc.). Little original language production is required. The materials are adapted realia (simplified adaptations and abridgements of Jack London's *World* and O. Henry's *The Last Leaf*, for example), which questions the authenticity of the reading task. The text can easily become a workbook for individual use with little or no intervention from an instructor (a list of correct answers, an idiom dictionary, and a recording of correct pronunciations are all that's needed to replace the teacher). From these details, I would conclude that the author's philosophy places the teacher into a technician role, and the student into a behaviorist [learning] paradigm.

Such a philosophy may be defensible if the text were used by an individual learner without teacher contact, but as a school text, this philosophy comes up short in utilizing teacher knowledge and limits student freedom. In addition, it fails to take into account the need to provide material to the learner that is authentic and connects to their lives outside of class. This does not make the text unusable. . . .

### Stated Goals and Objectives

Again, goals are absent from this text. However, from the publisher's Internet page, I found a list of objectives this text is meant to meet. *English, Yes!* is meant to introduce students to quality classic and contemporary authors, promote self-discipline through self-scoring exercises and encourage students to improve their productive and receptive language skills in English. . . . It is important to give some credit concerning a yet unmentioned goal. The publisher's web page states that *English, Yes!* is a flexible teaching format that allows varied teaching approaches to be implemented. This is very true [and may help account for the absence of] any philosophy statement or "How to use this book" section. . . .

### Organization of the Text

*English, Yes!* is organized in the following way: five adapted short stories are presented section by section, with each section not exceeding more than 50 to 60 lines of text. Immediately following each section, a series of multiple choice questions is provided that test comprehension of the story line as well as vocabulary and idioms from the text. After this, a series of several different grammar tasks are found. These tasks require a comprehension of the preceding story section as well as knowledge of English structure like question syntax, verb conjugation, and vocabulary meaning. Eventually, the exercises end with a task which asks one to three questions that [are intended to] connect the story to the learner's own lives. An example is, "A terrible dream is called a nightmare, Why does a nightmare always wake you up?" (p. 59). This pattern is then repeated starting with the next section of text, ultimately followed by the first text section of another story.

I call this organization a repetition within a linear structure. It is really nothing more than a patterned variation on adapted literary texts. It allows for the reader to move from the beginning to the end of one story and then on to another. . . .

### Quality and Justification of Content

[There is] evidence of hidden and null curriculum . . . Through the selections of the texts to be adapted, the author Burton Goodman implicitly provides instruction in American cultural norms. Stories like *Wolf, The Last Leaf,* and Stephen Crane's *The Hero* expose the reader to Goodman's view of what comprises quality writing. Because of Goodman's background, it is not surprising that the stories he has utilized are part of the American Literature canon. And as part of that canon, these stories reflect an American view of 'reality.' This is an argument I have regarding the judgment of what is considered good literature in general . . . [There is] an American ethno-centrist view of literature . . . In the . . . selection of which stories to use, this ethno-centrical view is taught to the learner. In effect, the student implicitly learns that all good literature is American or European literature and the cultural view of the world is only seen from that paradigm.

As far as a null curriculum, the production of original language is left to the last exercise in each section of *English, Yes!* and does not comprise a predominate part of this text. This implies that original use of the English language is not important. Again, this reflects a lack of connectivity between [the text] and the real-life experiences of the ESL learner.

### Role of Student

The role of the student is predominantly as a receptor of English and not a producer of the language. The only production they are asked to give through most of the text is to divulge a knowledge of the text and a mastery of grammatical constructs. Yet this book could be adapted by requiring the student to express their reactions to the story in discussion or writing, thus making the student interact more with the text and his/her peers in language production and practice. . . .

### Evaluation

The evaluation of student work in this text is basically left to whether they got the right or wrong answer. This reflects an idea that original language use is not important, especially for beginning learners. Students are asked to produce little bits in the beginning that are then built on with more advanced steps, presumably, in the other books in the ... series. In essence, evaluation exists solely to know what the learner has mastered, not what they are trying to express, their effort, or the meaning of what they have to say. ...

### Practical Use of English, Yes!

I am willing to use [the text] in my ESL classroom with some adaptation [until] a better book [is] located. To do so, I would have students use the stories provided in the text as jumping points to create their own stories. I might have students act out scenes from the stories in the text as a way for them to use language in more interesting ways and to think about ideas of adaptation, voice, and so on ...

## CONSIDERATIONS

Irene finds much that she likes about *Mathematics—Applications and Connections*, but as she begins digging through the text she discovers elements of it that are troubling, that suggest a hidden curriculum is at work. Two issues stand out: The presence of a significant amount of material that has nothing to do with mathematics but is included to grab student interest; and the implicit view of teachers as "stupid," a view communicated through the written text and its organization. It puzzles her why non-mathematics material would be included in the text when so much interesting mathematical material is available. Irene knows mathematics and assumes other math teachers do as well; she also assumes that other teachers have a measure of what she would consider common sense, that teachers know students need monitoring, for example. She rejects outright the possibility that some teachers might actually need such hints. Implicitly, Irene thinks of teachers as educated professionals capable of exercising judgment while it appears, at least to Irene, that the authors have a more limited view of their ability. This difference is a crucial one that would have a profound effect on how Irene would use the text. Returning to the concepts introduced earlier, because of her analysis the *implemented curriculum* of her classroom would likely be quite different from the *explicit curriculum* presented in the book.

For the most part, Irene liked the way her textbook organized and approached the content of mathematics and, especially, its emphasis on practical applications. She checked the text carefully to see if it attended to the curriculum standard generated by the National Council of Mathematics Teachers, and it did. It appears consistent with the best thinking in the field. Further, the topical organization also appealed to her understanding of mathematics. But she is cautious: "I don't think I have the experience necessary to [judge it]." Most of our students take the organization and structure of their disciplines for granted, and generally accept how they are presented in textbooks including "curricular form." Irene cautiously questioned them. The majority of our students tend to view the disciplines as stable, expert-driven discourses, where the central issues are identified and widely accepted. Few have taken courses on the philosophy of history or science, for example. Not surprisingly, we only occasionally receive papers that propose alternative conceptions of the disciplines and these arise from debates internal to the disciplines, as, for example, in art where there is a small challenge to the dominance of The Getty's view of discipline-based art education (DBAE).

Adam is unenthusiastic about *English, Yes!* He recognizes a hidden curriculum. He is troubled that so little emphasis is placed on language production and that a quest for right answers dominates the text and is embedded in the curricular form. But despite these difficulties he believes he can effectively adapt the text, at least until he finds a better one, using it less as a program for skill development than as a convenient resource for instructional materials. In this regard, its lack of a clear philosophy seems to be a virtue for Adam.

The hidden curriculum Irene discovers, unlike Adam's, is not all negative. As Eisner commented—and this is easily forgotten—the hidden curriculum can teach positive values. For example, Irene singles out for praise the inclusion by the authors of "differing strategies and different techniques for solving problems. . . . [E]ight different ways to estimate solutions are covered." For the authors, mathematics is not so much a matter of memorizing [rules] but of learning to think. They recognize that there are various good ways to solve any given problem, even in mathematics.

Irene and Adam's analyses share another characteristic: Although neither person has extensive teaching experience, both seek to get outside of themselves momentarily, to consider how students would engage the content. Such are the eyes of intelligent and critical consumers of curricula.

Both Irene and Adam's studies illustrate an additional point worth mentioning: Beginning teachers need not only questions but also concepts, like the "hidden curriculum," to help them analyze texts; otherwise, superficiality will inevitably result. But beginning teachers bring more than concepts to studies: Both Irene and Adam brought to their analyses rich background knowledge and experience. By drawing on this knowledge, public and private theories of teaching interact.

## EXTENDING THE CONVERSATION

In a sense, curriculum analysis is as old as schooling. Analysis is involved whenever the question is asked and answered, "What should be taught?" But perhaps never in the history of schooling has this question been more difficult to answer. Part of the difficulty centers on the growing awareness of the tentative nature of the disciplines themselves. Not only is knowledge changing, but what counts as knowledge is also much debated. Certainly since publication of Thomas Kuhn's *The Structure of Scientific Revolutions* (1962) awareness has grown that knowledge is socially constructed and forever tentative. In addition, the debate over the nature of knowledge has been influenced by the shifting demographics of America and the growing presence in the debate of citizens of diverse cultures and language traditions. As noted previously, the attempt to forge national history standards was much influenced by the cultural diversity of those who participated in the project, which included representatives from 33 national education organizations and more than 1,000 educators from all over the country. Recognizing the difficulty of producing consensus, one commentator wrote: "The national infatuation with commissions and task forces—architects of wry, uninhabitable structures—to resolve every difference is as ill considered as first love" (Morris, 1998, p. 13).

Recently interest has increased in curriculum analysis primarily because of growing concern over just what is being taught. The standards movement reflects this trend. Recall how Irene Tomsic looked for evidence of the standards for mathematics teaching generated by the National Council of Teachers of Mathematics in the mathematics textbook she analyzed. Irene used the standards as a basis for assessing the quality of the text. Having thought carefully about the standards, she knew and valued them. In addition to groups like the NCTM, there are also organizations, like the California Textbook League, which publishes *The Textbook Letter: A National Report on Schoolbooks and Schoolbook Affairs*, that are concerned about the quality of content. Not all those who have an interest in curriculum analysis are friends of teachers and teaching, however. Standards must be critically considered. Reflecting one or another political agenda, some groups are aggressively committed to curriculum censorship (Bullough, 1988). It is our view that despite the time pressures on teachers, it is best that they do their own thinking and their own analyses, which is a view supported both by Irene and Adam.

Given the growing complexity of the teacher's role and the ever present demands on teacher's time, it is likely that few teachers engage in careful analysis of the curriculum they teach or the guides and texts they are given. Teachers are simply overwhelmed by materials now as never before. While opening up vast and wonderful possibilities for curriculum enrichment, the internet has added to the problem. Consider, for example, that each state has curriculum guides, units, and lessons plans on-line. In addition, recently America On-line created AOL@School which is a free curriculum service that is rapidly expanding. AOL advertises its service with this claim: "Schools can quickly set up the software and integrate its content into classroom curriculum." No single teacher can possibly become a critical consumer of all the educational materials that are now available for use. Nevertheless the challenge remains: Teachers must become critical consumers of curricula. To do this teachers must help one another and make a concerted effort to share materials that are deemed educationally worthwhile and shun those found wanting.

The most difficult curriculum issue of all is not deciding what to teach, since there is so much worth learning and so little schooltime available, but what not to teach. When planning teachers generally make decisions based upon an implicit set of standards, a private theory of what is most worth knowing, and think about activities not aims or objectives. Experienced and skilled teachers typically work from a lively sense of what a good classroom looks like (see Copeland, Birmingham, DeMeulle, D'Emidio-Caston, & Natal, 1994), and it is this sense that informs their planning decisions. Lacking such a sense, beginning teachers need to make explicit the criteria that will be used when making curricular decisions, about what will be taught as well as how it will be taught. Questions like those we pose when conducting a textbook or curriculum analysis point in a direction but do not provide criteria for making curricular decisions. You make these decisions, one way or the other, wisely or not, based on your knowledge of students, yourself and your abilities, pedagogy, content, and school context. What makes the curriculum you plan to teach worthy of your students' time and energy? What vision of America is embedded in your practice? How do you understand your discipline and what view of it will you champion? What, in your judgment, is most worth knowing about your discipline and what will you dismiss and why? And finally, how will you communicate and defend your decisions to the parents of the young people you teach?

# Integrating
# Methodologies

---

✦

# ✦ 8 ✦

# Action Research

---

## INTRODUCTION

Action research links theory and practice. In action research, action and reflection, occur in a cycle, as Stephen Corey, one of the pioneers of action research, states:

> action research ... is a practice in which no distinction is made between the practice being researched and the process of researching it. That is, teaching is not one activity and inquiring into it another. The ultimate aim of inquiry is understanding, and understanding is the basis for improvement. (Corey, 1953, p. 3)

Approaches to action research differ (Rearick and Feldman, 1999). Writing in the wake of World War II, Kurt Lewin, for example, argued that action research is a means for diminishing the role of emotion in decision-making and elevating the place of reason. To engage in action research was to think systematically about one's practice.

> And again, it is not an accident that the first act of modern Fascism in every country has been officially and vigorously to dethrone this goddess [reason] and instead to make emotions and obedience the all-ruling principles in education and life from kindergarten to death. (Lewin, 1948, p. 83)

More recent advocates, such as Carr and Kemmis (1983), Kemmis and McTaggart (1988), and Gore and Zeichner (1991), utilize action research to enable participants to think systematically about their practice and to illuminate the values underlying seemingly technical teaching problems. Within this view of action research, an examination of classroom management, for instance, would raise questions concerning not only the effectiveness of a strategy or technique in keeping students on task but also the desirability of the technique viewed in light of its impact on the quality of teacher-student relationships and the kind of public world the teacher seeks to help create.

Still other scholars (e.g., Stenhouse, 1985; Elliott, 1991) view action research from a naturalistic perspective. These authors see the processes involved in action research as occurring naturally within the classroom as teachers grapple with the problems of teaching. The purpose of action research, then, is to make teaching, and the inquiry process that is part of teaching, explicit. As Stenhouse writes:

> The effect [of action research] is not unlike that of making the transition from amateur to professional actor. Through self-monitoring the teacher becomes a conscious artist. Through conscious art he is able to use himself as an instrument of his research. (pp. 15–16)

Because this approach seeks to make implicit processes explicit, it recognizes that teachers necessarily must determine the nature and focus of study when engaging in action research.

In this chapter we draw primarily on the naturalistic and more explicitly value-oriented approaches to action research. Studying teaching, as we have argued, requires digging into and criticizing private and public theories about teaching. However, it is your practice, not ours, that is the focus of research, and you may choose a different approach. In the final analysis you must decide the focus of your research if for no other reason than, as Stenhouse observes, "teachers are in charge of classrooms" (p. 15).

At this point, we need to broaden our discussion momentarily. One of the factors that influences what type of action research is undertaken is the structure or organization of the teacher education program within which you are enrolled. Full-time practice teaching for a single term will limit the types of questions that can be asked and the rigor of the project itself. Even with a student teaching seminar, the pressures of teaching under such conditions and time limitations seriously constrain what can be accomplished. Furthermore, the long-standing separation of preservice from in-service teacher education makes a continuing conversation about theories embedded in educational practice difficult. We mention this here because expectations for action research often run well beyond what can reasonably be expected of beginning teachers. Preservice teacher education should introduce you to the process of action research and provide opportunities for you to develop skill and understanding that will enable you to continue researching your practice once you assume a teaching position.

Finally, we should note that action research is an *integrative methodology* because it brings together inquiry about self and context. It is, after all, your concerns as they emerge in your classroom that are the focus of study. And it is an integrative methodology because it provides the opportunity to pull together and apply insights gained from each of the methodologies previously discussed in *Becoming a Student of Teaching*.

## WRITING

The action research assignment is laid out in three phases. In Phase One a concern or issue is identified, written up, and data collected. In the light of the data gathered, the problem is reconsidered, perhaps reformulated, and a problem statement written that will guide the study. In Phase Two an action plan is written and implemented, and again data gathered. In Phase Three the plan is assessed in the light of the data gathered and recommendations are made for future study and practice. We set due dates for each phase to nudge along the work and help with pacing. Pacing is important because the temptation is to let more immediate and obviously pressing teaching demands consume your energy.

This assignment has several parts:

### PHASE ONE

1. Describe in writing a concern or issue relating to some aspect of your teaching.
2. Gather data using one or a combination of the following methods:

A. *Peer observation.* Choose one or two of your cohort colleagues to work with. Prior to being observed, discuss your concern or problem with your colleagues. Observation notes should focus on this issue, but other significant events should also be recorded. Observation notes should be shared in a post-observation conference and discussed.

B. *Audio-taping.* Audio-taping is an easy and effective way to gather data. If you choose this option, make certain you tape relatively often, which will allow you to make comparisons. The difficulty with audio-taping is to make certain you set up a classroom situation and/or find an appropriate placement for the machine to make certain you record useful information. A trial run will be a good idea.

C. *Videotaping.* Although sometimes distracting to students and to beginning teachers, videotaping can be a powerful means for gathering data. If you decide to videotape your classroom, a practice run to get you and your students accustomed to the camera might be helpful. Make certain you give explicit directions to the operator to make certain it is understood what, specifically, you want captured on tape. As with audio-taping, it is a good idea to do multiple takes to allow for comparisons of activities or lessons.

D. *Student work/feedback.* You may wish to use student work of one kind or another as a source of data. More formally, you might want to conduct student interviews (or have someone in your cohort or your cooperating teacher conduct them), design a questionnaire, or have the students perform some task that will produce data useful for thinking about your problem or concern. If you design a questionnaire, have your cooperating teacher or instructor review it before it is used to avoid leading questions and to make certain you will obtain useful data. Be cautious in what you ask of students. Make certain you do not put your students in the position of betraying a confidence or of revealing information that later might adversely affect their relationships with peers or with teachers and administrators.

3. After gathering and reviewing your data, reconsider your initial written description of the concern or problem. Because other issues or concerns are likely to surface,

you may need to reformulate the problem or make it more specific. Write a problem statement.

### PHASE TWO

4. Write a plan for addressing or ameliorating your concern or issue.
5. Share your plan with your cooperating teacher, and if working with peers, your team. Based upon their feedback, revise the plan.
6. Implement the plan.
7. Gather data (see #2 above) to assess your plan. At this point you may wish to include your cooperating teacher in data gathering. If so, make certain he/she understands the purpose of the observations. All data gathered should be written, systematically gathered and sharply focused on the issue or concern.

### PHASE THREE

8. Review the data to determine the effect of your plan. With an eye toward your future work as a teacher, write up and share the results. Include recommendations for future practice.
9. Time permitting, engage in additional cycles of action research.

Before presenting two edited and much abbreviated action research projects, it is important to place these projects in context. These action research projects were conducted during full-time practice teaching. Because of this constraint, additional research cycles were not possible. These projects, then, are in some respects limited.

Although we refrain from determining what issues or concerns are identified for study, the students we work with often need assistance in forming researchable questions. "I'm having a difficult time deciding what my problem statement will be, but I'm quite sure that it will be something related to discipline and learning." Frequently, issues like classroom management are identified at first. Such issues are too broad to study; they need redefining and sharpening to become manageable: "What I would most enjoy solving is a problem that occurs when students show no desire for learning and no motivation." On the other extreme, some trivial problems are identified, the solution of which will have little impact on your development or understanding of teaching: "I use 'um' during transitions way too much. This gives an impression of being unsure on my part and the students get a little restless." Had this beginning teacher undertaken the study of his tendency to say "um," one wonders what, if anything, would have been learned about teaching.

It takes time to identify and usefully frame a problem for study. Be patient. Remember, the problems of teaching are interrelated, and no one can work on every problem or concern at once. What is important is that a beginning is made, recognizing that other concerns will emerge over time that will command attention in a continuous cycle of reflection and action.

The two edited and abbreviated studies that follow were written by two preservice teachers, Vicki Healy and Sonja. We use Vicki's name with her permission. Vicki's study was chosen in part because it represents an effort to link public theory—concepts studied in teacher education—with her teaching practice. The nature of her relationships with students is a primary concern. We should mention that both Sonja and Vicki taught English—and Vicki, low-level reading classes called "developmental reading"—in an ethnically diverse, working-class high school. Sonja, whose work is also included in the next chapter, addresses a range of issues common to beginning teachers, particularly those associated with establishing classroom authority, and engages in honest and open reflection. But what makes this study particularly interesting is that she initially poses a broad-value issue, "who she is as a teacher," which in the end is reduced to a set of technical concerns.

## VICKI'S STUDY: BUILDING REFERENT POWER

While studying classroom culture, attention was given within the program to various sources of teacher power or influence. Four sources were identified, and research relating to each was read: (1) Referent power is based on the teacher's personality, the connection that comes from knowing about and caring for one another; (2) expert power is tied to respect for a teacher's knowledge and expertise; (3) legitimate power flows from the teacher's position within the institution as teacher; (4) coercive power comes from a teacher's ability to punish and dispense rewards. Vicki was interested in increasing her referent power. What is significant about Vicki's problem statement is that she understands management as a relationship issue, and not merely as a concern arising because of the lack of teaching skill. We include portions of Vicki's study that followed her reformulation of the problem statement (the last part of #3 above).

**Problem Statement**

[I recruited] a fellow cohort member [to do] observations to help identify a problem. These observations did reveal some management concerns, and upon reflection I identified some students who seemed to be very alienated, others who were 'testing the limits,' and still others who seemed to be engaged very minimally if at all. I wanted to develop a plan which preferably would address all of these concerns.

At this point in student teaching, I am concerned with building referent power in the classroom. Amazing as it may seem, not every one of my students has come to love and adore me. Although I can live with this (I admit with chagrin that I don't love and adore every one of them, either), I sincerely believe that the establishment of referent power in my classroom will go a very long way toward preventing and/or eliminating most management problems.

I have arrived at the decision to concentrate on this issue after considerable thought and a review of [some of our class readings]. I still feel fairly confident in my ability to maintain expert power. I am a strong advocate of my content area and attempt in all my lesson plans to make the subject and content relevant to the students. I am less comfortable with resorting to legitimate power, and at this point completely reject the idea of resorting to coercive power [to influence students]. I believe that a combination of referent and expert power is the most desirable method for [creating the kind of classroom climate I want].

**The Plan**

One way that I plan to address the issue of referent power is through holding individual conferences with each student. Since I am experiencing what I would characterize as management problems most noticeably with my fourth-period . . . class, I plan to try the individual conference approach with this group first.

In these conferences, I plan to discuss several matters with each student. . . . First, I will discuss their grade so far this quarter, congratulate them on successes, make suggestions for improvement, and ask for their input and ideas. . . . I also plan to discuss the book they are currently reading in class and the type of books they enjoy reading and, if they would like, offer suggestions for future reading selections. I would also like to take this opportunity to find out more about each student, their attitudes, and interests and, if necessary, discuss any management concerns I may have. . . . I hope through this process to establish a more personal relationship with each student, thus bolstering referent power in the classroom.

I have discussed this idea with my cooperating teacher, and she agrees that it is a good strategy for addressing the issue of referent power. She feels that this method of discussing concerns individually would be very beneficial and that it would also avoid calling undesirable and/or negative attention to any student by making [him or her] feel singled out for such a discussion. She thinks that individual conferencing could be accomplished while the rest of the class is doing group work, silent reading, or individual seat work.

I have also had another cohort member do some peer observations of my fourth-period class to assist me in framing this problem. I plan to continue peer observations, particularly during the conferencing process. . . .

My hope is that this process will enhance my rapport with the students, decrease power struggles and management problems, and create a classroom climate more conducive to learning.

**Final Report**

Early in the quarter I identified the building of referent power as an objective for two major reasons. First, the establishment of referent power as opposed to legitimate or coercive power in the classroom is consistent with my philosophy of teaching and therefore comfortable and desirable to me. Second, I felt that the establishment of referent power in my classroom would go a very long way toward preventing and/or eliminating most management problems.

Although there were only two or three students in any given class whom I considered to be causing significant disruption in the classroom, the approach I decided upon to begin building referent power was to conduct individual conferences with each student. My hope was that this process would enhance my rapport with the students, decrease power struggles and management problems, and create a classroom climate more conducive to learning....

I had a fellow cohort member, my cooperating teacher, and one of my university supervisors do observations during the individual conferences in fourth period. All three observed that although many students seemed fairly nervous at the beginning of the conference, at some point in the conference most loosened up and seemed to realize that I was not just a 'teacher figure,' but a fellow human being who is genuinely interested in them, their concerns, and their interests. The observation notes which I received would seem to confirm this assessment. My own perception of the conferences was that each student with whom I had a conference at least left [it] with the impression that I sincerely wanted them to succeed in my class.

I was generally pleased with the outcome of the conferences. I observed most noticeably that the teacher/student relationship was altered in significant ways during these one-on-one conferences. We were able to relate to each other on a more personal and informal basis, and I feel that this really helped to build a more cooperative relationship with some of these students.

Other observations during the quarter noted a comfortable 'ambience' or 'atmosphere' in my class. To me, this constituted a major accomplishment and improvement from the way things were.... The environment in the class felt better to me, and this feeling seemed to 'rub off' on the students. I also noted that many management problems, particularly in the fourth and sixth periods, decreased.

During my planning and teaching, I attempted to keep the objective of referent power in mind while planning activities. . . . I did not want to build a positive personal relationship with the students at the expense of learning and academics. Some observation comments I received indicated that I was on the right track. From my cooperating teacher: 'I like your writing topics! They are thoughtful and interesting.' 'Everyone seems to be comfortable with you! Hooray! I heard some good ideas being discussed.' 'I think this is a really fun idea. They seem to understand the concept very well!' and 'I like the way you are always so positive with everyone. They seem to feel comfortable with you and the things you ask them to do.'

As a final phase of this project, I wanted to get some student feedback. I designed an evaluation form which I had students in fourth and sixth periods fill out anonymously. This was really an exciting and satisfying part of the project for me. The questions which I felt applied most directly to the issue of referent power were Question #3: 'The thing I liked best about Mrs. Healy's teaching was . . . '; Question #4: 'One thing I think Mrs. Healy could do to be a better teacher is . . . '; and Question #6: 'The thing I will remember the most about class this quarter is . . . "

Many of the responses I received to Question #3 are very gratifying and lead me to believe that I have in fact achieved some success in establishing referent power in these classes. Some [of the responses to Question 3 follow.]

The thing I liked best about Mrs. Healy's teaching was:

The way she taught that made it fun.

She makes reading class more fun.

Made me feel more comfortable.

She was so cool; she was kick[ed] back, but she had us get the work done.

She is so nice and she really likes to teach.

She was nice, she explained things well, she was patient.

She is very nice and is patient, to help you understand things better.

Cool, laid-back environment.

She seems to care about you and [is] willing to help you.

She is nice. She makes this class fun.

Although most of the responses I received to Question #4 (such as "I think she's a good teacher" and "Nothing," "She was the best," and "I hope she works at [this school] next year") were highly complimentary and positive, I did find some of the suggestions for improvement . . . enlightening.

One thing I think Mrs. Healy could do to be a better teacher is:

Get the kids [to be] more controlled.

Be more strict. (She's too nice!)

Be more strict and tell the kids they need to stay in their seats and do their assignment. Just be more strict.

Not be so lenient.

More stricter [sic].

These responses indicate to me that many students are more comfortable with [high] structure and limits. I do realize that referent power is not the whole picture and that it can only go so far in maintaining order in the classroom. I plan to take these comments to heart. . . .

I was also very gratified by many of the responses I received to Question #6.

The thing I will remember the most about class this quarter is:

It would be Mrs. Healy. She is cool.

Mrs. Healy and my friends.

I had a great teacher this quarter, Mrs. Healy.

I provided a space for additional student comments. Some I received were:

Mrs. Healy, I think you did a really good job. Thanks for being such a good teacher.

Mrs. Healy is an awesome teacher.

Mrs. Healy has been a great teacher. She made this class fun for me!

Needless to say, these comments made my day and did go a long way toward helping me see this project as a success. However, as mentioned above, I did not merely want to make ... class a 'fun' experience for the students. My desire was also that they actually learn something. Therefore, I also carefully perused the evaluation forms for indications that some learning had taken place and perhaps made a difference to the students. I was particularly interested in the responses to Question #1, 'What has been the best thing [about class] this quarter?' and Question #6, 'The thing I will remember the most about class this quarter is ... ' Out of 31 evaluation forms I received, 25 of them listed an item which we had studied or something we had learned in their responses to one or both of these questions. Although I am of course delighted by the students who stated that they liked me and referred to the enjoyable atmosphere in the classroom, I am exceedingly pleased that the majority of them also chose to remember and refer to some of the learning activities....

I am very glad I conducted this project. It helped me to reflect on my teaching in a way I know I would not have done otherwise. Although I am pleased with the progress I have made in achieving referent power in the classroom, I feel I still have a long way to go. As some of the student comments revealed, I need to 'fine-tune' my management style and achieve more of a balance between 'laid-back' and 'strict.' I want to be able to indicate a genuine interest and friendship for the students without being seen as a pushover or a patsy. In my first year of teaching, I would like to set some specific goals and objectives for establishing and maintaining both order and a comfortable ambience in my classroom (promoting learning all the while, of course).

## IDENTITY AND CLASSROOM PRESENCE: SONJA'S STUDY

### Initial Problem Description

As I have taught my junior and senior English classes, the one situation that continually concerns me is classroom management. I have gleaned many things already that have helped me to improve my management skills, such as better pacing ... speaking loudly and clearly, waiting for students to quiet down, and adjusting the curriculum to keep the attention of the class. I find that even as I teach, I think of some new way to better the lesson.... Sometimes I leave [the classroom] frustrated, but I realize that I am going through a process and learning what will work....

In trying to combat management problems, I have sought the advice of my cooperating teachers [but] they are very different and have different philosophies on student discipline. I have found much of their advice very helpful and have applied some of it. However, I began to realize that I needed to find my own philosophy and my own way of dealing with management problems.... On the one hand, I feel that I need to be firm and show the students I will not put up with nonsense. On the other hand, I want to have a caring and friendly relationship with students.

This statement was read by one of the cohort leaders, and on it written: "Gee, Sonja, these are huge, broad, issues. Can you focus more sharply on just a piece ... a small but crucial part of what troubles you?" A discussion followed to help Sonja begin to think through what a problem statement might be. She began to gather data that would help her focus her study. As a result of listening to audiotapes of her teaching and watching a videotape taken by her husband, and feedback from her cooperating and supervising teachers, Sonja reconsidered the problem. Management was not the central issue: Sonja was struggling with her identity as a teacher.

### Revised Problem Statement and Plan of Action

Although at times I am excited about my teaching, I am not completely the teacher I want to be. I feel that I am starting to find myself as a teacher. Before I started student teaching, I didn't realize how long it would take to develop an identity as a teacher.... Sometimes I have held back because I was afraid that if I demonstrated too many emotions or too much of a personality, the students would take advantage of me. I have also held back because I do not always know what type of [teacher] I want to be in front of the classroom.

In order to allow my personality to develop, I need to put myself more into the classroom and become a presence.... I am trying to use my voice more. It is difficult sometimes for me to walk among the students and come out from behind the pulpit or from behind the table. It takes a conscious effort for me to walk among the students; sometimes I forget that I need to reach out to them physically....

In order to further develop my ... presence in the class-room I have [made] a plan of action.... In order to make my presence felt in the beginning of class or during transitions, I [will] wait until I have every person's attention before I start to explain what is due or the lesson for the day. In each lesson, I [will] write, in bold letters, notes to remind me to move throughout the room and to better use my voice. I will continue practicing certain pieces of literature at home with expression before I [read] them in front of my class.... I will continue ... recording [my classes] in order to better evaluate my voice [which is weak and uncertain]. I will also have my husband videotape me [again] in order to assess my movement [throughout the classroom].

## Analysis

There is a great deal going on in Sonja's mind and in her classroom. She is uncertain who she is or wants to be. She feels uneasy with students, but is reluctant to engage them as a person. She recognizes that she is not seen by the students as an authority figure, nor does she see herself in that role. She observes that she acts differently depending on how the students respond to her. As she contemplates these discoveries and how she wants to address them, she determines that her first efforts must be directed toward engaging the students, toward becoming a "presence" in the classroom. She understood the issue technically; what she needed to do was to move around the classroom, speak up, and better plan her transitions. These actions, she thought, would increase her authority in the classroom. The crucial issue of identity, of who Sonja is as teacher, is lost, at least for the time being.

Sonja implemented her plan and continued to gather and analyze data. A few days after student teaching ended, she turned in her final report.

## ACTION RESEARCH RESULTS

My ... project consisted of better using voice and movement in the classroom to establish a stronger teacher presence [in the classroom].... I chose to use videotapes, feedback from students and my cooperating teachers ... as data to assess where I was and how I was improving.

The videotapes were especially revealing.... After watching the first videotape ... I realized how unauthoritative and weak I sounded at times. I was too tentative when I gave an assignment or when I asked for students' attention. My voice became weaker sometimes when I was making a request, not stronger as it should [have been]. One weak point that I noticed in the video was when I told [a] student to be quiet. I did not sound firm. It seemed that I was almost afraid of telling him to quiet down. I have worked on this area as well, and I have become more firm.

Frequently I did not wait for the class's full attention before I gave an assignment. Consequently I found myself constantly repeating directions for assignments. This wasted a great deal of time....

[After implementing my plan of action] I started waiting a little longer for the class to quiet down. I also began warning the class before I gave an assignment that I would only mention it once, and if they missed it, they would have to find out about it from someone else. Once they realized I was serious, they started to quiet down. I realize now that I cannot take responsibility for everything the student should do. If a student does not take the time to make up an assignment, I do not have the time to continually check with the student. I would help students in any way I could, but I feel by taking on the students' responsibilities, I only ... make them more dependent on me....

From the video, I realized that I had another problem with voice. I repeated the word 'OK' a lot, which seemed to demonstrate that I was tentative about giving the lecture or the assignment. It definitely did not add to sounding more authoritative. I also paused several times in my speech adding an 'umm,' 'uh,' or such. This also gave the appearance of being unorganized although I had carefully planned the lesson.

I also realized that I needed more movement in the classroom. I didn't realize how much I stayed to the front of the classroom or how isolated I looked until I watched the first videotape. I stayed in front of the classroom the entire time and frequently my back was to the students because I was writing on the board. I would talk while I was writing on the board, and it sounded a little mumbled.... I now realize how important eye contact is between the teacher and students.... As I viewed this tape I realized how important it is that when a student answers a question, I give feedback clearly by looking directly at the student and responding ... promptly. This too, I now realize, is an important part of teacher presence.... By isolating myself at the front of the classroom, I was unaware of how much talking was going on while I was giving a lecture. I was stranded in front of the classroom because I had to write constantly on the board.... I was surprised how much extra talking the video showed was going on. I realized from watching it that there were times when I was competing with it. [Handouts helped.] ...

[Students] lost an increasingly large amount of interest in the subject matter because the lesson was too long. I should have broken the grammar down into chunks [and varied my instruction to increase interest]. I later did this and found more success in so doing.

Before I had the students turn their papers in at midterm, I had them write an evaluation of their goals and things that we could do in class to help them. [This was part of the data I gathered]. I received a great deal of good feedback. One student said that she felt it would be better if I broke the period down into different lessons so she could better stay attentive.... Based on this evaluation ... [I adjusted my plan].

After trying to improve ... my teacher presence by better using my voice and movement, I [was videotaped again]. After watching this video I could see a great deal of improvement. Immediately I realized how much stronger my voice was.... I sounded much more firm and authoritative. I noticed that in the first video it seemed that I felt embarrassed to walk among the students. I looked much more confident.... I moved a great deal more.... I saw more life in my face. [Wanting] to make the material come alive for the students [I varied my instruction].... Overall, I was greatly improved.

In this video there were several times when the students wanted to know about previous assignments that they had missed, but I quickly told them to speak with me after class, and I moved on with the lesson. This kept me from losing my train of thought.... I didn't have as many 'umms' and 'uhs' in my voice. I had more eye contact with students, and I picked on a variety of students rather than completely allowing only a few students to speak out. I made an effort to include all the class.

... [W]e read ... together. Instead of allowing the students to volunteer, I picked several of the students. Frequently I chose a student who was not paying attention. I also moved around the class as the students read and checked to see who was reading [along]. I noticed that as I walked by some students, they suddenly appeared more interested. I also saw myself wake up some students that were falling asleep.... I glanced several times around the room to see if the students were following along.

## CONSIDERATIONS

Sonja's study illustrates nicely how problem definitions evolve. She begins with a very general and common problem, classroom management. By gathering data she comes to see her management problems as associated with other problems, insecurity and lack of a clear teacher identity. Lack of identity is tied to a lack of classroom presence, and presence, in turn, is linked to her lack of enthusiasm, lack of movement in the classroom, and "weak voice." These latter issues are ones she can address directly, and the results of her efforts are quickly apparent.

The decision to gather data through videotaping proved crucial for Sonja. She could see her face, hear her voice, and witness herself hiding behind the desk and avoiding students. This data, along with the observations of her cooperating teachers, helped her focus her energies. Although it is not fully apparent in either Sonja's study or Vicki's, ongoing and extensive conversation about these issues with peers, cooperating teachers, and supervising teachers was extremely important to understanding their problems and, ultimately, to how they addressed them.

Sonja's study also illustrates, however, how some very important issues can be lost if care is not taken. Sonja's concerns for identity and to build a philosophy of management are overwhelmed by the quest to gain greater classroom control. She appears frightened of the students, fearful of revealing herself to them. Rather than risk revealing who she is, Sonja explores techniques for being more "teacherlike." Questions of philosophy introduced in the initial problem statement, where she sought a balance between an approach to management that was "caring" and one that was "firm" and no-nonsense, are set aside for learning techniques of control, ways of getting students to, as she puts it, "quiet down." Firm wins out. Sonja wants to sound "authoritative" and this is her aim.

Sonja's concerns are legitimate ones. We would not want to discount the importance of various teaching skills to producing a productive and engaging learning climate. The issue, however, is one of purpose. The study illustrates that Sonja did become more of a "presence" in the classroom and, apparently, students were more respectful of her, but for what purpose? Classroom control and classroom management are not ends in and of themselves. And one wonders if the firm, no-nonsense presence Sonja began to create was one that represented an authentic expression of who she is as a person and wants to be as a teacher. Sonja needs to address these issues if action research is to be something more than a way to accommodate to institutional role demands.

Vicki's study presents an important contrast. She too is concerned about management, but management, as she conceives of it, is about relationships not control. Rather than seek to withdraw into a teacher presence, Vicki seeks means for breaking down barriers in the belief that the more she can relate to students as persons, the more likely learning will take place. The few students who want a "more strict" Mrs. Healy illustrate the power of institutional roles and relationships to shape teacher and student behavior. Because Mrs. Healy does not fit the strict teacher role the students are used to, they encourage her to change, and perhaps she will adjust somewhat. But it is uncertain what the students actually mean when they request more strictness. This would need to be explored before any changes were undertaken. In the light of this additional information, Vicki would need to decide if she will or should change. However, the study does illustrate that Vicki desires a different role, one more consistent with her view of herself as a person. The tension Vicki feels is also felt by Sonja, but Sonja seeks technical rather than interpersonal means for increasing her power. One wonders if, in the process of accommodating, she will form the authentic identity she wants.

The ultimate question for Sonja is who she will be as a teacher and whether or not the context of schooling will allow her to be that kind of teacher. Perhaps eventually she will be able to shape the context in ways necessary to achieve an authentic teaching self. Until this question is answered, the context of teaching will prove overpowering.

Both teachers honestly and openly explore their teaching. They seem committed to the ongoing study of their practice even though they realize that at times the struggle to improve will be painful and compromises necessary. Both studies contain strong evidence of increasing understanding about teaching, of a willingness to listen to and to learn from students and others, and of growing confidence about their ability to become effective teachers and direct their own development. This said, both realize that they are just beginning their professional journeys and that much remains to be learned. Sonja ended her study with these words: "I feel that I am making progress in my profession. . . . I realize, though, that I need to carry this self analysis on when I have my own classroom. . . . I want to continue to be a student of my [practice]."

## EXTENDING THE CONVERSATION

There are comparatively few studies of the use of action research in preservice teacher education. From what is known, action research helps beginning teachers be more thoughtful about their teaching, "aware of their own practices and of the gaps between their beliefs and their practices . . . and . . . of their pupils' thinking and learning " (Gore & Zeichner, 1991, p. 131). These are very positive outcomes evident in the two studies we presented in this chapter. However, and referring to their own work, Gore and Zeichner (1991) suggest there is a disappointing lack of evidence that action research addresses contextual, political, and ethical issues. Beginning teachers, like Sonja, are generally consumed with practical questions and only rarely address wider contextual issues. We generally agree, although there are exceptions (see Atweh, Kemmis, & Weeks, 1998). Some of our students, like Vicki, consider wider issues. Student teachers in our program have studied the moral implications of teacher bias and favoritism: "I knew without a doubt that I tended to favor smart white girls, and was biased against loudmouthed boys of any race." Student power: "Who really runs the classroom?" Student dependency: "I felt the students were too dependent on my opinion of their work or progress on an art project. They are not talking to each other about art questions." The nature of evaluation: "For those of us raised in an industrialized society the tendency to apply ourselves to a simple standard of measure is overwhelming. We have been eager to buy unconditionally the economists' pitch that innovation and competition would solve our problems. . . . To serve the interests of the simple economic standard of productivity, we have been waging, and winning, a war against our own people and our own land. . . . I find myself all too easily succumbing to an all too simple standard of measure." Class size and student learning: "There seems to be an ongoing debate over the effects of class size on the classroom and student performance. . . . Teachers contend a class with fewer students is a better atmosphere for [teaching] and thus leads to better learning." These are among the many issues that reach beyond the more common technical issues and concerns of beginning teachers and in which contextual, political, and ethical questions are posed. They might be issues worthy of your attention.

The knowledge that Sonja and Vicki have produced as part of their action research projects represents a departure from the way novice teachers typically make decisions. As opposed to Sonja and Vicki's considered study of practice, most beginning teachers engage in a process of trial and error. In this process they draw heavily on their prior experience, including their experience as students. The focus on prior experience and use of trial and error approaches to problem-solving should come as no surprise given the conditions under which teachers work. Having accommodated to the culture of teaching, both novice and more experienced teachers generally reject research of all kinds as legitimate sources of insight into teaching. Seen as originating in the "ivory tower," research—public knowledge—is judged irrelevant to the concerns of teachers and disrespectful of teachers' knowledge (Gitlin et al., 1999). Potentially, action research challenges these conclusions by underscoring the role of teachers as researchers, as students of their practice.

While action research challenges the relevance question and provides the means for linking private and public theories, making the transfer from preservice teacher education to in-service teaching is difficult. Transfer will become easier only as teachers come to value the process of studying their practice and seek to create institutional conditions that support teacher inquiry.

Through their action research projects Sonja and Vicki have not only moved beyond the common practice of using only prior experience and a process of trial and error to make teaching decisions, but have become convinced of the value of teacher research to quality teaching. As they move into their first year of teaching we believe it is important for them to consider means by which they can continue to study their practice. Certainly, like you, they can gather data about their teaching on their own. However, we believe the full power of action research comes when teachers join together to inquire into teaching. Potentially, such studies have the power to alter departmental and school cultures as well as to build and strengthen teacher relationships. When planning to engage in action research, it would be helpful to explore the following questions, questions of importance to chapter ten on collaborative teacher research: What is the attitude of administrators and department chairs toward teacher research?

Are there other teachers within the department or school that share an interest in teacher research? Do members of your department know of teachers who currently are engaged in the systematic study of their practice? Who are they, and are they willing to share the results of their study with you? Are their departmental or school resources available to support inquiry? What are the issues that are most likely to engender interest and to facilitate teacher interaction and community building?

# ✧ 9 ✧

# Creating
# a Personal Teaching Text

## INTRODUCTION

Throughout *Becoming a Student of Teaching* we have sought to provide an alternative to training views of teacher education and development. The methodologies described have the potential to enhance beginning teacher reflectivity and the development of a professional community. This potential, however, will be lost if the methodologies are viewed as disconnected and discrete techniques to be laid out sequentially, side by side, like a row of hurdles. Instead, they need to be connected, and closure needs to be provided at crucial transitional points in the program. As Buchmann and Floden (1992) remind us, teacher education is unlikely to have much impact on beginning teacher development if it lacks coherence and remains fragmented.

The cohort organization, where students stay together in a group, is an important but partial step toward overcoming fragmentation and providing program coherence. This administrative arrangement, which puts beginning teachers and teacher educators together for extended periods of time, must be complemented with changes in the form and content of the teacher education curriculum. Clearly, unless content is carefully integrated and efforts are made to provide closure, fragmentation will remain a problem despite the cohort organization.

The creation and use of a personal teaching text (PTT) has proven to be a powerful means for addressing this problem and for helping beginning teachers to reflect on their experience. The PTT builds on a number of innovations currently being explored in teacher education, including portfolios and student journals (Valli & Rennert-Ariev, 2000). Like portfolios, PTTs encourage beginning teachers to put together an array of products that in some fashion represent their teacher education experience. In contrast to portfolios, which originated in the tradition of the visual arts and over which there is a great deal of confusion (Meyer & Tusin, 1999), the concept of the personal teaching text taps literary traditions. Our desire is to emphasize writing and reflection on teacher development over time and process over product. In education, portfolios are mostly viewed as a product created for the purpose of demonstrating to some external body, like a certification agency, panel, or board, that a standard of one kind or another has been met (Naizer, 1997). Indeed, this trend has accelerated as performance-based accreditation of teacher education and performance-based certification have come to dominate the conversation about teacher education reform (see Wise, 2000; Yinger, 1999). We recognize the importance of this change in emphasis toward performance and meeting specific "outcomes" and away from what are called program "inputs." But our interest is first and foremost in helping beginning teachers like yourselves to "hear the voice" of your own experiences and to respond to that voice (Munby & Russell, 1993, p. 11). It is this difference in emphasis, on process rather than outcomes, and the place of self-evaluation in the process of teacher development, that distinguish PTTs from portfolios.

All written assignments generated by the methodologies presented in the preservice section of *Becoming a Student of Teaching*, along with any additional written work deemed appropriate, are placed chronologically in a binder which forms a case record (Yin, 1984), a text, of each student's development over the course of our program. Throughout the year the students are encouraged to read and review all of the materials contained in the PTT and consider what they have written and where they are in their development and thinking about teaching. Following a careful re-reading, they write periodic reviews, self-assessments, of the PTT including at year's end. The written reviews are occasions to critically examine one's development as a teacher, to celebrate accomplishments, to identify areas of concern that need attention, and to plan for the future.

WRITING

One of the recent end-of-year review assignments read as follows:

> Reread the contents of your personal teaching text for the entire year. Based upon this reading, assess your development as a teacher. Are you pleased with what you have accomplished this year? Any disappointments? Has your resolve to become a teacher strengthened or weakened? Why? Has your view of yourself as a teacher changed during the course of the year? If so, what has prompted the change? If not, why not? Are you on track for becoming the kind of teacher you imagine yourself capable of becoming? Be specific, and give examples.

Each written review encourages the beginning teacher to think carefully about his or her professional development—past, present, and future. Comparing the reviews enables beginning teachers to see the progress made over the course of the year, progress that sometimes seems fleeting but is not.

Three edited and abbreviated reviews follow. Each was written at different times of the year by the same beginning English teacher, Sonja, whose work was included in the previous chapter. These reviews were chosen for inclusion in *Becoming a Student of Teaching* for three reasons: Sonja addresses a range of issues common to beginning teachers; they show a beginning teacher seriously examining her experience during the program; and they indicate growth and change in thinking, but uncertainty remains.

We should note that for writing some beginning teachers choose to organize their reviews around specific program activities and their impact, while others organize them around the specific questions we ask. Capturing the spirit of the task, still others write essays that range rather widely, reaching well beyond the PTT entries but touching on issues and questions of genuine concern. Regardless of the approach selected, the purpose of the reviews is to reflect on one's experience in relationship to one's personal and professional teaching ideals and development.

## FIRST REVIEW: FADING INNOCENCE

[December 10, prior to winter break:] As I review my personal teaching text and the experiences I have had as I have studied to become a teacher, I realize that I have developed and changed my philosophy [about] what type of teacher I am going to be. I have seen some approaches [to teaching] work and many approaches I thought would work, fail. I have become aware of many negative aspects of teaching which would have been very discouraging if I had not also [encountered many] positive aspects [of teaching] that overshadowed the negative.

[The] life history . . . was an important assignment for me because I was able to reflect on the reasons why I have chosen to become a teacher. Prior to this paper I had reminisced about my life history, and reflected on how certain events had changed my life, but I had never pieced together several episodes in my life in order to assess why I had chosen [this] particular path. Once I started writing my life history, the words flowed. I felt such emotion that I even started to cry as I wrote about some of the events of my life. Sometimes memories dim, but through writing them down I was able to recapture how I felt.

[My] life history was what inspired me to choose my teaching metaphor. I started to reflect on the times when I had no one to turn to and no one to defend me from the cruelties of other students. I chose the metaphor of "defender." As I visited the classrooms of my cooperating teachers, I began to realize that I could not simply sit with a stick in my hand and ward off every attacker. . . . I realized that I would have to teach them to defend each other. After doing my classroom study . . . I realized that in order to teach them to help each other, they first must learn to defend and value themselves. I added the metaphor of "nurturer" to that of defender. I now realize that I must fill my classroom with caring in order to nurture the students. I am beginning to understand how carefully I need to construct not only the intellectual and emotional characteristics of the classroom, but the physical environment as well. I noticed in my [classroom study] how the physical appearance of the classroom had been altered to provide a nurturing atmosphere. I feel that I am obligated to help the students by providing ways for them to develop self-esteem and self-motivation. Once students are empowered with these qualities, they will be more prepared to defend and protect others.

As I considered seriously becoming a teacher, I thought that I would take the role of a friend to the students, an equal, someone who understood what they were going through. I could see myself joking with them and being a part of their groups. Because I was close to the age of the students, not long out of high school myself, and because I had siblings their ages, I felt that I could treat them as equals. After observing . . . classes for the classroom study . . . and watching videos of other [beginning teachers], I realized that if I tried to be too friendly I would soon lose control of the classroom. When I substituted for [my cooperating teacher] on December 1st (this was part of an assignment), I realized that I could not have a "peer" relationship with the students. As I substituted. . . I had to constantly monitor the students in order to keep them on task. I had previously assumed they would work hard for me because I could relate to them as a "peer." I was surprised at how obstinate one particular girl was. . . . When I walked up to her and asked if she was working on the assignment, she said she had completed it. I told her [that the teacher's] instructions were that they were supposed to [keep working on the text]. She replied that she was tired of doing it. I told her she had better work on it. I was surprised by the resentful, almost hateful look she gave me. I didn't anticipate this kind of reaction when I had fantasized about myself as a teacher or when I had observed other classrooms. I think I partially developed this notion of being a "peer" to the students because several times when I had done observations I had been mistaken for a student by other students and some adults. I felt like I was one of them. Also, as a student myself, I could relate to [them].

When I did my Shadow Study, I picked an honors student. She was much more mature than many other students, and I was able to relate to her more on an adult level. She reminded me of myself and the type of people I formed relationships with in high school.... [She] felt I was "one of them." Contrary to these assumptions ... I found that it was quite a different feeling to be up in front of the class. Once in front of the class, the students treated me differently....

While preparing to become a teacher, I encountered some disappointments.... I found pessimism and skepticism in some of the teachers I interviewed. Some teachers were burned out with teaching.... I realized that some students were antagonistic towards school, but I had the impression that these teachers felt that the majority of students did not enjoy learning in school, and that they constantly had to "force feed" them. During my teacher interview with [one of my cooperating teachers] I was dismayed when I realized how she felt about some aspects of teaching. Her question to me was troubling: "Can I do this for the next 25 years of my life?" I was fearful of developing [a negative attitude] as a beginning teacher. I dreamed of walking out of the classroom each day [after teaching] feeling rewarded for the things that I had accomplished and knowing the students appreciated my efforts. Instead, in my interview, I confronted a teacher who told me that the students would take advantage of me whenever they had the opportunity....

My other cooperating teacher... told me that the only way he could survive teaching and the stress that goes with it was to have fun. When I did my classroom study... I began to understand what he meant.... He would make jokes with [students] and talk to them about their lives. This alleviated stress for the students because they felt more relaxed and thus opened up; it also alleviated the stress on [him] because he was able to develop a relationship with the students based on humor which allowed him to shape and guide the students without the tensions and rebellions that [usually] follow.... I have always wanted to have a sense of humor while interacting with students. I feel that because I am younger [than most beginning teachers], it may be more difficult for the students to take me seriously and therefore I need to be firm and control the relationship that I have with them. I am concerned about finding a balance between establishing a firm classroom and creating a relaxed climate in which students feel they can participate openly and freely.

I am pleased with the progress I have made towards becoming ... a good teacher. Although some of my idealism has been [lost], I feel that some of the more negative responses I have heard about the "reality of teaching" are only realities in the minds of those who speak them. I feel that I am capable of being a good teacher. As I watch the videotapes of former student teachers (used as a means for thinking about teaching and exploring teaching strategies), I realize that the purpose of [teacher education] is to discover new ways and objectives of teaching, improve what I already know, and change that which I feel is detrimental to myself and my students. I feel that as I have probed my past, reflected on my present state, and projected myself into the future, I have become more secure in what type of teacher I want to be.... I know that I am on the right track for becoming the kind of teacher that I want to be, I just need to go through a few more towns.

## SECOND REVIEW: GETTING TO KNOW STUDENTS

[March 11, following the "short course" (a three-week unit taught to a single class during the winter and prior to practice teaching in the spring):] After reading through my personal teaching text, it is as if it has been several years since I first wrote my educational life history. I have changed so much. As I read through the work from fall quarter to the present, I realized that I see my role as a teacher from a "real" perspective versus an "artificial" perspective. I see myself less idealistic and more practical, although I feel even more excited to delve into teaching.

After reading my writings before [the] short course, I found myself wanting to make comments in the margins of my own papers and express to myself all that I had learned. Everything that I had put in my papers to that point was merely observations of an outsider. Now I really am starting to feel that I am a real teacher, and I feel that I have a right to consider myself part of the teaching profession.

As I read through my life history I realized that I did not always see in each of my students a reflection of myself during the short course. A couple of the girls I had were "jocks." This type of student has always bothered me throughout my own educational experience, and I found myself judging [such] girls through my experience.... I didn't have much patience with them, although I never voiced this.... I didn't realize before how difficult it can be not to be judgmental and compare these students to others who were troublesome to me in my secondary school years. On the other hand, there was another student for whom I felt a great deal of compassion. I think I felt this way mainly because he was so shy. I was a very shy student. He never gave me any problems. Throughout the course I found myself really wanting him to succeed.... I wanted all of my students to succeed, but I felt more compassion for him. His image haunted me....

I am really beginning to see the reality of what [my cooperating teacher said in my interview with her]. I remember her talking about her relationships with her students. I feel a bond with the students I taught even though I only taught them for three weeks. I also remember [her] talking about the more negative aspects of teaching. She said she was tired of the games the students played and how they would try to take advantage of her. I did find this to be true, even in the short time I taught.... [Still,] I am very anxious to go back into the classroom and teach them....

After reading through my other assignments such as the mundane models [where we described how our cooperating teachers accomplished the mundane tasks of teaching, like collecting homework and handling late papers], I realized how little I really understood the realities of paperwork.... I didn't realize how makeup work could become such a problem. In my short course it seems I had more makeup work than the actual work I had assigned.... When I read about the distractions that teachers often face in the classroom, I had no idea how irritating they could be.... I was interrupted several times by people pulling students out, announcements, late students, and students who had to be excused from class for one reason or another. Each time I would lose my train of thought and my lesson would suffer. . . .

I am pleased with what I have accomplished. I now know that I can stand in front of a class and teach a lesson and that I can do it competently. I am pleased about the relationship that I have been able to develop with my students. I am excited about developing my sense of humor and presence in the classroom. Before, when I only read about these concepts, I really didn't understand what it meant to have a "presence" in the classroom. With each day of teaching I developed that presence more. I am realizing that although I have not changed my initial personality, I am also developing another aspect of my personality, one that is only revealed in the classroom. I am pleased with this personality so far, although I realize that I need to develop more discipline and management [skills].

My biggest disappointment came from students who did not do the homework and who tried to cheat or get away with doing as little as possible. . . .

My initial teaching metaphor has not necessarily changed, but I have expanded it. I feel that a teacher is many things. When I first wrote about metaphors, I saw myself as a defender [of students]. I think a great deal of this stemmed from my experiences in education and my review of those experiences in my life history. I did not have anyone to defend me in some of my darkest times during my junior high school experience, and I really felt that I needed to be there for my students. As the quarter progressed, I started to see myself as a nurturer. As I observed the teachers and the way they nurtured their students through joking with them and helping them to feel important, I realized that in order to defend my students and to teach them to defend others, they would have to be nurtured first. As I began winter term and began working with my cooperating teachers, I realized that a [student] could not benefit from nurturing if he or she was not motivated to accept the nurturing. Finally, after my short course my perspective changed because I became a part of the students' environment, not just an observer of that environment. I developed a feeling of concern for my students and also a responsibility for teaching them that they are important. My metaphor then expanded to include the roles of "caretaker" and "self-esteem lifter." ... As I look back on my experience now, I also see other metaphors emerging. Although I am not a parent, I think that the way I feel about my students is similar to the feeling of a parent [for his or her] children: although I was often disappointed because I knew they could do better, I still was concerned about them and felt responsible to help them succeed. I didn't expect to get attached to them so quickly.... During the ... short course, I ran into students on two different occasions outside of class. It was kind of neat to see them outside of class....

I think my greatest concern right now is putting together a policy for classroom management [for student teaching] that I can give to the students. I have an idea of how I will do it already....

## THIRD REVIEW: TEACHING IS DIFFICULT

[Saturday, June 5, a day after completing practice teaching:] After reviewing my personal teaching text for the year and reflecting on my experience, I have realized that I have really changed and developed throughout the ... year.... I have undergone a complete transformation....

My ideas of what a teacher was and what a teacher did when I first stepped into the program were very naive compared to what I now know. Of course, I realize that when I read [these words] after a few years of teaching, I will think of this writing as only [preliminary and incomplete].

[A]t the beginning of the [teacher education program] I felt that with the help of other future teachers like myself, I could transform the nation. Although I still feel that I would like to be part of improving our nation through teaching, I now see it [differently]. I hope that many students will find new insights from my teaching, but I also realize that many will not be significantly changed by being in my class, because they are unwilling to [change]. Throughout my student teaching I felt so much responsibility for the students. I felt responsible to entertain, uplift, and inspire them. I felt that if they missed any assignments, it was my responsibility to see that they made them up. . . .

During my practice teaching, I began to realize that. . . . I could not be responsible for [seeing that every student does every assignment]. I spent hours grading and talking to the students about what assignments they were missing. I soon found that the time I spent trying to help some students with their grades was wasted by the student arguing about his/her grade and not about what he/she could do to improve it. These students wanted me to be responsible for [their performance]. . . . Earlier in my grading practices description (an assignment that required them to meet with their cooperating teacher and discuss grading and then write a description of how their cooperating teachers assessed student work), I decided that I would follow a portfolio format [as a way] to deal with late and makeup work. I felt that much of this problem would be eliminated by the portfolio format. I decided, however, that I needed to have the students turn in the portfolios more frequently in order to assess their [work]. During student teaching I found that I no sooner had the students turn in the folders for midterm [grading], [than] it was time to turn them in again for finals. . . .

I realize that in order to become a better teacher and further develop myself, I need to learn to adapt to each situation. Sometimes this adaptation requires developing a defense mechanism so as not to allow students to destroy the identity that the teacher has created. . . . In the beginning, I identified my first personal teaching metaphor as that of a defender. . . . [Since then] I found that I had to defend myself against the games and tactics of the students. Certain students would continually attack my curriculum. I had one girl in particular who would whine at everything. When I had the class do a unit on short story writing, she complained continually. One day she walked up to me before class and asked me why we were writing in this English class. I told her that it was an English class and that writing was important because it would help her in all aspects of her life. She said that she had never had to write in class, that she only had read.... Although I feel that many students benefitted [from what we did], this girl still continued to complain about everything. When I finally gave out grades, she complained that she was getting a "D." She felt that if she simply turned everything in, she would receive a high grade. I explained that the quality was important and that if the assignment was half done, it was not going to receive the full points.

At times I wondered if my expectations were too high.... Sometimes I allowed myself to believe that the rest of the class felt the same way [as she did], and that I was [overly] strict and defensive [as a result]. [Learning] what the other students felt [helped] me to overcome this feeling.... I had them write evaluations of the class [as part of my Action Research project].... Many of the students gave critical but positive feedback about things that I could do that would help, such as doing several activities during the long period rather than one the entire [time]. After reading [their comments], I sat down with the class one day and talked about the problems we were having and [shared] what I expected from them and what I would try to do to better the situation. From that point on, I found that I had the support of several of the students. In fact, when the one girl continually whined about the assignments, other students would tell her to be quiet....

I am a perfectionist, and I always felt that everything had to be very precise in my grading practices. I still feel that [I must keep track of] everything.... But I realize that I need to learn shortcuts and time-saving techniques. My cooperating teacher told me not to stress so much over the little things. I think that with time I will be able to define what the little things are and what the big things are. I have improved in this area. During my short course I felt that I had to keep track of who was absent each day and personally give the student the assignment. Toward the end of student teaching, I had copies of the assignments and passed them out to those missing them. When I begin teaching, I will have folders that will have each assignment for each day, and the student will only need to go to that folder to find what he/she is missing. Many of the improvements I will make will be in the area of [getting better organized].... I feel that part of my organization problem was not feeling that I really owned the classroom and not feeling that I could organize my things in the classroom. Toward the end of practice teaching I created a space for a box in which to turn in makeup work and extra credit. I realize now the importance of the [classroom study]. [A classroom has a culture] and it is important [for me] to take ownership of the classroom, [to take responsibility for setting] the atmosphere....

With [better] organization and understanding, which I will continually develop, I will be able to attend to the needs of my students. I simply found myself so tied up in ... management [problems] and [the] whining of a few students that I felt that to some degree I neglected the needs of other students. [I did little nurturing]....

I didn't realize how difficult it would be to motivate students. I felt that if I had enthusiasm for the subject matter, the students would also be motivated.... I often had a difficult time maintaining enthusiasm because I felt so run-down from ... disciplining [students] and dealing with problems. My fifth period class was wonderful, and so I tended to allow myself to relax too much.... Just because they were quiet and well behaved did not mean that they were motivated to learn the subject matter, [I discovered]. I began to realize that although I didn't have management problems with [this class, unlike the others], I [still] had to motivate them because they often weren't paying attention when they appeared to be.

One problem that really concerned me was the difficulty of relating to the students. I realized [from class reading] that there were [different student groups], and intellectually ... I felt that I would be able to respond to and help each group. However, this was a difficult matter.... I sometimes had a difficult time understanding [student] personalities.... Some were very aggressive and mouthy. Although I related to the quiet students, I found myself giving more attention to the aggressive students at times. I feel that this happens quite frequently and that, unfortunately, some of these quiet students slip through the cracks. The more aggressive students were always hovering around my desk demanding to know about their grades or wanting an explanation of everything. Toward the end of student teaching, I started to spend less time with these students. . . . In the future I will make an attempt to give equal time to all, including those who do not demand it. . . .

I made many mistakes. I have learned from those mistakes and now have the knowledge to start building my own career. . . . Earlier in the year I thought about teaching students, but I never realized how much more was involved [in teaching]. . . . Both of my cooperating teachers frequently told me that they are continually changing and trying new ways to do things. I think that this is one of the most exciting things about the teaching profession: there are endless possibilities for bettering the situation and learning. I feel that the greatest thing perhaps that I have learned this year is that the best teacher is the best student of his or her [teaching]. . . .

## CONSIDERATIONS

After having read a good many reviews over the past few years, one gets a sense that there is a rhythm or pattern to the certification year. The problems that demand attention in the first review are often not of concern later. This is important for beginning teachers to keep in mind. The pattern also reflects an increasing sophistication about teaching and appreciation for the complexity of teaching. Knowledge of this complexity must be joined by greater sophistication in knowing how to respond to it. Naive conceptions of teaching, and particularly about students' and teachers' work, begin to be replaced by more sophisticated conceptions. The talk is about the loss of idealism, but a more accurate description is a loss of innocence. Beginners like Sonja commonly talk about facing "reality" and of struggling from time to time to avoid discouragement particularly because of management problems or difficulty establishing authority within the classroom as they move from one side of the desk to the other. But typically, our students end the year on a cautiously optimistic note. This said, how Sonja and many other beginning teachers use the word reality, the "real world" of teaching, is disturbing. At times it seems she assumes that there is a fixed world of teaching and that her charge is to fit into it regardless of the personal costs; she is powerless in the face of the "realities" of teaching, and ideals such as the desire to care and nurture students are set aside. But Sonja does not always talk this way. Other times she writes as though she can shape the context of teaching and make it more educable for herself and the students, which is an insight and aim we wish to cultivate. She talks of "realities" when she is most discouraged; the danger is that discouragement will get the better of her. As we have suggested in *Becoming a Student of Teaching*, a key to overcoming discouragement is to reach out to other teachers and become actively engaged in building a professional community, as will be discussed in chapter ten.

Sonja's reviews illustrate why we consider the personal teaching text an integrating methodology. Taken together, the reviews present snapshots of Sonja's story of becoming a teacher. In them she links activities to one another and applies public theory learned in class to practice and to her private theory. She links, for example, her written life history with the tendency to prejudge students and her desire to reach out to quiet, shy students. She confronts her own bias. She is troubled by her impatience with and bias against the "jocks," and hopes to be responsive to all students. Similarly, her initial teaching metaphors come directly from her life history. Recalling her "darkest times" during junior high, she concluded that some students needed defending and it was her job to be a "defender." Again, the power of biography to shape experience is revealed. Presence, a concern noted in the second review, is featured prominently in her action research project as are other concepts taught in class and explored within classrooms.

Like the action research project, the personal teaching text brings self and teaching context together, and the reviews enable their exploration. This is well illustrated by Sonja's ongoing exploration of teaching metaphors and her struggle to realize these metaphors in the light of contextual constraints like paperwork and worrisome students. Generally, she likes the job of teaching, but like many experienced teachers some aspects of the work get frustrating. She discovers that her future as a teacher may well rest on her ability to manage the mundane and technical concerns of teaching before they become consuming. We sense in Sonja's criticism of the conditions under which teachers work the beginnings of a cultural and structural critique of schooling.

From the first to the last review we see Sonja's understanding of teaching becoming increasingly complex and her knowledge of herself becoming deeper and richer. She adds metaphors indicating recognition of additional teaching responsibilities and she confronts, as all thoughtful teachers must, some of the contradictions of teaching, the paradoxes that make teaching simultaneously interesting and perplexing (Palmer, 1998). For a time responsibilities proliferate until she seems to stagger under the burden, finally concluding that there are limitations on what a teacher can and should do. She realizes she cannot "transform the nation" nor get every student motivated to do her assignments. What, then, is her responsibility as teacher? She is uncertain but wants to give all types of students "equal time" and nurture and care for them, but she cannot. She does not yet realize that to give "equal time" to all students may mean that many students do not receive the assistance that she so desperately desires to give each student. Here is one of the paradoxes of teaching: Equality does not mean sameness.

Sonja does not settle into an authentic teaching role, but then not all beginning teachers do. Like many beginning teachers she looks ahead to when she will have her own classroom as a time to settle. Given the culture of teaching found in many schools that promotes teacher isolation, she may not get it. That this danger exists underscores the importance of linking preservice with in-service teacher education, as we have argued in *Becoming a Student of Teaching*.

Among the themes of Sonja's reviews, a couple require special attention. During much of her practice teaching Sonja's relationship with students was the most crucial indicator of her teaching success. Many beginning teachers desperately want to be liked by their students; Sonja wanted to be seen by her pupils as one of them even though in her first review she claims otherwise. This was a source of her initial problem with identity and authority that figures so prominently in her action research study. Over the course of the year she discovered that she could not be one of them, a buddy, no matter how young she looked or felt. Still, Sonja's sense of self-worth was heavily dependent on their views of her as a person, which was understandable. Criticism was personalized, and she had difficulty distinguishing important from unimportant events. Complaints about the curriculum, for example, were personal attacks. Feeling defensive, she was strict and distant yet still in need of student affection. Finally, unhappy with her relationship with students and frustrated with management problems, Sonja had the students give her written feedback on her teaching and invited one class to help her create a more positive climate. This was a risk that paid off handsomely. She begins to think of the students in less adversarial terms. They can and will help her create an engaging learning climate if she provides the means for their involvement; the class is, after all, theirs too. Potentially, this is a very significant development, one that may eventually lead to insights that will fundamentally alter her views about teaching and further deepen her already lively sense of the ethical responsibilities of teachers.

From the first to the third review there is a subtle shift in Sonja's relationship with her cooperating teachers. Concern for teacher negativism gives way to understanding the frustrations of teachers. She also becomes frustrated. One would hope that these feelings would be taken as occasions to engage other teachers in open and honest explorations of teaching with the aim of altering work conditions. Too often they only lead to withdrawal and disillusionment. What was striking about Sonja's relationship with her cooperating teachers was that both expressed appreciation for being able to work with her and to talk about their work. It was for this reason, in part, that her relationships with them deepened and became more caring, a core aim for Sonja. Each cooperating teacher profoundly influenced how Sonja thought about teaching, and through them she comes to see herself as connected to the wider profession even while she struggles to establish herself in the classroom. She also influenced them. Through experiences shared with other teachers in the school, particularly her cooperating teachers, Sonja concludes that the key to becoming a great teacher is to continually study one's own practice and, we believe she would add, reach out to other teachers.

## EXTENDING THE CONVERSATION

At the beginning of the chapter we presented some of the background out of which the idea of the personal teaching text arose. Here we add a little more background information. In addition to drawing on insights from recent developments in the use of portfolios in education when creating the PTT concept, we also drew on the use of student journals as a means for encouraging writing and thinking about one's experience within teacher education (Berry et al., 1991). The aim of student journals is usually to further development of some kind by identifying and describing significant events on a somewhat regular basis. In this sense, they have much in common with PTTs. However, the writing contained in journals is often narrowly introspective and unfocused, and seldom are attempts made to critically consider the relationship of one entry to another and to the direction of one's development as a teacher. Furthermore, as Knowles (1991) observes, beginning teachers often find the time demands of journal keeping prohibitive. Our acute awareness of these problems prompted consideration of alternatives. An additional source of insight came from the use of cases in fields other than education, especially medicine. Nurses, for example, are taught to construct case records of their patients, histories of treatment and of patient response to treatment, that enable decision-making. But in nursing, those who gather the material and assess it are different from those whose records or materials are included in the record; again we encounter the problem of external evaluation. In contrast, personal teaching texts require those gathering the data to assess it. In our view, learning ought to be the aim of assessment.

Beginning teachers often do not think their teacher education has had much of an impact on their learning. This is a disturbing outcome. We have realized that being swamped by the many and varied demands of the first year or two of teaching, beginning teachers need help to gain and maintain perspective on their development, where they have been and where they are tending. The personal teaching text has proven a helpful means for assisting beginning teachers to be more aware of their development as teachers and a means for better directing it.

Reconsidering Sonja's writing points in the direction of an issue that deserves careful thought by beginning teachers. All beginning teachers struggle to know young people who have backgrounds very different from their own. Obviously, the range of differences is extensive and not just a matter of age, social class, or race and ethnicity. For Sonja social class antagonisms seemed to rear up. Importantly Sonja eventually accepted that her experience was limited as a means for understanding the experience of others and realized she needed to transcend her background if she was to connect with students in productive ways and create a setting that facilitated learning. Sonja's difficulty illustrates well the limitations of private theories and the need to openly test them, as we have argued.

Edmund Gordon and his colleagues (1990) coined the phrase "communicentric bias" to describe this problem. We humans tend to think that the way we have lived and experienced the world is normal and shared, that everyone else thinks and experiences as we do. Second language learners know the fallacy of this kind of thinking. Many people are able to live comfortably within the boundaries of their world-experience, but not so teachers who are committed to facilitating student learning. Students of teaching are skilled boundary crossers, people who are able to suspend their prejudices and who know about how others' worlds are constructed and are able to build bridges of understanding across worlds. This is what is meant by "responsive" teaching (see Villegas, 1997). Sonja wanted to be responsive. Knowing one's content area and having practiced pedagogy are important elements to becoming a student of teaching. However, one must also know one's students from the inside, and this takes not only experience but also desire and hard work. Student populations vary dramatically, and one cannot assume success with one group of students will necessarily translate into success with another, as teachers who have transferred schools quickly learn. Will you seek to cross boundaries? Will you carefully attend to how your students respond to your teaching, ever seeking better ways of linking their experience with the subject area you teach? Will you find pleasure in challenging your own understanding of the world as you seek to better connect with those living in very different worlds? There probably is no greater challenge to teachers than this one.

# Section 2

✦

# In-Service
# Teacher Education

# ✴ **10** ✴

# Collaborative Teacher Research

## INTRODUCTION

This chapter, on teacher research, is a bit different from previous chapters. In many ways it represents a transition from your preservice experience to a time when you will have your own classroom and become a certified teacher. While somewhat daunting, this transition provides a number of opportunities, including the possibility of using your experience with the methodologies presented in *Becoming a Student of Teaching* to take a much more active role in knowledge production as a beginning teacher. This shift requires a number of changes in our approach to this chapter. Specifically, we will present a set of assumptions which underpin a particular approach to teacher research, rather than provide an exact accounting of how to "write" teacher research. Because assumptions do not specify how to put a methodology into practice, this approach invites you to interact with and perhaps challenge the value positions embedded in each of the assumptions.

During this transition time, you will be faced with a difficult dilemma. On the one hand your primary and immediate concern, quite rightly, will be on your practice. On the other hand, it is also the case that becoming a good teacher is a continuous journey, not an apprenticeship that ends after a specified time. To walk on the road less traveled, to engage in a continuous journey of practice, development, and insight, you will need to consider how to both practice teaching and step back from practice to raise questions and engage in the study of teaching, to be a student of teaching.

In some ways, there is no easy time to begin this transition. Student teaching is a very intense time, as is the first year or two of teaching. Yet, even during this intense period, there are ways to mediate the pressures and demands, not the least of which is to enter this journey with others as co-collaborators.

Our focus on collaboration points to an important difference between this methodology and the action research methodology described earlier. While action research and teacher research have much in common, most centrally the linkage of conceptual insight with practice, collaborative teacher research, as we conceptualize it, is centered on the possibilities of having teachers work with others in small professional learning communities. It is our hope that these communities embrace differences among collaborators (e.g., orientation to education, experience, position in the educational community) such that the group enters into an inquiry process where much can be learned about teaching. Unfortunately, working across differences can also lead one down a slippery slope where those in positions of authority impose their views onto others. For this reason, it is crucial that before we address the assumptions that inform this approach to teacher research, we account for one central difference in the educational community, the gap between academic and school cultures.

## ACADEMIC/SCHOOL COMMUNITIES

When it comes to producing knowledge, the academic (i.e., those working in universities and colleges) and school (i.e., those working in schools district and state offices of education) communities are quite different. Advocates of teacher research argue forcefully that keeping a journal of one's experiences, oral inquiries, conversations with other teachers about teaching, and even teachers' interpretations of the assumptions and characteristics of the classroom are legitimate ways to produce knowledge (Cochran-Smith & Lytle, 1993). The focus on one's own practice poses a challenge to the way knowledge is typically produced in the academic community. Where academic researchers typically "gaze" on the experience of others from an "outsider" point of view, teacher researchers examine their own practice and therefore produce knowledge that reflects an "insider" point of view. What teacher researchers seem to imply is that "insider" knowledge should be valued as highly as outsider knowledge. Ironically, neither teachers nor academics typically adopt this point of view. A careful accounting of many teacher research reports indicates that the knowledge produced from an "insider" point of view rarely is linked in substantial ways with traditional academic forms of research. The same type of divide can also be seen when viewed from the perspective of academic research, which deems teacher research as "soft" (Labaree and Pallas, 1996). While academic research has become more diverse over the last few decades, this research rarely if ever references teacher research, except where the academic research is focused on a teacher research project. The separation of insider and outsider points of view should not come as a great surprise. Teachers consistently express concerns about the practicality, accessibility, and value of academic research (Gitlin et al., 1999). Conversely, university-based researchers often gain distinction by producing work that is removed from teacher experience, the life world of practice (Gitlin and Burbank, 2000).

These two communities have interests, and points of view, which do not necessarily meld into a singular point of view. While important, this difference in point of view on knowledge production is not cause for alarm. Instead, it is a point of reference that must be considered as you proceed to do teacher research, hopefully in ways that will cut across the divide that separates these education communities. The teacher research assumptions that follow reflect our desire to bridge the gap between these communities and strengthen them in ways that acknowledge the value of both insider and outsider knowledge. More specifically, we want your insights on teaching to be informed by public theory and knowledge, as we want academic research and knowledge production to be informed by teachers' insider points of view.

## OUR BASIC ASSUMPTIONS FOR TEACHER RESEARCH

The assumptions that follow are informed by a long-term collaboration between one of the authors of this text and a group of six teachers and teacher educators interested in collaborative teacher research. This group emerged from a graduate class on teacher research and continues to meet voluntarily to produce knowledge, alter practices, and further professional development. While the group worked together, each member identified individual research questions.

*Collaboration*

Collaboration of one sort or another appears to play an important part in many teacher research projects. While generally endorsed, collaboration is not a concept with a singular meaning. The multiplicity of meanings attached to collaboration suggests that it is important to clarify this concept.

Some forms of collaboration, such as contrived collaboration (Hargreaves, 1994), have teachers work together, but the collaboration is required or imposed by administrators. In contrast to contrived collaboration, other forms of collaboration emerge from the desires of those participating in the collaborative process. Typically these forms focus on the possibilities of teachers and others talking with each other (Hong, 1996). Still other types of collaboration attempt to transform relations of power between those participating in the collaborative arrangement. The focus of this approach to collaboration is on the identification of social justice issues (Smyth, 1991). In sum, collaboration can reinforce relations of power (contrived collaboration) or try to transform those relations. In some approaches the centerpiece of the collaborative process is talking to others on whatever issues are deemed desirable, while others focus on issues of social justice.

While some of these approaches to collaboration have great potential to enable you to extend your conversations about teaching, produce new knowledge, and develop deeper insights into teaching, collaboration should not be seen as a universal good. If we are to collaborate, we must go into the process with our eyes wide open so we can see any potential stumbling blocks or potholes to be avoided.

One pothole is that the collaborative process (if a form of contrived collaboration) may actually conflict with one aim of teacher research: to provide a forum for teachers to express their educational views, to have a voice in public educational matters. If teacher research is to provide teachers with an opportunity to share their insights about schooling in public forums, the process used to facilitate those insights cannot and should not be imposed on teachers. Contrived collaboration is likely to contradict the central aim of teacher research.

A second stumbling point you may encounter as you enter a collaborative process is that the knowledge produced may be conserving. Just because you get together with others interested in education and school improvement does not mean that you will not simply reinforce your perspectives, values, and understandings of teaching. Unless there is a push within the collaborative process to see anew, to be open to differing possibilities and points of view, collaboration may evoke Sarason's (1971) refrain concerning educational reform that the more things change, the more they remain the same.

A final crack in the pavement that should be noted is that collaboration almost always involves local actions—actions between you and one or several individuals. While these actions can have a significant influence on the decisions you make and your understanding of educational issues, it is important to remember that what happens in your classroom is also influenced by institutional constraints and commonsense points of view. For example, when the State Office of Education (S.O.E.) determines that teachers must attend so many in-service seminars to maintain certification, this helps shape what it means to engage in teacher development. If it is commonly assumed that teachers entered teaching because they "love kids," this perspective may influence teacher status, pay, and what sort of supervisory controls are put into schools. Any local collaboration, by itself, cannot alter these influences. Collaboration, therefore, is *part of* a wider process of change that must be complemented by other collective actions if significant possibilities for change are to emerge from the linkage of knowledge production and practice.

Understanding the potential stumbling blocks associated with collaboration ought not to be discouraging. Recognizing these challenges encouraged us to rethink collaboration. The result is an alternative approach to collaboration that you might want to consider as you proceed to engage in teacher research.

Our approach to collaboration begins with a recognition of differences between those participating in the collaborative process. If you are working with a teacher educator, for example, the fact that you will receive a grade from your "collaborator" creates a difference between the two of you. If you are working with another teacher who is more experienced, such as your cooperating teacher, or an assigned mentor, the experience of that teacher and her/his supervisory role creates a difference between the two of you. And even if you are working with another teacher who has the same experience as you do, your orientation to teaching and schooling is likely to be a source of difference. Of course, you will also have much in common with your collaborator. Our point is that differences among collaborators are not a problem to be overcome, but rather a source of potential advantage to be utilized in seeing the educational landscape in new ways. In this type of collaboration, the aim is not to become one, to make sure that everyone is on the same page, but rather to utilize differences in perspectives and contexts to challenge the assumptions which guide decision-making in the educational world. For example, at the beginning of our teacher research collaboration, the academic often started the conversation and made some suggestion about a theory that might be helpful to understand a certain issue. This privilege of speaking first was initially accepted by the teachers in the group. In time, however, questions emerged about why the academic had the privileged position of talking first, and how his focus on theory was related to institutional priorities between academic institutions and schools. With this conversation as a backdrop, the teacher research group altered its practice to make sure the conversation could be initiated by any member of the group and that theory was linked to practice, without prioritizing theory as a privileged form of knowing. Based on these alterations, we were able to rethink our positions or at least understand them more clearly. We did not, however, assume that such a move transformed our relations; rather; these actions showed how "differences" could lead to an understanding of the way we produce knowledge and approach knowledge production within an academic context.

*Posing Questions*

One of the strengths of teacher research is that this form of knowledge production challenges the silence of teachers in the public educational domain. Certainly, those most closely connected to students should have a say in the policies and practices that help shape schooling. This strength, however, also comes with some limitations. One such constraint is the relation between voice and the limits of those voices. Teachers, as is true of all groups, do not speak from a singular point of view (Hargreaves, 1996). Teachers' views on education vary in some dramatic ways in terms of desired practices and aims. Nevertheless, those views are not free floating. Teachers' views cannot be separated from the context in which they work, the school culture in which they operate, and broader institutional influences. The context that enables teachers to "see" education in ways that those outside schools cannot, also bounds and narrows what teachers do "see" as educational issues, problems, concerns, and solutions. Teachers' voices must be listened to and heard at the same time that they are also examined and questioned.

To address this dilemma, our teacher research group did not simply start off with a question to be researched. Instead, we started composing autobiographies, what we have referred to in this book as life studies (see chapter two). The members of the teacher research group also conducted a mini-institutional study of their work context. By considering both the autobiographical and institutional texts, members of the teacher research group were encouraged to be self-reflexive about the relation between the question posed and the way self and context enable possibilities and bound views and practices (Bullough and Gitlin, 1995). Put simply, this process enabled the questions posed to be part of an inquiry process that acknowledges the voice of teachers but provides a way for teachers to look critically at the questions they pose for study.

Because everyone in the group went through this question posing process, individual questions and perspectives could also be reconsidered in relation to others'. Based on this type of relational analysis, initial research questions were revised and in certain instances reformulated in dramatic ways. For example, one teacher in the group set out to examine the nature of collaborative relations in the math department at her school. The initial question for the study was to see how well the math faculty could match their practice to the standards established by the S.O.E. (State Office of Education). This question directly related to the researcher's context: She was under pressure to meet state standards because of her recent appointment as chair of the math department. After much reflection on self and context she realized that the question was not her "own" but rather one encouraged by the contextual pressures of her new appointment. Based on this understanding of the question, she decided that her goal for collaboration was much broader than matching practice with state standards. Put differently, she was not willing to let the context dictate the emphasis (on state standards) of her teacher research project. Instead, she wanted to consider how collaboration could lead to changes between men and women faculty as well as how collaboration could enable teachers to raise critical concerns with each other.

*Academic Knowledge and Teacher Knowledge*

As mentioned, the knowledge produced by academics reflects an outsider point of view. Members of the teacher research group felt that they could better understand their own experiential stories, their teacher research, by looking at them in relation to the "academic" body of knowledge. To help achieve this aim, the group represented their studies as two stories that were woven together. One story focused on the experience of doing research and the issues and concerns that emerged from inquiry, and the other story considered how the data and the academic research literature might inform and be informed by our accounting of these experiences. In this sense, the group tried to combine insider and outsider points of view. The differences between insider and outsider knowledge encouraged a type of reflectivity that forced the group to reconsider the assumptions which guide our world views and, more specifically, our educational goals and professional ambitions. The following edited section from a field based teacher educator in our teacher research group suggests how the group tried to move back and forth between teacher and academic knowledge:

> "Reflective practice" seems to be a key term in the field of teacher education. Teacher education programs often seek reflective practice as a goal of their program. However, as a supervisor of student teachers I was not sure how I supported this reflective practice or what it even looked like. I also struggled with the issue of power with my student teachers. The current relationship places me in a position of authority over the student teachers. I evaluate their performance, which affects their future. I have struggled with this relationship because it did not match my goals. I am a university supervisor and evaluator, yet I want my student teachers to have the opportunity to voice their experience and knowledge as teachers. After a year and half of struggling with these issues, I took on a teacher research project to look at how I could promote and increase reflective practice with my student teachers.
>
> Members of our group pushed me to think about what research approach I should use and the way I should analyze the data. I also reviewed the academic literature and various

models of supervision—traditional, clinical, etc.—in order to consider what approach to take in my project. In the final analysis, I used a combination of my experience and the suggestions found in the academic literature to think through how to [better] work with student teachers. For example, I knew from the outset that I did not want to use traditional models of supervision because of their emphasis on standards and efficiency (Bolin and Panaritis, 1992, p. 34). However, when I looked at clinical models of supervision (the model that my university subscribes to), I still felt like the student teachers' voice was missing from the supervisor-student teacher relationship. In order to develop that student teacher voice, I looked to research on peer observation/evaluations—a totally different model of supervision. The use of academic research has informed my practice and caused me to look at different paths to improve my practice and ultimately my student teachers' growth. This search eventually led me to important research on promoting reflective practice with student teachers, some of which my experience challenges. (Zeichner, 1987)

Note that the story, the teacher research experience, still occupies center stage. However, this teacher educator uses academic research both to support some of her assumptions, such as the one's concerning traditional models of supervision, and as a way to extend her own thinking about supervision by considering Zeichner's insights on promoting reflective practice.

### Beyond Neutrality

Most academic research tries to avoid any sort of bias which would limit the "truth" of the reported findings. We reject this stance of neutrality in our teacher research projects because we feel this stance is a charade. The "charade" is that researchers in the human sciences can somehow bracket all their perspectives, views, and understandings of the world and leave them at the door as they do research. While it is extremely important to be open minded and not predetermine the findings of a study, or manipulate the data to achieve a desired end, it is also important to acknowledge the perspectives one brings to teacher research.

We want those who read the results of teacher research to understand the perspectives, orientations, and background experiences and beliefs that shape the questions posed and the analysis conducted. Put differently, we want to replace the charade of neutrality with a more *authentic* approach to research. One teacher addressed this challenge when she wrote as part of her project:

> It is generally held that good students work consistently while in school on whatever they are assigned to do. This is referred to as "on-task" behavior. Carefully watching my students as part of this project has challenged this commonsense view. I found that students accomplished more work, of better quality, when they had more freedom to determine the type of work they were engaged in. I came to realize that improving my practice was only part of the "solution." I also needed to examine the structures of schooling if I wanted to fundamentally alter my students' educational experiences as well as my own educational experiences.

The standpoint from which this teacher researcher approaches her study is clearly and openly articulated and therefore the reader can examine and understand the perspective that informs the questions she asked and the type of analysis that she conducted. This openness about the values that the teacher researcher enters the study with also allows the teacher researcher to talk candidly about any changes in perspective that have occurred because of the inquiry process.

Our teacher research group has also tried to go beyond neutrality by recognizing that many analyses of schooling are reduced to a "technique": Utilize cooperative learning when you work with "at-risk" students; maintain high expectations, especially for minority students; employ group activities with African-American students because they come from a collective culture. All these statements contain a bit of truth. A problem arises, though, when we focus on these teaching techniques without unmasking other value questions. Without considering these values, educational techniques appear neutral—appear to reside "outside" of one perspective or another. One teacher in the teacher research group exemplifies this move away from neutrality by talking about the values that inform a teaching technique:

> When I began teaching, my one concern was covering the required curriculum as specified by the State. I presented the material and those [students who] did their work were rewarded with good grades. I had done my part, I had sorted them as required by the system. Since working on this research project, I have come to view the structure of schooling through a different lens. Covering the curriculum and then sorting [students based] on this information, is simply a way to determine the "haves" and "have nots." Engaging students without altering the sorting function of schooling, I now believe, is like putting the cart before the horse.

This teacher is suggesting that techniques to engage students as a way to cover state requirements may be nothing more than a ruse to sort students. According to this teacher, the sorting process must be altered before educational practices "that keep students on task" are put into place. Values hidden within the teaching technique of keeping students on task are exposed.

*Teacher Research in Practice*

To get a sense of what the assumptions articulated in the previous section look like in practice, it may be helpful to provide an example of a project that developed as part of the teacher research collaboration. The following project was developed by an experienced sixth grade teacher, Marcie Peck, who had become somewhat disenchanted with her teaching and was searching for alternative ways to engage her students. In particular, she wanted to consider what would happen if she put into practice a student generated curriculum.

> After teaching for a number of years, I got to the point where I no longer worried so much about classroom control and content, so that I actually had the presence of mind to notice what my students were doing while I was teaching. As I looked out at my students, they mostly looked bored and disinterested. Blaming their passivity on laziness and lack of commitment only worked for so long as I noticed that even the "good" students were less than enchanted within the classroom

environment. They would do their work, but only because they wanted good grades, not because they were engaged in what they were doing. I was feeling bored myself and I wanted to know why. First, I questioned my practice: "What was I doing wrong? Should I try more group work?" I then evaluated my curriculum as well and wondered why the students usually didn't appear interested in what they were doing, even when it was a project that should have engendered some enthusiasm. I even considered my students and tried to determine why some succeeded and others failed. As time went on though, I mostly began to question the educational process itself. Working on this teacher research project provided answers to some of my questions, while also leading me into further exploration of not only what occurs in my classroom, but the structures of school as well.

To encourage more student engagement, I decided to alter the traditional teacher/student relationship where teachers teach and students supposedly learn. Instead, I wanted to collaborate with my students to plan not only what we were going to learn, but also how we were going to go about it (Apple & Beane, 1995). To accomplish this, I used a method called student generated curriculum in which students generate questions about their world and about themselves and then structure categories of study organized around these questions. Just as teacher research attempts to challenge the silencing of teachers in the educational process, this project challenged the silencing of students by allowing them a voice in the educational process. An unforeseen benefit of this collaboration for me was the mutual respect that developed. I found that as students felt that their voices were respected and valued, they were more inclined to respect my voice.

As collaboration began between teachers and students, there existed a real tension between the teacher's "academic" knowledge and students' "experiential" knowledge which had to be addressed for collaboration to occur. The behaviorist belief that students are empty vessels waiting to be filled by the omniscient instructor could not exist in this context. As a teacher, I had to believe that my students possessed not just knowledge, but valuable knowledge which could be used to enrich everyone in the learning environment, including myself (hooks, 1994). Before this teacher research project started, I felt there was a general devaluing of the knowledge of the "other" [teacher knowledge and student knowledge] with neither side believing the other had anything important to contribute to their understanding. For example, I felt I obviously had superior knowledge and it was my duty to impart that to my deficient students. My students, on the other hand, expressed through their actions and statements that they knew everything they needed to know about English already and were just "doing their time" until they got their freedom at graduation. My research demonstrated that students have much to teach me and their classmates, if we were both willing to address the issue of legitimate knowledge and begin to listen to each other.

When I began my teacher research project, my goal was to increase student engagement in the learning process. As I analyzed the data (e.g., interviews with students on how they felt about the student generated curriculum) from my research, I discovered that students were much more engaged in their work when allowed to be active participants in a caring, supportive learning community, and I began to look at improving my practice accordingly. At the same time, though, I unexpectedly encountered the hidden curriculum in schools and its impact on what I and my students did. For example, there is a belief in my school and I suspect many others about what constitutes acceptable school work. It is generally held that good students work constantly while in school on whatever they are assigned to do. That is referred to as "on-task behavior." Watching my students work during my project challenged this belief. Students were allowed to plan their time each day and that plan usually involved a mix of work, socializing and reflection. Surprisingly, students accomplished more work, of better quality, during the research period (one school year) than in a traditional classroom when they were directly under the control of the teacher and expected to be producing all the time. This phenomenon can only be understood when we uncover the messages we send to students when we demand traditional schedules of work. While we may claim to value engagement, creativity, and self-directed learning, we instead are teaching compliance, passivity and a factory-labor mentality, and that is usually what we get (Marcie, 1998).

## CONSIDERATIONS

One telling aspect of Marcie's teacher research project is that she approached the project with a degree of openness. Her notion that blaming the students for their lack of engagement could only take her understanding so far suggests that posing questions about teaching requires looking at all aspects of the process, including the character-istics of students and the perspectives and practices of teachers. Because Marcie chose to focus on her practice, her aim was to alter her part of the relationship to see if her efforts influenced students' engagement with the curriculum. The question she posed as part of her research project clearly comes out of an in-depth consideration of her teaching self—what that self is like, what she wants it to be, and how she wants to relate to young people.

Marcie makes an important observation early on in the question posing process—she is bored. As teachers, we often are so focused on our students we forget that if teaching, and being in school, becomes a rote, boring activity for us that children's learning will be negatively impacted. Part of the wonderment of this human realtionship is lost. Marcie poses a question that reflects a fundamental realization—she is losing steam. Her teacher research question emerges from the core of Marcie's teaching—her relationship with students.

As you develop your questions, we can not stress enough how important it is to slow down and not simply grab hold of the first ques-tion that pops into your head. While the question posing process can be difficult and time consuming, reflections on self and context, in whatever form you choose, can enable you to get to a core issue as opposed to one you select because it is convenient or emerges from another's passions.

As Marcie begins to consider her question, she makes an interest-ing observation: What she is doing with her students, a collaborative planning process focusing on both what and how they learn, mirrors the type of collaborative process she is engaged in with the research group. She is not trying to become one with her students but rather work across differences to come to some alternative "place" with students where learning again emerges as an engaging passionate activity. Instead of approaching this collaborative process with students from a neutral point of view, where her values, perspectives, and goals are hidden from the reader, her point of view is stated clearly: "I had to believe that my students possessed not just knowledge, but valuable knowledge." Stating her position on students and the knowledge they possess, however, is only a first step in moving away from a so-called neutral stance to an authentic stance. What is also needed is a judgment by the reader that the articulated position(s) did not overly skew the findings and that the findings have influenced the positions articulated. One indication that Marcie's findings influenced her thinking is the degree to which unexpected results are reported. Where unexpected results are reported, the reader is more likely to view the author as open to the implications of the findings (not everything came out the way the author anticipated). For Marcie, the unexpected result was her discovery that planning in a collaborative way was unlikely to make a major difference in the teacher-student relationship unless what counts as "acceptable school work" is also transformed. You may not view Marcie's teacher research as authentic, but at least she identifies some unexpected results that show her openness to move beyond initial assumptions and perspectives.

We should mention, in closing this Consideration section, that Marcie struggled to tell two stories—her own, which focuses on what she found as she put into place a collaborative planning intervention, and the way this story interacts with the academic research literature. Our reading of this teacher research project is that Marcie's experiential story dominates the landscape of her research project. This is neither good nor bad. For some teachers the experiential story may dominate, for others the academic research literature may be more prominent. Where a study falls on this continuum really depends on the research aims, how you learn, and your audience. Our only recommendation is that you keep in mind how the two stories come together and then consider how this mix relates to your aims, goals, and audience.

## EXTENDING THE CONVERSATION

Collaborative teacher research is a process fraught with difficulties. Even though Marcie's project exemplifies the assumptions of our approach to teacher research, all members of the group ran into substantial difficulties as we worked our way through this complex process. What follows emerged from an audio-taped conversation by group members that was recorded after the teacher research projects were finished (e.g., the conversation was recorded to help us reflect of the year long process of doing collaborative teacher research). This conversation illuminates some sense of the pitfalls and stumbling blocks as well as the benefits that can come from doing collaborative teacher research.

*What Do You Want Us to Do?*

As mentioned, the roots of this collaborative teacher research group began in a graduate class. While classes differ in almost infinite ways, it should come as no surprise that both professor and student positioned the professor as knower, as one who would tell the "other" what to do and how to conduct teacher research. At this time, the quality and character of the interactions between professor and student were captured by the question, "What do you [professor] want?" As was noted in our taped discussion occurring after our teacher research projects were concluded:

> You remember how frustrated we got at times in the beginning? Trying to figure out how everything fit together . . . I mean there were times where we were like "What do we do?, What do you want?, What is it that you are trying to do with us?"

This type of interaction, while common to many or most classes, really is at odds with the goal of teacher research, which is to enable teachers to see value in and examine their own experiential knowledge. For the process of teacher research to achieve this goal, the professor/student relationship must be reconsidered. There is no recipe for such a change. In our case, the change in relationship seemed to go hand in hand with our move to a voluntary group that would continue to meet outside of class. Put simply, when we operated within a "classroom discourse," we acted out traditional teacher/student hierarchical roles without deviation. When we came together as a matter of choice, outside of class, the roles and relationships became less certain. Given our attempt to move outside of the classroom discourse, new possibilities emerged that made the production of knowledge a more personal and meaningful experience. As was stated by one of the teachers in our group:

> I really don't know how it [our relationship] shifted away from an assignment for class which you do, hand it in, and don't care about it anymore, to something that is personal and meaningful to me. Just a different setting, a classroom setting, is so hierarchical that even though we had some authority when we moved outside the classroom it became a more cooperative type of venture. That is why we were able to express ourselves because it wasn't "here is the professor and we the humble students."

If collaborative teacher research is to become an authentic process that is more than an assignment to be handed in and forgotten, our experience suggests that explicit attempts must be made to examine the way contexts, such as the classroom, shape the relationships that occur among participants. Undoubtedly, many teacher research groups will not begin in a class format. However, it is likely that many teacher research groups begin in a setting which can be easily reshaped as a classroom. Members of the group should attempt to become aware of the influence of dominant discourses, such as the classroom discourse, and find ways to challenge these discourses where they are found to be limiting.

## What Can You Do to Enable Us to Achieve Our Goals?

Pushing up against the boundaries of the classroom discourse is not an attempt to have the "teacher" wither away (Shor, 1987). Even though the traditional relations of power between teacher and student conflict with the aims of teacher research, in our experience a leader of some sort is much needed. A member of our research group put it this way:

> If someone else was to try to duplicate this [our approach to research] I think they would need some assistance. I think you would need to have a leader because at the beginning we didn't know what we were doing.

The group's desire to have a leader differs from their initial view that the teacher is one who determines the terrain for knowledge production and inquiry while the "student" tries to find ways to please the teacher. For our group, the initial agenda was the professor's. The students' role was to try to satisfy that agenda, although they could do so in various ways. As the group moved outside the classroom context, the members of the group started to determine their own agendas.

> Until it [this process of teacher research] becomes a personal thing, you don't become passionate about it. We have had to learn some things about research but in time we felt that we owned the project. It was something we were doing for us. I had some vested interest and then the project becomes meaningful, and I was willing to make something of the project.

In our experience, for the original leader to alter her/his role from one where the students find ways to please her/him to one where the leader guides and assists "others" in achieving goals that have become meaningful and personal to them, it is critical that the leader value the opinions of others in the group.

> I think the relationship that we [teachers] have with you [academic] is quite different than what I have with other professors at the university. I mean, it is a whole lot different and one of the things that made that possible is that you showed early on that you did value our opinions and our views. We could voice our views and someone was going to listen and it was going to make a difference; without that stance I don't think we would have gotten anywhere.

What this statement implies is that typically teachers have neither been heard nor is their experiential knowledge valued (Goodwin, 1987). If the process of teacher research is to challenge this dominant positioning, those in leadership roles need to put in place practices that value the knowledge of teachers and allow that knowledge to make a positive difference.

Valuing the knowledge of teachers, however, is different from suggesting that their knowledge and perspectives are beyond reproach. The voices of teachers, as is true of the voices of all "cultural" groups, are filled with contradictions, limitations, and even narrow stereotyped views that have the potential to silence others. For this reason, the reconceptualized role of leader, in our experience, must not only value the views of teachers but also provide a stance where critique and criticism become an everyday part of knowledge production and professional development.

> I think sometimes we [teachers] get in our little worlds or our own classrooms and there is little criticism. We are not used to being critical, being critical in our profession turns into personality conflicts; . . . people won't talk to each other. I finally realize that being critical is going to make the project better. It is not that you are a bad person, it [the criticism] allows you to start looking at your project and yourself from differing points of view and it makes you stronger. That was a huge lesson for me that [I learned].

While the leader can encourage others to take a critical stance toward teaching, this role is not without its contradictions. For while the leader can lay the foundation for such a stance, it is also the case that often "leaders" are very poor at looking critically at themselves.

> In some ways professors might be even worse than [those teachers who resist any sort of critical feedback]. Professors not only tend to teach the same way throughout much of their careers, but in journals that have a dialogue between professors how often do you see one professor say, "that is a good point I will have to consider that seriously?" Instead, it is a game of one-upsmanship. I think professors should look at themselves and instead of saying why don't teachers take criticism and change, ask why don't they [professors] want to take criticism and why don't they change?

Clearly, if critique is to play a role in a teacher research group it must be a two-way process where those in dominant positions look critically at their stances as well as encouraging "others" to do so.

The process of collaborative teacher research, for our group, was a process of reconceptualizing the notion of classroom. Finding ways to please the teacher gave way to having the leader (in this case the professor) assist and guide other members of the group to achieve their own agendas. By doing so, group relations and experiences became more authentic and meaningful. In part, this change was facilitated by moving materially and discursively outside the classroom. Once "outside," a double move was made whereby the voices of those traditionally marginalized were heard and responded to and at the same time a critical stance became a normal part of our interactions. Whatever has been accomplished in our work with teacher research is a direct result of challenging the boundaries of the classroom discourse and of putting into practice a new array of roles and relationships which continue to be made and remade even as we write.

As you create or enter your own teacher research group you may want to extend the conversation by asking questions about how the context, such as the classroom or school, influences the relationship found in the teacher research group. You might also question if some group members are acting to please others, or acting to address core issues that lie at the heart of their teaching self. Finally, you will also want to ask about how teacher experience will be shared and how it will be scrutinized for blindspots, limitations, and distortions.

# Appendix:
# Notes to Teacher Educators

## A NOTE TO TEACHER EDUCATORS ON CHAPTER TWO, LIFE WRITING

For a variety of reasons, not least among them the training orientation of teacher education, teacher educators frequently ignore what they tacitly understand: As with other teachers, what they teach will be filtered through and made more or less meaningful based upon a set of biographically embedded assumptions, beliefs, or preunderstandings held by their students. These are now taken as the common tenets of constructivism. Some of what is taught will be ignored and discarded as meaningless because it does not fit current understanding, and recognized as self-confirming, other content, perhaps even less significant content, will be embraced eagerly. Ignoring the past does not make it go away. It lingers, ever present and quietly insistent.

Recognizing that all learners pick and choose what they will learn, all teachers, us included, use a variety of means— grades, tests, rewards, and punishments—to increase the likelihood that the content presented will be learned in the manner desired. Learning to teach, however, is not merely a matter of engaging or being forced to engage content—to know, for example, what is involved in putting together a comprehensive unit or even what are the most common reading errors of children. It is also a matter of learning how to direct one's professional development intelligently and to express one self in a way that builds desirable and educationally defensible relationships with students and increases the enjoyment of teaching.

Many beginning teachers come to teaching with relatively clear, but likely not fully articulated, conceptions of teaching and of themselves as teachers. Perhaps their parents or grandparents were teachers, and their conceptions of teaching are overlaid with the feelings of admiration felt for them. Perhaps an especially inspiring teacher challenged them in ways they would like to share with others. Maybe they hated school and desire to "fix things" so others won't suffer as much. Or, maybe they played school as little children and feel "called" to teaching like Carla. In addition to these experiences, each beginning teacher has spent literally thousands of hours sitting in classes as students, engaged in what Daniel Lortie (1975) called an "apprenticeship of observation." They are familiar with schools and feel more or less knowledgeable about teaching. Taken together, these kinds of experiences and the understanding and attitudes that come from them are the bedrock of professional development, of who the beginning teacher thinks he or she is and wants to become as a teacher (a professional vision or "dream") and—swapping images—the seeds of socialization to teaching.

For beginning teachers, switching to the other side of the desk may bring some surprises, however. It certainly did for Carla, J.B., and John. Teaching looks quite different to a student about to become a student teacher from how it looks to an experienced teacher. Teachers and students see different things and, to a degree, have different concerns. Preunderstandings about teaching and about self as teacher borne of student experience and brought to teacher education are inevitably naive, perhaps misleading, and sometimes blatantly false. Prejudices blind. Prejudices cripple. Prejudgments— judgments lacking explicit justification—blind by cutting off other, perhaps more fruitful, sensitive and responsible ways of understanding and framing a problem or building a relationship; they cripple by unnecessarily constraining opportunities to learn and by truncating one's professional growth.

To confront preunderstandings, we have argued that a turn inward toward self is required. But turning inward can be a risky business, and sharing the results of the turn even frightening. Fearing retribution or a bad grade, the beginning teacher may not wish to uncover, let alone reveal, some views or beliefs. This is a difficult problem. Ethically, teacher educators must not and cannot compel students to disclose more about themselves than they wish. We are not, after all, in the "molding" business. Teacher educators can only invite, not compel, the "good." More about this issue follows. At this point, we need to underscore the importance of trust and of an honest and sincere effort to explore self, of which life writing in its various forms is a part. Without trust, risk is unwise, yet risk is essential to maximizing the educational value of each of the methodologies presented in *Becoming a Student of Teaching*.

We turn now to a set of specific questions and issues related to using life histories or autobiographies in teacher education.

### Sharing

Once the life histories have been written, we often ask our students (either in small groups or in a large group) to share briefly the "high points" of their stories. What they do not wish to share with their peers they need not share. We are careful to remind them of this, just as we are careful to remind them of the importance of being respectful to presenters.

As noted, themes—shared concerns or issues—are identified. Typically, themes are of two kinds: particular and general/common. Particular themes, of the kind discussed earlier such as Carla's tendency to dominate others, relate to patterns of belief and action embedded in an individual's story that have a bearing on their work as teachers. General themes, ones that cut across stories like the feeling of being an outsider, also impact classroom performance but represent commonalities among stories and, therefore, tend to reflect wider, contextual issues. General themes are of interest here.

A decision will need to be made about how to best pursue commonalities. One approach we have used is to identity general themes or problems, to group the beginning teachers according to commonalities, and have them explore one or more of these in depth and in relationship to teaching, school contexts, and the conditions of teachers' work. This approach requires that students be helped to turn their shared concern into a researchable problem statement, be connected with appropriate literature, and then be assisted in ways that will enhance and broaden their understanding. The results of these inquiries should be shared with the entire group. Although time-consuming, this has been a useful and powerful way of assisting students to confront aspects of their past (in particular, constraining influences on their development), to identify alternatives, and to build a sense of community within the group.

A second approach, used because of time constraints with Carla's group, is to treat the general themes and problems less directly. Instead of becoming the basis for a specific inquiry, they become ongoing threads to which we periodically return. Some assignments, for example, may include one or another aspect of the concerns raised. We have found the student teaching seminar to be a particularly fruitful arena for this activity. Instructionally, the outsider theme was powerful, in part because it was related closely to the study of student culture which was about to begin. The feelings associated with being an outsider provided a means for connecting emotionally and intellectually to students who felt excluded and who formed oppositional cultures. This theme opened access to the ways in which school structure and teacher behavior relate to, and in some ways sustain, student categories and, through categories, affect. A second theme that emerged in Carla's cohort focused on the victimization of young people. This also proved to be a powerful theme, especially given the political context of early twentieth-first century America. These are a few of the many possible themes that life writing may open.

A third approach is to avoid commonalities altogether, and to treat the stories as simply personal statements that will be returned to from time to time. In this instance, the focus is on particularistic rather than general themes.

### Ethics

As noted previously, students should not be compelled to reveal more about themselves than they wish to reveal. It is extremely important that the classroom be characterized by a climate of trust, where risk taking is not only accepted but honored. This is especially important when values associated with the "core" self are at stake; these are values and beliefs that represent a significant personal investment. To accomplish this aim, we have found it necessary to downplay evaluation. If sorting of students is institutionally required, and often it is, the burden should be placed on quizzes or other assignments unrelated to revealing self. Written comments on the life histories should encourage and honor student effort and honesty, not bear judgment. Moreover, students need to be assured that what they have written will be held in confidence. Thus, the three education-related autobiographies we have included were published with written permission and with the understanding that with the first two fictitious names would be used.

By not formally evaluating the education-related life writing, some students have mistakenly understood that the work is unimportant. A few are pleased to discover that a page or two of superficial writing will receive full credit. This has been an ongoing dilemma. A good many students, however, will produce rich and interesting documents *provided* they fully understand that they are writing *for themselves* and that a good piece of work, an authentic expression of self, will prove most valuable over the course of their certification program and perhaps into the first years of teaching. This claim is based upon data gathered from beginning teachers who were asked to evaluate the quality of the certification program and their experience within it.

The education-related life history becomes the first entry in the *personal teaching text*. It serves as the backdrop against which the beginning teachers will assess much of their development over the course of the year we are together because it is the source of one's ideals. Periodically, as part of reviewing their development, they are asked to reread their life writing and, in a review of the personal teaching text, assess their development in writing. Thus, a poorly written, inauthentic, and superficial life history haunts them. This, too, we carefully explain.

We have found that reading our students' life writing affects how we view them. In some instances, where our experiences blend with theirs or where a story represents a particularly touching or compelling tale of self-discovery, empathy develops and bonds build. Knowing our students in this way has forced us to review perhaps with greater care than otherwise the possible implications of our actions on our students. Moreover, knowing our students in this way has compelled us to reveal more about ourselves and our backgrounds to students than perhaps might otherwise have been the case (see Bullough, 1994). Knowing them encourages intimacy, as does working with them over the course of an entire year. Finally, knowing something about the background of our students has enabled us to make our programs more responsive, and especially allowed us to function in more sensitive and, we believe, more effective ways as supervisors during practice teaching.

## A NOTE TO TEACHER EDUCATORS
## ON CHAPTER THREE, METAPHOR ANALYSIS

Implicitly, teacher educators have long recognized the intimate relationship between metaphors and teacher identity. Some years ago Earl Pullias and James Young (1968), for example, created a list of teaching roles that took the form of: "A teacher is . . ." A teacher is a "guide," they said, "an example," and so on. Surprisingly, "one's relation to the world can often be reduced to a few words describing how one thinks and feels" (Norton, 1989, p. 1). Moreover, as we have suggested, there is a strong link between metaphor and narrative, thus between chapters two and three. Metaphors often form a story's theme or plot line (Bruner, 1990; Bullough & Baughman, 1997; Parks, 1996); they stand between story and image. As such, they provide a promising means for clustering images for exploration and analysis of teacher thinking and provide an avenue for self exploration. It is for this reason that the practice of metaphor analysis is growing in teacher education: "In courses for the professional development of teachers, especially in preservice courses, it is now common to attempt to get teachers to identify their own metaphors for teaching, the classroom, learning etc. as part of a reflective process of helping them to reconceptualize the processes of teaching and learning through self-critique and through appreciation of multiple perspectives. The development of alternative metaphors related to evaluating actual practices is part of this" (Cortazzi & Jin, 1999, p. 172–173).

Perhaps the most powerful teacher role is embedded in the metaphor that a teacher is "one who knows," a master or expert. It is this metaphor that seems to come to mind most readily as representing the essence of "teacher" and is institutionally most supported in secondary schools where it is often taken as being commonsensical. Of the three sets of metaphors we included in chapter three, both Martha and Terry were tied to such views of teaching and of learning. The institutional strength of this understanding is remarkable, as evident not only in how school is organized structurally but also in student, teacher, and parent expectations.

Clearly, for a teacher to be master or subject matter expert, it is necessary that students, as "other," become disciples, imitators, or mimics of those in the know. And here's the problem: As Terry noted, a good many students do not want to be cast as disciples, yet disciples they must be if teachers are to be masters. But this is not all. For the master, teaching is telling, or shifting images, a matter of filling a "dry-well" (Sternberg & Martin, 1988, p. 557); and filling a dry well, as Martha discovered, is often no fun at all. As each teacher discovered, metaphors reach out, interact, and define one another and simultaneously define the other. Yet, they also change over time as the social context changes and new demands, or rediscovered old demands, of schooling are embraced by policy makers and the public. The recent arrival and growing importance of market metaphors in educational discourse may signal that a change is on the horizon.

One change has been particularly dramatic over the past few decades. Societal expectations for schooling have expanded beyond reason and with them teacher roles have changed. Other non-academic metaphors have arisen to compete with expert teacher metaphors. For good or ill teachers find themselves functioning as social workers, therapists, confidantes, and surrogate parents, and often expectations are contradictory. Some role expectations are troubling for many beginning teachers, and they need help to understand and respond to them. Clearly, teaching has been made more difficult by role expansion, and the challenge of establishing a satisfying and productive teacher identity is more complicated and demanding than ever before.

There is more at stake to exploring self through metaphors than just the inner workings of self. For beginning teachers, coming to terms with who they are as teachers and the assumptions that underpin their thinking about teaching requires coming to terms with that which is not self: the institution of schooling and, most importantly, students. Exploring teaching metaphors is not, then, only important because it is a means for assisting beginning teachers to articulate and consider who they think they are as teachers and what they want to be but also because it simultaneously enables exploration of co-evolving conceptions of other: students, the disciplines of knowledge, one's colleagues and building administrators. It is particularly important to note that the metaphors held by teachers both enable and limit student opportunities to learn. Their consideration, then, necessitates that the ethical and moral implications of different conceptions of self as teacher, as well as different relations with the other, be confronted and criticized. And, exploring metaphors is a means for considering the ways in which different contexts enable some meanings while they inhibit others. In secondary schools, it easy, almost natural, to think of teaching as telling than as the exchange of cultural capital or even as mothering, for example. As such, the identification and analysis of teaching metaphors is a means for gaining perspective on one's own socialization and institutional life, as we have suggested. We turn now to a set of issues and a few problems related to metaphor analysis.

### Getting Started

We stress to our students that they should reread their life histories when seeking a metaphor or metaphors that capture their views of themselves as teachers. Also, we introduce the topic by discussing the centrality of metaphors in thinking and draw on the work of Lakoff and Johnson to do so:

> Just as in mutual understanding we constantly search out commonalities of experience when we speak with other people, so in self-understanding we are always searching for what unifies our own diverse experiences in order to give coherence to our lives. Just as we seek out metaphors to highlight and make coherent what we have in common with someone else, so we seek out personal metaphors to highlight and make coherent our own pasts, our present activities, and our dreams, hopes, and goals as well. A large part of self-understanding is the search for appropriate personal metaphors that make sense of our lives. (1980, p. 232–233)

In teaching, as in life generally, metaphors are central to the process of sense making.

We explore with our students how coming to think of the heart as a "pump" made open heart surgery possible. Pumps can be repaired. Consider E.L. Thorndike's concept of learning, and its derivation from the switch board used to direct telephone calls or research currently underway that is grounded in the metaphor that the mind is a computer. Each metaphor opens up and simultaneously closes down possibilities for meaning making. We share our own metaphors for teaching, one of which is "teaching is conversation," and explore by way of example the implications of our metaphors for practice as guiding theories. We have also discovered that for some students visualization is helpful; we encourage them to close their eyes and imagine their ideal classroom. We ask them to focus on how that classroom feels, what they are doing, and what their students are doing while in the room. Then, they write.

*Generating Metaphors*

Some students, like Mary, have difficulty identifying metaphors. We have found that for the vast majority of our students, authentic metaphors do eventually emerge and a little patience coupled with a measure of determination are all that is necessary. For a few, however, metaphors never come. A very few students never quite understand what a metaphor is. And, some do not want to reflect on their conceptions of themselves as teachers because they either think they "have it" and they see no purpose to the exercise or they are generally unreflective. Additionally, for a variety of reasons a small group of students have difficulty because they assume there is a right answer, a single metaphor that is them and that will endure.

To address these problems we encourage a few students, after the first writing, to rethink what they have written or to expand on it. We urge them to turn inward, be patient, and focus on naming their images of themselves as teachers. For those who do not understand what a metaphor is we talk individually, and this seems to help. Often they "know" but are unfamiliar with the label. With those (and there are a very few) who produce silly metaphors that indicate an unwillingness to seriously think about their views and commitments, we prod gently and seek to better explain the purpose of the methodology. And finally, we stress over and over again that there is no universal, single, best teaching metaphor. We remind them that all metaphors have limitations and break down as comparisons are made, an outcome we demonstrate in class. Moreover, we suggest that as their thinking becomes more complicated, other metaphors may become more compelling than those initially generated, and that this is the way it is supposed to be; it is a sign of development as a teacher.

*Student Reactions*

We have sought through interviews and questionnaires to gather data that would help us better understand the strengths and weaknesses of the methodology. Some students do not find the methodology helpful, but clearly most do, particularly during the early stages of teacher education (Bullough with Stokes, 1994). A few of our students find that by the end of teacher education the value has lessened because they have settled on a comfortable role and self-understanding albeit often a more complex understanding. This is to be expected, and celebrated, provided the role generated is ethically and educationally defensible. Our questionnaire included the following question: "Was the focus on the identification and exploration of personal teaching metaphors helpful?" Typical comments included: "Yes. Because of the written metaphor updates I was able to see where I was (mentally, developmentally) at certain times during the year. The updates forced me to think about, and put into words, my ideas and assumptions." Another wrote: "I thought the metaphors were very helpful. When I started the cohort in the fall, I was very nervous about what it meant to be a teacher. I certainly couldn't imagine it then. The metaphors worked for me because they made me examine my feelings about myself as a teacher, which helped when I began teaching." A third student wrote: "Yes, very much so. It allowed me to re-evaluate myself periodically and be self-critical. . . . Through the metaphors I was able to look back on my progress and realize I was beginning to think like a teacher. . . . I was able to look at what I was becoming as a teacher and decide whether I was headed in the direction that I wanted to go." And a negative comment, which illustrates some of the difficulties noted above: "Not really. I hate to compare myself in a metaphor. Each of us is different in terms of our personalities. Each of us is unique and will teach in a different manner. I think the metaphor is actually restrictive in describing ourselves. Maybe a multiple metaphor?"

## A NOTE TO TEACHER EDUCATORS ON CHAPTER FOUR, INSTITUTIONAL STUDY

One difficulty in doing successful institutional studies is that they require a number of skills that need to be developed and supported before the process begins. The three phases of the institutional study process will serve as a framework for discussing how these skills can be cultivated.

### Phase One: Problem Formation and Data Gathering

One of the challenges of producing institutional studies is data collection. While our intent is not to produce sophisticated research studies, it is important to become familiar with a few ways to conduct observations and interviews and develop questionnaires. The way we support these activities parallels many of the assumptions that underlie the methodologies discussed in *Becoming a Student of Teaching*. You may want to begin by having the students do a very short pilot study. To begin such a study, the students literally wander around the school and talk to teachers, students, and administrators. These informal observations and chats, which can be accomplished in a few short visits, help establish a tentative focus for the institutional study. Once an issue or problem is set by the members of the study team, observations, interviews, and questionnaires are planned to gather data systematically. The questions that will structure the questionnaires or interviews are shared with us to get feedback, as are issues concerning the observation of classroom practice. Once feedback is given, team members might try one interview or observation session. The advantage of using a team format is that each member of the team can concentrate on doing in depth interviews and observations as opposed to having an individual conduct a large number of "surface" observations or interviews. The purpose of these trials is not so much to collect data, but rather to identify problems associated with conducting observations and interviews and using questionnaires. Again, problems are shared with us and with other beginning teachers to generate possible solutions. Part of the feedback that needs to be given involves advice about situations that might put the beginning teacher at risk. For example, if a beginning teacher asks questions of teachers on the staff in the school within which they will student teach, and asks these questions in ways that alienate these faculty members, the institutional study can create problems for the novice without producing much insight. Teacher educators must steer novices away from confrontational questions that will put the school staff on the defensive. Feedback should also be solicited from faculty working with student teachers to make certain they understand and support the process.

*Phase Two: Description*

Transforming data into description, a story, is difficult. We find that students often summarize the data in a short list, such as how respondents answered interview questions, and then write the description without any supporting evidence. Links between data collection and the story told are not clear. Others will use so much data that the story or description never comes through. The challenge is to find a balance between the data provided and the story told. The following institutional study focusing on a middle school seems to capture this balance.

> The mission of Northeast Middle School is to provide a safe positive learning environment which encourages and recognizes active learning.... Terri King, a social studies teacher, was mentioned by six students as being their favorite teacher. When asked why she was their favorite teacher, they noted that she taught with activities and a hands-on approach. During one observation, she used political cartoons from the newspaper as a way to help students understand the current presidential election and allowed students to come to their own conclusions as to the meaning of a chosen cartoon.

One way we have found that helps encourage balance is to have students go through their observations and interviews several times and then, without the data in front of them, simply describe the event or perspective expressed. Once a tentative description is written, the student is encouraged to go back to the data and insert quotes or excerpts from field notes that support the story told.

*Phase Three: Interpretations and Themes*

The interpretive phase is the most difficult. The first challenge is to identify themes. Having students look at the types of themes developed in well-organized published qualitative studies can be helpful. We have also spent time looking at the author's point of view and how his or her arguments are constructed. Discussion of these issues provides some insight into the difficult but important activity of making sense of data.

Another vital part of this phase is the integration of outside readings into the study. Some students are not sophisticated in doing library searches. It is helpful, as a consequence, to begin any consideration of "outside" readings with a trip to the library and a discussion of the types of resources that can be obtained. We then have a follow-up session which helps beginning teachers make choices about which scholarly work to focus on and how to quickly summarize the arguments found in a particular article, research paper, or text. While this is time consuming, if an aim of teacher education is to foster students of teaching, knowing how to locate and summarize literature is important.

A final point about institutional studies needs further elaboration. As noted, sharing insights is important in part because changing the school context often requires group discussion and action. Generally speaking, neither teacher education programs nor the school context supports such discussion. One way to challenge this trend, particularly within preservice education, is to use institutional study texts as a forum for discussion. Through them, common concerns and interests can be identified and built upon.

Given that emergent communities are never formed overnight, and that institutional studies are complex projects that require a considerable amount of time, these studies are likely to be most effective if they are conducted in phases over a quarter or semester, or seen as an integrating methodology that summarizes and focuses what has been learned about self and context. If the methodology is used over a quarter or semester, beginning teachers could be working on this long-term project as they are utilizing other methodologies. For example, the Shadow Studies (see chapter five) or the Textbook Analysis (see chapter seven) could easily be part of the institutional study. The only change required would be to make certain these methodologies, in part, speak to the question or questions central to the institutional study. On the other hand, if the institutional study is seen as an integrating methodology, it could occur at the end of the preservice program and be used as a way to pull together insights gleaned from other methodologies. In either case, what is most important is that beginning teachers be given the time to take on the difficult work of understanding the school context.

## A NOTE TO TEACHER EDUCATORS ON CHAPTER FIVE, SHADOW STUDY

### Preparing to Conduct the Study

Prior to conducting the Shadow Study, our students are given selected readings that address student cultures and particular ways in which the institution shapes and responds to those cultures. Because of their power within schools to shape interaction and understanding, special attention is given to labeling and tracking (Oakes, 1985). It has been our experience that many of our students are too comfortable with schooling labels and the norms associated with them, and use them too easily as means for accounting for how pupils and teachers make sense of school life. It is important to note that young people have different relationships with school and with teachers and respond to norms and make and use their wiggle room differently. Young people may be "cowboys" or "burnouts," for example, which signify an unfriendly institutional relationship (see Bullough, Knowles, & Crow, 1992, chapter nine). Other students have labels (like "gifted") placed on them by the context of schooling, which signal institutional acceptance and the promise of a high degree of conformity to established norms. We stress the importance of attempting to look beyond and under labels—the institutional and cultural shorthand that so seductively defines reality by prejudging it—and that beginning teachers need to become wary of them as a means for relating to young people and for understanding their behavior.

### Sharing the Studies

The three Shadow Studies presented are based upon spending only one day shadowing a student. Lengthening the time spent will produce richer data, but not necessarily more useful interpretations. Aside from getting to know students better, the value of the Shadow Studies is centrally tied to the discussions about them and, later, the classroom study. We have organized these discussions around a cluster of questions which we will share, along with a few reactions to them, noting that they are more suggestive than definitive. You may find other questions more helpful than these.

First, what was the day like for the student? How much was your shadowed student's experience of schooling like your own as a student? What was different? Where differences are noted, they are explored. For example, Veronica notes that she did not recall school being so boring. Others shared her recollection, while many disagreed. Teachers were identified as the critical variable, underscoring their power and educational responsibility. But differences in school contexts, and especially in tracks, were also mentioned as important. Different tracks reflect different norms. Social class and culture often surface as well as reasons for differences in experience as does gender.

Second, what was most important to the student? What were the sources of his/her greatest pleasure and disappointment during the day? How was the student treated by teachers and other students? Answers to these questions also present occasions to compare and contrast experiences. A common perception is that academics are less important to the shadowed students than they were to the beginning teachers. This is not surprising, since most of the beginning teachers were very able students and a large percentage of those shadowed are from lower tracks, as one would hope, given the assignment. Inevitably, a discussion follows of how important social interaction is to young people, how hard teachers and the institution of schooling work to constrain rather than build on the gregariousness of youth, and how school cuts off and opens up opportunities to different types of young people based upon criteria that seldom have anything to do with ability: School norms favor some young people over others. Exploring why this is so and how students respond is crucially important.

Third, who holds power within the school? How powerful are students to shape their educational experience? What are the sources of their power? How powerful are teachers? What are the sources of their power? How do students come to terms with teacher power? These questions direct the students to consider teacher-student relationships and the teacher's role and responsibilities. In his ability to play one set of school norms off against another, Jamal illustrates some of the covert and overt aspects of student power. In principle, young people always have the power to refuse, to resist institutional demands, but in practice refusal to conform either leads to withdrawal from the institution, and perhaps expulsion as in Ed's case, or finds expression in institutionally nonthreatening ways: Students sluff class, do only portions of their work, and talk when they are supposed to be working. Power may also come from collaborating with teachers: Jamal cuts a deal, and teachers "wink" at his "misbehavior." Sharing norms with teachers and invested in serving institutional interests, student body officers are allies who are granted privileges and become functionaries of the corporate school. In all cases, student power must be understood in relationship to teacher power and to the costs and benefits of compliance or resistance.

It is the abuse of teacher power by failing to exercise it for the sake of student learning that prompts Veronica to conclude that lunch period ought to be extended. But Veronica hints at a more radical relationship of teacher and student power when seeking to preserve Janie's voice. She seems to want teachers to share power, to hold it *with* rather than *over* students. Perhaps this is a reflection of still thinking of herself as a student primarily and not yet as a teacher, but we think not. If young people are to become active participants in their own education, then there is no alternative but for teachers to share power, and for this to happen different institutional norms may need to be created. As an aside, the same argument is now being made for teacher-administrator relationships: Power ought to be shared.

Inevitably, discussion leads to the exploration of the role and responsibilities of teachers, and in relationship to the institutional, social, and political context of teaching. A beginning teacher asked, after Mick shared his study, whether it was reasonable for him to expect that he, or any teacher, should have known what was going on in Ed's life that led to drug usage? This type of question is crucially important to beginning teachers who are thinking seriously about who they are as teachers and the kind of relationship they want to have with pupils, and are beginning to discover the limits of teacher power.

As mentioned, you may find other questions more useful than these for guiding discussion. And you may wish to include some of these or other questions as part of the written assignment. This decision is related to what work comes before and after the Shadow Study, how much time is available, and whether greater emphasis is placed on written interpretation and evaluation than on description. We have emphasized description. We see the Shadow Study as a continuing foray into a set of issues to which we will often return throughout the program.

Finally, we should mention the Shadow Study can be part of a case study of a student. Case studies provide a very effective means to explore in depth how a student learns. The addition of a focus on student learning broadens the range of instructional and curricular issues available for discussion. The disadvantage of the case study is, once again, that a good study requires investment of a great deal of time that our students do not have. There are alternative means for exploring student learning, among them various forms of authentic assessment that require teachers to explore student performance and attend to reasons for variations in learning (Darling-Hammond, 2000).

## A NOTE TO TEACHER EDUCATORS ON CHAPTER SIX, CLASSROOM STUDIES

As noted previously, good classroom studies require a tremendous amount of time to produce. It is not only that time needs to be spent in the classroom, but also that time is needed to make sense of the data gathered. Since we are not conducting a class in educational anthropology, our expectations are relatively modest ones. We are more interested in having our students explore culture and test some tentative hypotheses than produce tightly argued and polished papers. Still, we want papers that have meaning for our students, that will generate useful insights. To this end, and in recognition of time constraints and the limitations associated with being novices to the study of teaching and culture, when we introduce the assignment we include, in addition to sharing sample studies, tips on note taking and on making sense of the notes taken. We also include a warning to avoid what Teitelbaum and Britzman dub the "rush to judgment" (1991, p. 174) to which Mark may have fallen prey. Time constraints are a major factor behind the rush. One needs to slow down and in a sense let the data speak.

Prior to conducting a classroom study, the students have not only formally interviewed their cooperating teacher but also spent a good deal of time with them and in their classroom. We urge our students to select a class for study that seems interesting, and one that they will most likely be teaching when practice teaching. We tell them to pick a location in the classroom that is unobtrusive but that allows them to see what is going on. And we urge them to review the assignment with their cooperating teacher to make certain they understand what is being done and why. At first we suggest that a running record of classroom events be kept, perhaps with time counts in the margins (e.g., "8:45 A.M., class begins when . . ."). As they record—as they learn to see—we encourage them to write "memos" to themselves, marginalia, when an event stands out as interesting, exceptional, or puzzling or when they have a flash of insight about the meaning of events. Later, but certainly sometime the same day of an observation, we urge them to review their notes. At first the purpose of the reviews is to flesh out gaps in the notes and especially to respond to and perhaps amplify the memos, which generally serve as the basis of the interpretations that will emerge. "What is going on?" is the question to be asked. Soon the purpose of the reviews shifts somewhat, and the quest begins for patterns. A second question is posed: "What is going on, and why?" Finally, the focus narrows and hypotheses are proposed to account for the patterns that are observed. Lastly, hypotheses—tentative interpretations—are tested through additional observation, adjusted, and sometimes rejected.

These phases of analysis, loose to be sure, are evident particularly in Mark and Laura's studies, although Mark rather quickly jumps to an interpretation—the social contract—and it is somewhat difficult to tell how he got there. Laura's study contains evidence not only of proposing hypotheses but also of testing them. For example, to test her hypothesis that lack of student participation in first period was due to the early hour of the day she observed other classes, at first through a fortuitous turn of events but later intentionally. By observing these additional classes, she began to better understand the nature of student power within the classroom, its operation, and its influence on her cooperating teacher's practice. Other better and more compelling hypotheses followed that most certainly will inform her understanding of classroom events come practice teaching.

In addition, we urge our students to test their tentative interpretations by checking them out with their cooperating teachers and the pupils. Sometimes surprising results follow. As Laura discovered, a teacher's perceptions of classroom events and those of an observer may be quite different. Depending on the nature of the beginning teacher and cooperating teacher relationship, these differences can provide the occasion for a rich and lively discussion of teaching. Unfortunately, such discussions are not always possible and interpretations must be kept to oneself. In any case, perceptions should be checked, for more complex and interesting understandings will often result. We should also note that when interpretations differ, the beginning teacher should not necessarily assume that his or her interpretation is incorrect. After all, reality comes in many forms!

Pupil interviews are a useful way of checking some interpretations. For instance, Laura could have checked out her conclusion that competition among groups was a crucially important cultural element in one of the classes she observed. Time constraints and her interest in many other aspects of culture prevented her from doing so. Interviews are not the only means for obtaining pupil input, however. Some of our students have designed questionnaires to gather data and test hypotheses. A few have even conducted whole-class discussions, with cooperating teacher permission and without their presence. What is important is that data be gathered by means that will enable interpretations to be assessed.

Nicole had difficulty moving beyond description in her study. She seemed nearly overwhelmed by all that was going on in the classroom and unable to find and frame a question or issue for exploration. Put differently, no events stood out or challenged her to ask, "Why? What is going on here?" Because discipline problems are readily apparent, many of our students who feel adrift grab hold and study them, and sometimes they prove to be a productive avenue for uncovering and exploring norms, but not always. But what does one do when no genuine discipline problems appear, as when Nicole observed the geometry classes? It is for this reason, among others, that memos are of such importance. When observing, an idea or question will pop into one's head and, if not immediately recorded, quickly be lost. These flashes of insight, like Mark's uneasiness when being introduced as "Mr. Pendleton," often prove to be rich avenues for beginning to understand the meaning of events. For students who struggle to get an "angle," discussions with other students or with you, the teacher educator, may prove helpful. If such meetings take place, it is important to remember that the purpose is to pose questions and nudge along understanding and not to impose an interpretation. One important way to further understanding and to help the students find an angle is to recommend readings that elaborate themes or patterns found in the qualitative studies of schooling. While this can lead to imposition, the alternative of trying to remain neutral places the students in an intellectual vacuum that encourages surface or commonsensical explanations. We have approached this task in different ways. Sometimes we have required readings that help orient the students to the study of culture and help them frame questions for exploration, as noted by Mark. Other times we have suggested readings and had the students locate their own readings that speak to the issues that concern them. In either case, we encourage them, through open criticism of the readings, to be wary of the conclusions of others. It is important that an angle be found, a beginning made, but it need not be one that we, or the authors of the studies we have the students read, think is the central or most significant focal point. As we have seen from the studies presented, there are perhaps an infinite number of interesting angles awaiting exploration that will shed light on classroom norms and their operation.

Finally, the studies are discussed in class, sometimes in groups and sometimes they read and criticize one another's work. Within the groups they test interpretations, and the opportunity is given to write a postscript (see Teitelbaum & Britzman, 1991).

## A NOTE TO TEACHER EDUCATORS ON CHAPTER SEVEN, TEXTBOOK/CURRICULUM ANALYSIS

An additional cluster of concepts relating to the teacher role and teachers' conceptions of teaching undergird our work with the analyses, besides those associated with the explicit, hidden, null, and implemented curriculum and curriculum form. One of the sure signs of training is the commonly held view that teachers do not develop curriculum, someone else does; teachers instruct, "tell," but do not produce curriculum (Sardo-Brown, 1988). This is a serious problem not only because it represents a constricted view of teachers' abilities (see Zumwalt, 1988), but also because it places the burden of content development on experts who are generally little involved in classroom work. Teachers are experts, and their talent is desperately needed in curriculum development, as our analysis questions suggest.

Beginning teachers need assistance to understand that the commonly held view and form of curriculum, what Goodson labels CAP (curriculum as prescription), bring with them a teacher role based upon the assumption that "we can dispassionately define the main ingredients of the course of study and then proceed to teach the various segments and sequences in systematic turn" (Goodson, 1991b, p. 168). This is the view that nonteacher curriculum developers often support; it runs throughout commercially produced texts and curriculum materials. It devalues teachers and teachers' work and emphasizes control of teacher behavior in order to achieve externally established outcomes.

A good many beginning teachers feel compelled to come to terms with the role of teacher as "implementor of a predetermined body of knowledge" (Zumwalt, 1989, p. 174) that comes with CAP. For beginning teachers struggling to define who they are as teachers, this can be a frustrating and discouraging experience.

> Not only must [the beginning teacher] implement a curriculum generally developed by others and with which they are unfamiliar but simultaneously they must negotiate a satisfying teaching role. At times the two demands are contradictory: The adopted curriculum prohibits establishing a satisfying role; and the desired role makes it difficult to implement the established curriculum. (Bullough, 1992, p. 239)

Recognizing this problem and relationship is an important step toward addressing it. And it is an important reason for engaging in the critical analysis and reconstruction of curricula.

As we have had students engage in curriculum analysis we have run into some difficulties that require mention: A few of our students have had difficulty identifying a textbook or curriculum guide for study. Sometimes this is a problem related to the subject matter they will teach, like art or music. We urge our students to analyze material that is in wide use and available and that they likely will teach. When a cooperating teacher uses more than one guide or text, we suggest the most frequently used one be analyzed.

A second problem has occasionally arisen: Some of our students resist being critical of the texts or guides. This problem is rooted in several sources. We will mention only two: Some of our students have had little experience in criticism and need a bit of help and encouragement. In a sense, they are victims of training's emphasis on "teaching as telling," which elevates the importance of public over private theory. Also, a few are hesitant to criticize because they do not feel they know the subject area well enough. Sadly, school content and university majors often have little in common. One of our students succinctly captured the problem when she said, "I don't know enough about the content to say whether or not what the book presents is any good." Under such conditions it is little wonder that so many beginning teachers find themselves depending on a textbook for much of the curriculum. With these students we suggest that in the textbook analysis they pay particular attention to those questions that address teacher and student role, and downplay those addressing content issues. A good analysis, as we have said, need not attend to all or even most of the questions we present. For these students a side benefit of the analysis is that by working carefully through the textbook, they learn a great deal of content.

Finally, we should note that what distinguishes a good analysis from a poor one is not length but the willingness of the beginning teacher to question the text seriously; to probe it for insights into authors' conceptions of teaching, learning, and content; and then to think carefully about the results of the probing in relationship to their own thinking and values.

## A NOTE TO TEACHER EDUCATORS ON CHAPTER EIGHT, ACTION RESEARCH

Critics of action research have raised a wide range of issues. Goodson (1991a), for example, observes that if teachers and teacher educators seek collaborative relationships, action research may disappoint. Goodson's concern is that by placing teacher practice at the center of action, action research "focuses on the maximum point of vulnerability" (p. 141). He suggests that "a more valuable and less vulnerable entry point would be to examine teachers' work in the context of teachers' lives" (p. 141). The point is a good one, as Sonja's project suggests, and underscores the importance of thinking about the methodologies presented in *Becoming a Student of Teaching* in relationship to one another and to in-service teacher education. Action research comes after our students have engaged in a good deal of self and context study and after a reasonably good level of trust, a feeling of community, has been developed within the cohort group.

*Issues: Beginning Teacher Frustration*

Sometimes beginning teachers are put off by the word "research" and are a bit threatened by the term "theory." This uneasiness is not unusual, as Garth Boomer observed a few years ago:

> We cannot remove the semantic dye into which "research" has been plunged. It is almost impossible to give it the "small r" meaning. It has accumulated connotations of validity, generalizability, objectivity, and control, which get in the way of those of us who want it simply to mean "finding out in order to act more effectively." (1987, p. 7)

Additional difficulty, as we have noted, arises because of the pressures associated with practice teaching. Student teachers are tired, stressed, and often frustrated. Given these feelings, many resist the idea of formally studying their practice. They want to teach, and teaching is not about researching practice, or so some assume. *Becoming a Student of Teaching* is based on a different and contrary view, that teaching, as Stenhouse suggests, is researching.

Despite many of our students' initial resistance to action research, once the process gets underway their attitudes usually change. "Once again," one of our students wrote in her final action research report, "you have pushed me to do something I did not want to do, and I am grateful. Yes, student teaching is a lot of work [even] without having to [do] other projects, but I would have not learned as much [as I did]." Another initially disgruntled student wrote: "As I look forward to [my first year of] teaching next fall, I continue to have many concerns about my development as a teacher; the experience [of conducting an action research study] has helped me to see that I need to continually study . . . teaching. I need to think critically about how I prepare lessons and the effects [of my teaching] on students. I think it is necessary to continue gathering data on how I teach. If this assignment has done nothing else, it has taught me to view my [work] critically and to look for ways to improve daily."

Action research is a lot of work, especially when it is understood as an addition to teaching and not integral to it. Yet, action research represents, formally, what reflective teachers or teacher researchers do informally, and that is study their practice. It is part of the quest to become self-conscious about teaching. Understood as a cyclical and ongoing process, as Elliott (1991) characterizes it, action research is a means for beginning teachers to more quickly escape the vicissitudes and frustrations attendant to trial-and-error approaches to learning to teach, to muddling through, that are commonly associated with the first years of teaching (Bullough, 1989).

*Issues: Data Gathering*

The data sources we listed could easily be expanded: Field notes, anecdotal records, diaries, logs, portfolios, photographs and slides, and cooperating teacher observations are all useful sources depending on the problems being addressed. Whatever sources of data are identified, it is crucially important that ethical issues about data gathering be addressed beforehand and that careful consideration be given to potential dangers inherent in some sources of data and their use. In addition, some sources of data are intrusive and potentially disruptive. Already we have mentioned that videotaping is sometimes disruptive to a class, but also to a teacher.

> I chose [to] videotape my teaching, and I can assure you it was frightening! I am glad [I did it], as it was very interesting and helpful; however, I feel that the experience was somewhat negative because of the affect of the camera in the classroom. I felt slightly intimidated by the camera, as did the students such that normal classroom behavior was altered, and the "natural" rapport between the students and myself "stiffened."

Videotaping is a rich source of data, but students and teachers need to get used to the camera's presence.

*Issues: Plan Implementation*

Once a plan is made, some of our students have difficulty implementing it. Again, the pressures of practice teaching get in the way.

> I would like to speak of a major difficulty I have encountered with [my study]. . . . The difficulty is that once I [made my plan] of self-examination, it [was] extraordinarily difficult to remember to [implement] it. I would begin class . . . and, typically, within about 20 seconds I would have forgotten to do it. It is absolutely extraordinary what little willpower I have. . . . Indeed, the realization of just how unconscious I am of what I am [doing] is shocking. This explains the "video effect" that occurs when one sees a videotape of oneself and exclaims, "Who is that?"

For some of our students, more careful planning has helped ameliorate this difficulty, including written reminders, like Sonja's, of what actions are supposed to be undertaken. For others, cooperating teachers have been invaluable sources for making certain the plans get implemented and that habits are set aside. Half-time practice teaching also helps.

*Issues: Sharing Results*

It is crucially important that time be made available, perhaps in the student teaching seminar, for sharing the studies as they unfold and not just the results. Assuming a reasonably good level of trust, sharing is a means for helping identify and usefully frame problems for study, for exploring issues associated with data gathering and use, for reconsidering initial hunches and results, and for strengthening community. Our experience has been that, generally speaking, beginning teacher concerns are more common than not and that much can be learned by openly and honestly exploring them. Minimally, beginning teachers are reminded that they are not alone, as they sometimes may feel, that they are not the only ones struggling, and that others can and will help. Sharing final projects is a time for celebration.

## A NOTE TO TEACHER EDUCATORS ON CHAPTER NINE, CREATING A PERSONAL TEACHING TEXT

As noted previously, if the personal teaching text and the reviews are to have the desired results of increasing program coherence and of enhancing student reflectivity in particular, careful planning is required. Students need to be encouraged to organize their PTTs carefully, as one recently observed in a year-end review:

> I really didn't know if I wanted/could teach. Anyone who picks up my personal teaching text could probably see this. It was poorly organized. Papers were thrown in haphazardly. There was no rhyme or reason to its order.... I kept the text because I was expected to. My attitude toward my text was, "I'll keep these papers stuffed in this folder in case I ever do teach." The folder was a source of irritation because it was always in a place where I needed to dust. [But now, after student teaching], I'm proud of my text. It symbolizes more than activities that have taken place over the last year. It serves as a reminder of all the doubts I had about myself.... Yet it also serves as a source of confirmation: "Yes, I can teach and do a pretty decent job of it."

Careful plans need to be made for when and how students will return to them for analysis. As a form of guided inquiry, you may discover that the questions we use may or may not be the ones you will find most beneficial. Different contexts may require different questions. We have found that some questions—for example, "Are you on track for becoming the kind of teacher you imagine yourself capable of becoming?"— are good ones to include in each review. We mention this because including some of the same questions in each review facilitates comparison and helps tie content and activities together, which enables careful thinking about one's development as a teacher. In addition, we try to balance our questions so that each beginning teacher will be encouraged to identify and celebrate accomplishments while simultaneously uncovering areas of weakness. Celebration and criticism ought to go hand in hand.

Reading the reviews has proven very helpful to us as we think ahead about the program and about our personal relationships with students. Strong, caring relationships between teacher educators, cooperating teachers, and students are essential to program continuity. Occasionally problems will emerge with a beginning teacher's relationship with a cooperating teacher. The negativism of one of Sonja's cooperating teachers, for example, was a worry, and a conversation with the teacher followed. When concerns raised in the reviews have been shared by more than a few students, we have addressed them in class. The reviews, generally speaking, are relatively good barometers for gauging program success.

An additional word should be said about the relationship between program coherence and the PTTs. Coherence, that sense of wholeness that one hopes to provide beginning teachers, comes only partially from having clear purposes, stable and caring relationships, and well-sequenced activities and assignments. In reality coherence represents an achievement of each beginning teacher who makes the program more or less meaningful in his or her own way. Ultimately, coherence arises out of the flow and direction, the feeling of purposefulness, of each beginning teacher's individual and idiosyncratic story of professional development and its resonance with one's life story. The PTT reviews are crucial to achieving cohesiveness and to bringing about a sense of closure. The reviews present occasions to stop and think about who the beginning teacher is and where he or she is tending as a teacher and to consider alternative endings to the story. In interviews and through questionnaires our students consistently support this conclusion and add, as Sonja's reviews indicate, that they are a valuable means for reflecting on their professional development for the purpose of better directing it.

## A Final Comment

The speed with which teacher education is moving toward outcome measures as the basis for both program accreditation and student certification decisions may make it necessary to think of the PTT in relationship to summative evaluation and performance reporting (see NCATE, 2000). INTASC (Interstate New Teacher Assessment and

Support Consortium) underscores the importance of mentoring beginning teachers who are to complete a portfolio as a means for demonstrating outcomes mastery (see recent issues of *INTASC in Focus*, which are available on the internet). INTASC is in the process of establishing classroom performance standards for beginning teachers in a variety of areas, and we fully expect that when completed these standards will rapidly find a place in teacher education. The emphasis on summative evaluation is not contradictory to our emphasis on beginning teacher development although we fear balance may be lost in pursuit of demonstrated skill mastery. Skills also need to be thought of developmentally (Diez & Hess, 1997). In our view, established performance outcomes can be included in the PTT. However, when included, like all other components of the PTT, they ought to become data for reflection about development. When proof of performance, an exhibition, is required for external audiences, like a certification panel or board, a different form of reporting is required that may necessitate a reorganization of some materials included in the PTT along with additional materials, a written summary evaluation, a performance log, sample lesson plans, examples of pupil work, assessment checklist, and teaching observations, for instance. In any case, it is our view that the form chosen and the materials included need to allow for a comprehensive and holistic exhibition of abilities, one that attends to the context of teaching (see Darling-Hammond & Snyder, 2000).

# Bibliography

∴✦∴

## ARTICLES, BOOK CHAPTERS, PRESENTATIONS AND DISSERTATIONS

Apple, M. W. What Correspondence Theories of the Hidden Curriculum Miss. *Review of Education* 5(2), 101–112, 1979a.

Apple, M. W. Curricular Form and the Logic of Technical Control; Building the Possessive Individual. In M. W. Apple (Ed.), *Cultural and Economic Reproduction in Education: Essays on Class, Ideology and the State*, pp. 247–74. London: Routledge & Kegan Paul, 1982.

Berry, D. M., Kisch, J. A., Ryan, C. W., & Uphoff, J. K. The Process and Product of Portfolio Construction. Paper presented at the American Educational Research Association Conference, Chicago, April. 1991.

Bolin, F. S., & Parantis, P. Searching for Common Purpose: A Perspective on the History of Supervision. In C. Glickman (Ed.), *Supervision in Transition: The 1992 Yearbook of the ASCD*, pp. 30–43. Washington, D.C. 1992.

Boomer, G. Addressing the Problem of Elsewhereness: A Case for Action Research in Schools. In D. Goswami & P. R. Stillman (Eds.), *Reclaiming the Classroom: Teacher Research as an Agency for Change*, pp. 4–13 Upper Montclair, N.J.: Boynton/Cook Publishers, Inc., 1987.

Buchmann, M. & Floden, R. E. Coherence, the Rebel Angel. *Educational Researcher* 21(9), December, 4–9, 1992.

Bullough, R. V., Jr. Accommodation and Tension: Teachers, Teacher Role, and the Culture of Teaching. In J. Smyth (Ed.), *Educating Teachers: Changing the Nature of Pedagogical Knowledge*, pp. 83–94. London: Falmer Press, 1987.

Bullough, R. V., Jr. *The Forgotten Dream of American Public Education*, Ames, Iowa: Iowa State University Press, 1988.

Bullough, R. V., Jr. *First Year Teacher: A Case Study*. New York: Teachers College Press, 1989.

Bullough, R. V., Jr. Exploring Personal Teaching Metaphors in Preservice Teacher Education. *Journal of Teacher Education* 42(1), 43–51, 1991.

Bullough, R. V., Jr. Beginning Teacher Curriculum Decision Making, Personal Teaching Metaphors, and Teacher Education. *Teaching & Teacher Education* 8(3), 239–252, 1992.

Bullough, R. V., Jr. Case Records as Personal Teaching Texts for Study in Preservice Teacher Education. *Teaching and Teacher Education* 9(4), 385–396, 1993.

Bullough, R. V., Jr. Personal History and Teaching Metaphors: A Self-Study of Teaching as Conversation. *Teacher Education Quarterly* 21(1), 107–120, 1994.

Bullough, R. V., Jr. Becoming a Teacher: Self and the Social Location of Teacher Education. In B. J. Biddle, T. L. Good, & I. F. Goodson (Eds.), *International Handbook of Teachers and Teaching*, pp. 79–134. Boston: Kluwer Academic Publishers, 1997a.

Bullough, R. V., Jr. Practicing Theory and Theorizing Practice in Teacher Education. In J. Loughran & T. Russell (Eds.), *Teaching about Teaching*, pp. 13–31. London: Falmer Press, 1997b.

Bullough, R. V., Jr. & Baughman, K. *First Year Teacher—Eight Years Later*. New York: Teachers College Press, 1997.

Bullough, R. V., Jr., & Gitlin, A. Beyond Control: Rethinking Teacher Resistance. *Education and Society* 3(1), 65–73, 1985.

Bullough, R. V., Jr. & Gitlin, A. Toward Educative Communities: Teacher Education and the Quest for the Reflective Practitioner. *Qualitative Studies in Education* 2(4), 285–298, 1989.

Bullough, R. V., Jr., Gitlin, A., & Goldstein, S. L. Ideology, Teacher Role and Resistance. *Teachers College Record* 86(2), 341–358, 1984.

Bullough, R. V., Jr., Goldstein, S. L, & Gitlin, A. Ideology, Teacher Role, and Resistance. *Teachers College Record* 86(2), 339–358, 1984.

Bullough, R. V., Jr., Kauchak, D., Crow, N. A., Hobbs, S., & Stokes, D. Professional Development Schools: Catalysts for Teacher and School Change. *Teaching and Teacher Education* 13(2), 153–169, 1997.

Bullough, R. V., Jr. with Stokes, D. K. Analyzing Personal Teaching Metaphors in Preservice Teacher Education as a Means for Encouraging Professional Development. *American Educational Research Journal* 31(1), 197–224, 1994.

Calderhead, J., & Robson, M. Images of Teaching: Student Teachers' Early Conceptions of Classroom Practice. *Teaching and Teacher Education* 7, 1–8, 1991.

Clark, C. M. Asking the Right Questions about Teacher Preparation: Contributions of Research on Teacher Thinking. *Educational Researcher* 17(2), 5–12, 1988.

Cole, A. L. Personal Theories of Teaching: Development in the Formative Years. *Alberta Journal of Educational Research* 36(3), 203–222, 1990.

Collins, E. C., & Green, J. L. Metaphors: The Construction of a Perspective. *Theory into Practice* 29(2), 71–77, 1990.

Copeland, W. D., Birmingham, C., DeMeulle, L., D'Emidio-Caston, M., & Natal, D. Making Meaning in Classrooms: An Investigation of Cognitive Processes in Aspiring Teachers, Experienced Teachers, and Their Peers. *American Educational Research Journal* 31(1), 166–196, 1994.

Cortazzi, M., & Jin, L. Bridges to Learning: Metaphors of Teaching, Learning and Language. In L. Cameron & G. Low (Eds.), *Researching and Applying Metaphor*. Cambridge, UK: Cambridge University Press, 1999.

Darling-Hammond, L. How Teacher Education Matters. *Journal of Teacher Education* 51(3), 166–173, 2000.

Darling-Hammond, L., & Snyder, J. Authentic Assessment of Teaching in Context. *Teaching & Teacher Education* 16(5–6), 523–545, 2000.

DeBoer, J. J. Organizing the Program of Professional Education. In G. E. Axtelle and W. W. Wattenberg (Eds.), *Teachers for Democracy: Fourth Yearbook of the John Dewey Society*, pp. 256–289. New York: D. Appleton-Century Company, 1940.

Dewey, J. (1904). The Relation of Theory to Practice In Education. In C. A. McMurray (Ed.), *The Third NSSE Yearbook*. Chicago, IL: University of Chicago Press.

Dickmeyer, N. Metaphor, Model, and Theory in Education Research. *Teachers College Record* 91(2), 151–160, 1989.

Diez, M. E., & Hass, J. M. No More Piecemeal Reform: Using Performance-Based Approaches to Rethink Teacher Education. *Action in Teacher Education* 19(2), 17–26, 1997.

Diggins, J. P. The National History Standards. *American Scholar* 65(4), 495–522, 1996.

Elbaz-Luwisch, F. Narrative Research: Political Issues and Implications. *Teaching & Teacher Education* 12(1), 75–83, 1997.

Elliott, J. Educational Theory, Practice and Action Research. *British Journal of Educational Studies* 35(2), 149–169, 1987.

Feiman-Nemser, S., & Floden, R. E. The Cultures of Teaching. In M. C. Wittrock (Ed.), *Handbook of Research on Teaching, Third Edition*, pp. 505–526. New York: Macmillan, 1986.

Fenstermacher, G. D. A Philosophical Consideration of Recent Research on Teacher Effectiveness. In L. S. Shulman (Ed.), *Review of Research in Education*, pp. 157–185. Itasca, Illinois: F. E. Peacock Publishers, Inc., 1978.

Fenstermacher, G. D. On Narrative. *Teaching & Teacher Education* 13(1), 119–124, 1997.

Fenstermacher, G. D. Agenda for Education in a Democracy. In W. F. Smith & G. D. Fenstermacher (Eds.), *Leadership for Educational Renewal*, pp. 3–27. San Francisco: Jossey-Bass Publishers, 1999.

Florio-Ruane, S. Social Organization of Classes and Schools. In M. C. Reynolds (Ed.), *Knowledge Base for the Beginning Teacher*, pp. 163–172. New York: Pergamon Press, 1989.

Gitlin, A. School Structure, Teachers' Work and Reproduction. In M. W. Apple and L. Weiss (Eds.), *Ideology and Practice in Education*, pp. 193–221. Philadelphia: Temple University Press, 1983.

Gitlin, A. Common School Structures and Teacher Behavior. In J. Smyth (Ed.), *Educating Teachers: Changing the Nature of Pedagogical Knowledge*, pp. 107–120. London: Falmer Press, 1987.

Gitlin, A. Educative Research, Voice and School Change. *Harvard Educational Review* 60(4), 443–466, 1990.

Gitlin, A., Barlow, L., Burbank, M. D., Kauchak, D., & Stevens, T. Preservice Teaches Thinking on Research: Implications for Inquiry Oriented Teacher Education. *Teaching & Teacher Education* 15(7), 753–770, 1999.

Gitlin, A. & Burbank, M. Academics'/Teachers' Views on Research: Implications for the Restructuring of Educational Institutions. Paper presented at the Annual meeting of A.E.R.A. held New Orleans, 2000.

Gitlin, A., & Teitelbaum, K. Linking Theory and Practice: The Use of Ethnographic Methodology by Prospective Teachers. *Journal of Education for Teaching* 9(3), 225–234, 1983.

Goodlad, J. I. Why We Need a Complete Redesign of Teacher Education. *Educational Leadership* November, 4–10, 1991.

Goodson, I. F. *Teachers' Lives and Educational Research*. In I. F. Goodson & R. Walker (Eds.), *Biography, Identity & Schooling: Episodes in Educational Research*, pp. 137–149. London: Falmer Press, 1991a.

Goodson, I. F. Studying Curriculum: A Social Constructivist Perspective. In I. F. Goodson & R. Walker (Eds.), *Biography, Identity & Schooling: Episodes in Educational Research*, pp. 168–181. London: Falmer Press, 1991b.

Goodwin, G. Humanistic Sociology and the Craft of Teaching. *Teaching Sociology* 15(1), 15–20, 1987.

Gordon, E. W., Miller, F., & Rollock, D. Coping with Communicentric Bias in Knowledge Production in the Social Sciences. *Educational Researcher*, 19(3), 14–19, 1990.

Gore, J. M., & Zeichner, K. M. Action Research and Reflective Teaching in Preservice Teacher Education: A Case Study from the United States. *Teaching and Teacher Education* 7(2), 119–136, 1991.

Griffiths, M., & Tann, S. Using Reflective Practice to Link Personal and Public Theories. *Journal of Education for Teaching* 18(1), 69–84, 1992.

Grimmett, P. P., & MacKinnon, A. M. Craft Knowledge and the Education of Teachers. In G. Grant (Ed.), *Review of Research in Education*, pp. 385–456. Washington, D.C.: American Educational Research Association, 1992.

Grossman, P. L., & Stodolsky, S. S. Considerations of Content and the Circumstances of Secondary School Teaching. In L. Darling-Hammond (Ed.), *Review of Research in Education*, pp. 179–222. Washington, D.C.: American Educational Research Association, 1994.

Gudmundsdottir, S. Introduction to the Theme Issue of Narrative Perspectives on Research on Teaching and Teacher Education. *Teaching & Teacher Education* 13(1), 1–3, 1997.

Hargreaves, A. Revisiting Voice. *Educational Researcher* 21(1), 12–19, 1996.

Haynes, N. M., & Johnson, S. T. Self- and Teacher Expectancy Effects on Academic Performance of College Students Enrolled in an Academic Reinforcement Program. *American Educational Research Journal*, 20(4), 511–515, 1983.

Hoff, D. J. Standards at the Crossroads after a Decade. *Education Week* 19(3), 1, 9, 1999.

Huberman, M. Working with Life-History Narratives. In H. McEwan & K. Egan (Eds.), *Narrative in Teaching, Learning, and Research*, pp. 127–165. New York: Teachers College Press, 1995.

Johnston, R.C. Test Scores in East St. Louis Raise Hopes of a Turnaround. *Education Week*, 19(40), 7, 2000.

Johnston, S. Images: A Way of Understanding the Practice Knowledge of Student Teachers. *Teaching and Teacher Education* 8(2), 123–136, 1992.

Keith, S. *Politics of Textbook Selection*. NIE Project Report No. 81 A7, April 1981.

Knowles, J. G. Journal Use in Preservice Teacher Education: A Personal and Reflexive Response to Comparisons and Criticisms. Paper presented at the annual meeting of the Association of Teacher Educators, New Orleans, February 1991.

Knowles, J. G. Models for Understanding Preservice and Beginning Teachers' Biographies: Illustrations from Case Studies. In I. F. Goodson (Ed.), *Studying Teachers' Lives*, pp. 99–152. New York: Routledge, 1992.

Korthagen, F. A. J., & Kessels, J. P. A. M. Linking Theory and Practice: Changing the Pedagogy of Teacher Education. *Educational Researcher* 28(2), 4–17, 1999.

Labaree, D., & Palas A. The Holmes Group's Mystifying Response. *Educational Researcher* 25(5), 31–47, 1996.

Liston, D. P., & Zeichner, K. M. Reflective Teacher Education and Moral Deliberation. *Journal of Teacher Education* 38(6), 2–8, 1987.

McCutcheon, G. How Do Elementary School Teachers Plan? The Nature of Planning and Influences on It. In W. Doyle & T. L. Good (Eds.), *Focus on Teaching: Readings from the Elementary School Journal.* Chicago: University of Chicago Press, 1982.

Measor, L. Critical Incidents in the Classroom: Identities, Choices and Careers. In S. J. Ball and I. F. Goodson (Eds.), *Teachers' Lives and Careers*, pp. 61–77. London: Falmer Press, 1985.

Metz, M. Sociology and Qualitative Methodologies in Educational Research. In B. Brizuela et al. (Eds.), *Acts of Inquiry*, pp. 37–49. Cambridge: Harvard Education Review Press, 37–49, 2000.

Meyer, D. K., & Tusin, L. F. Preservice Teachers' Perceptions of Portfolios: Process versus Product. *Journal of Teacher Education* 50(2), 131–139, 1999.

Morris, J. How Not to Set National History Standards. *Civreviews* 2(2), 1–14, 1998.

Munby, H., & Russell, T. The Authority of Experience in Learning to Teach: Messages from a Physics Methods Class. Paper presented at the Annual meeting of the American Educational Research Association, Atlanta, April, 1993.

Naizer, G. L. Validity and Reliability Issues of Performance-Portfolio Assessment. *Action in Teacher Education* 18(4), 1–9, 1997.

National Center for Education Statistics. Trends in Educational Equity for Girls & Women. Washington, D.C.: U. S. Department of Education, 2000.

NCATE. NCATE Releases New Performance-Based Standards. *American Association of Colleges for Teacher Education Briefs* 21(7), 2000.

Olsen, L. Worries of a Standards "Backlash" Grow. *Education Week* 29(30), 1, 12–13, 2000.

Parks, J. G. The Teacher as Bag Lady: Images and Metaphors of Teaching. *College Teaching* 44(4), 132–136, 1996.

Pinar, W. Life History and Educational Experience. *The Journal of Curriculum Theorizing* 2(2), 159–212, 1980.

Pinar, W. Life History and Educational Experience: Part Two. *The Journal of Curriculum Theorizing* 3(1), 259–286, 1981.

Presidential Task Force on Psychology in Education, American Psychological Association. Learner-Centered Psychological Principles: Guidelines for School Redesign and Reform. Washington, D.C.: American Psychological Association and Mid-continent Regional Educational Laboratory, January 1993.

Raymond, D., Butt, R., & Townsend, D. Contexts for Teacher Development: Insights from Teachers' Stories. In A. Hargreaves & M. G. Fullan (Eds.), *Understanding Teacher Development*, pp. 143–161. New York: Teachers College Press, 1992.

Rearick, J. L., & Feldman, A. Orientations, Purposes and Reflection: A Framework for Understanding Action Research. *Teaching & Teacher Education* 15(4), 333–350, 1999.

Rhodenbaugh, S. One Heart's Canon. *The American Scholar* 61(3), 389–398, 1992.

Riordan, T. A View of Self in the Teaching-Learning Process: Self Development as an Approach to the Education of Teachers. Unpublished doctoral dissertation. The Ohio State University Columbus, Ohio, 1973.

Riseborough, G. F. Pupils, Teachers' Careers and Schooling: An Empirical Study. In S. J. Ball and I. F. Goodson (Eds.), *Teachers' Lives and Careers*, pp. 202–265. London: Falmer Press, 1985.

Rist, R. C. Student Social Class and Teacher Expectations: The Self-Fulfilling Prophecy in Ghetto Education. *Harvard Educational Review* 40(3), 411–450, 1970.

Rosenholtz, S. J. Workplace Conditions That Affect Teacher Quality and Commitment: Implications for Teacher Induction Programs. *Elementary School Journal* 89(4), 421–439, 1989.

Sardo-Brown, D. Twelve Middle-School Teachers' Planning. *Elementary School Journal* 89(1), 69–87, 1988.

Shuell, T. J. The Two Cultures of Teaching and Teacher Preparation. *Teaching & Teacher Education* 8(1), 83–90, 1992.

Shulman, L. Knowledge and Teaching: Foundations of the New Reform. *Harvard Educational Review* 57(1), 1–22, 1987.

Sternberg, R. J., & Martin, M. When Teaching Thinking Does Not Work, What Goes Wrong? *Teachers College Record* 89(4), 555–578, 1988.

Stokes, D. K. Called to Teach: Exploring the Worldview of Called Prospective Teachers During their Preservice Teacher Education Experience. Unpublished doctoral dissertation, University of Utah, Salt Lake City, Utah, 1997.

Syrjala, L., & Estola, E. Telling and Retelling Stories as a Way to Construct Teachers' Identities and to Understand Teaching. Paper presented at the European Conference on Educational Research, Lahti, Finland, September 22–25, 1999.

Taylor, W. Metaphors of Educational Discourse. In W. Taylor (Ed.), *Metaphors in Education*, pp. 4–20. London: Heinemann Educational Books, 1984.

Teitelbaum, K., & Britzman, D. P. Reading and Doing Ethnography: Teacher Education and Reflective Practice. In R. B. Tabachnick & K. Zeichner (Eds.), *Issues and Practice in Inquiry-Oriented Teacher Education*, pp. 166–185. London: Falmer Press, 1991.

Valli, L., & Rennert-Ariev, P. L. Identifying Consensus in Teacher Education Reform Documents: A Proposed Framework and Action Implications. *Journal of Teacher Education* 51(1), 5–17, 2000.

Viadero, D. High-Stakes Tests Lead Debate at Researchers' Gathering. *Education Week* 19(34), 2000.

Villegas, A. Assessing Teacher Performance in a Diverse Society. In L. Goodwin (Ed.), *Assessment for Equity and Inclusion: Embracing All Our Children*, pp. 262–278). New York: Routledge, 1997.

Waller, W. *The Sociology of Teaching*. New York: John Wiley & Sons, Inc., 1932.

Wertsch, J. V. *MIND as ACTION*. New York: Oxford University Press, 1998.

Wideen, M., Mayer-Smith, J., & Moon, B. A Critical Analysis of the Research on Learning to Teach: Making the Case for an Ecological Perspective on Inquiry. *Review of Educational Research* 68(2), 130–178, 1998.

Wise, A. E. Performance-Based Accreditation: Reform in Action. *Quality Teaching: The Newsletter of the National Council for Accreditation of Teacher Education* 9(2), 1–2, 4–5, 8, 2000.

Witherell, C. The Self in Narrative: A Journey into Paradox. In C. Witherell & N. Noddings (Eds.), *Stories Lives Tell: Narrative and Dialogue in Education*, pp. 83–95. New York: Teachers College Press, 1991.

Wolf, A. Minorities in U.S. History Textbooks, 1945–1985. *The Clearing House* 65(5), 291–297, 1992.

Woodward, A., & Elliott, D. L. Textbooks: Consensus and Controversy. In D. L. Elliott & A. Woodward (Eds.), *Textbooks and Schooling in the United States, Eighty-Ninth Yearbook of the National Society for the Study of Education, Part I*, pp. 146–161. Chicago: National Society for the Study of Education, 1990.

Yinger, R. J. The Role of Standards in Teaching and Teacher Education. In G. Griffin (Ed.), *The Education of Teachers, Ninety-Eighth Yearbook of the National Society for the Study of Education*, pp. 85–113. Chicago: University of Chicago Press, 1999.

Zeichner, K. Preparing Reflective Teachers: An Overview of Instructional Strategies Which have been Employed in Preservice Teacher Education. *International Journal of Educational Research* 7, 565–575, 1986.

Zeichner, K. M., & Liston, D. P. Teaching Student Teachers to Reflect. *Harvard Educational Review* 57(1), 23–48, 1987.

Zeichner, K. M., & Liston, D. P. Traditions of Reform in U. S. Teacher Education. *Journal of Teacher Education* 41(2), 3–20, 1990.

Zeichner, K. M., & Tabachnick, B. R. Are the Effects of University Teacher Education "Washed Out" by School Experience? *Journal of Teacher Education* 32(3), 7–11, 1981.

Zumwalt, K. Are We Improving or Undermining Teaching? In L. N. Tanner (Ed.), *Critical Issues in Curriculum, Eighty-Seventh Yearbook of the National Society for the Study of Education, Part I*, pp. 148–174. Chicago: National Society for the Study of Education, 1988.

Zumwalt, K. Beginning Professional Teachers: The Need for a Curricular Vision of Teaching. In M. C. Reynolds (Ed.), *Knowledge Base for the Beginning Teachers*, pp. 173–184. Oxford: Pergamon, 1989.

## BOOKS

Agar, M. *The Professional Stranger: An Informal Introduction to Ethnography*. New York: Academic Press, 1980.

Apple, M. W. *Ideology and Curriculum*. London: Routledge & Kegan Paul, 1979b.

Apple, M. W. *Teachers & Texts: A Political Economy of Class & Gender Relations in Education*. London: Routledge & Kegan Paul, 1986.

Atweh, B., Kemmis, S., & Weeks, P. *Action Research in Practice: Partnerships for Social Justice in Education*. New York: Routledge, 1998.

Ball, S. J., & Goodson, I. F. *Teachers' Lives and Careers*. London: Falmer Press, 1985.

Apple, M., & Beane, J. *Democratic Schools*. Alexandria, VA: ASCD, 1995.

Berger, P. L., & Luckmann, T. *The Social Construction of Reality*. Garden City, N.Y: Anchor Books, Doubleday, 1966.

Beyer, L., & Apple, M. *The Curriculum: Problems, Politics, and Possibilities*. New York: State University of New York Press, 1988.

Bode, B. H. *Democracy as a Way of Life*. New York: Macmillan, 1937.

Britzman, D. P. *Practice Makes Practice: A Critical Study of Learning to Teach*. Albany, New York: State University of New York Press, 1991.

Bruner, J. Acts of Meaning. Cambridge, Mass.: Harvard University Press, 1990.

Bullough, R. V., Jr. *The Forgotten Dream of American Public Education*. Ames, Iowa: Iowa State University Press, 1988.

Bullough, R. V., Jr. *First Year Teacher: A Case Study*. New York: Teachers College Press, 1989.

Bullough, R. V., Jr., & Baughman, K. *First Year Teacher—Eight Years Later: An Inquiry into Teacher Development*. New York: Teachers College Press, 1997.

Bullough, R., & Gitlin, A. *Becoming a Student of Teaching: Methodologies for Exploring Self and School Context*. New York: Garland Publishing, 1995.

Bullough, R. V., Jr., Holt, L., & Goldstein, S. L. *Human Interests in the Curriculum: Teaching and Learning in a Technological Society*. New York: Teachers College Press, 1984.

Bullough, R. V., Jr., Knowles, J. G., & Crow, N. A. *Emerging as a Teacher*. London: Routledge, 1992.

Carr, W., & Kemmis, S. *Becoming Critical: Knowing through Action Research*. Geelong: Deakin University Press, 1983.

Clandinin, D. J., & Connelly, F. M. *Narrative Inquiry: Experience and Story in Qualitative Research*. San Francisco: Jossey-Bass Publishers, 2000.

Clift, R. T., Houston, W. R., & Pugach, M. C. (Eds.), *Encouraging Reflective Practice in Education*. New York: Teachers College Press, 1991.

Cochran-Smith, M., & Lytle, S. *Inside Outside: Teacher Research and Knowledge*. New York: Teachers College Press, 1993.

Corey, S. M. *Action Research to Improve School Practices*. New York: Teachers College, Columbia University, 1953.

Darling-Hammond, L. *The Right to Learn*. San Francisco: Jossey-Bass Publishers, 1997.

Dewey, J. *Influence of Darwin on Philosophy and Other Essays*. New York: Henry Holt and Company, 1910.

Diamond, C. T. P. *Teacher Education as Transformation*. Milton Keynes: Open University Press, 1991.

Dollard, J. *Criteria for the Life History*. New Haven, Conn.: Yale University Press, 1935.

Eisner, E. W. *The Educational Imagination: On the Design and Evaluation of School Programs, Second Edition*. New York: Macmillan Publishing Company, 1985.

Elbaz, F. *Teacher Thinking: A Study of Practical Knowledge*. London and Canberra: Croom Helm, 1983.

Elliott, J. *Action Research for Educational Change*. Milton Keynes: Open University Press, 1991.

Freire, P. *Pedagogy of the Oppressed*. New York: Seabury, 1970.

Gergen, K. *The Saturated Self: Dilemmas of Identity in Contemporary Life*. New York: Basic Books, 1991.

Gitlin, A., Bringhurst, K., Burns, M., Cooley, V., Myers, B., Price, K., Russell, R., & Tiess, P. *Teachers' Voices for School Change: An Introduction to Educative Research*. London: Routledge, 1992.

Gitlin, T. *Twilight of Common Dreams: Why America is Wracked by Culture Wars*. New York: Metropolitan Books, 1995.

Goodlad, J. I., & McMannon, T. J. (Eds.), *The Public Purpose of Education and Schooling*. San Francisco: Jossey-Bass Publishers, 1997.

Goodlad, J. I. *Teachers for the Nation's Schools*. San Francisco: Jossey-Bass Publishers, 1990.

Goodlad, J.I. *Educational Renewal: Better Teachers, Better Schools*. San Francisco: Jossey-Bass Publishers, 1994.

Goodson, I. F. (Ed.). *Studying Teachers' Lives*. New York: Routledge, 1992.

Goodson, I. F., & Walker, R. *Biography, Identity & Schooling: Episodes in Educational Research*. London: Falmer Press, 1991.

Habermas, J. *Knowledge and Human Interests*. Boston: Beacon Press, 1971.

Habermas, J. *Legitimation Crisis*. Boston: Beacon Press, 1975.

Hall, G. S. *Aspects of Child Life and Education*. Boston: Ginn & Company, Publishers, 1907.

Hargreaves, A. *Changing Teachers Changing Times: Teachers' Work and Culture in a Post-modern Age*. New York: Teachers College Press, 1994.

Hargreaves, A., & Fullan, M. G. (Eds.). *Understanding Teacher Development*. New York: Teachers College Press, 1992.

Hoff-Sommers, C. *The War Against Boys*. New York: Simon & Schuster, 2000.

Holmes Group. *Tomorrow's Teachers: A Report of the Holmes Group*. East Lansing, Mich.: Author, 1986.

Holmes Group. *Tomorrow's Schools: A Report of the Holmes Group*. East Lansing, Mich.: Author, 1990.

Hong, L. *Surviving School Reform: A Year in the Life of a School*. New York: Teachers College Press, 1996.

hooks, b. *Teaching to Transgress: Education for the Practice of Freedom*. New York: Routledge, 1994.

Kemmis, S., & McTaggart, R. *The Action Research Planner, Third Edition*. Victoria, Australia: Deakin University, 1988.

Kohl, H. (1984). *Growing Minds, On Becoming a Teacher*. New York: Harper Colophon Books.

Kozol, J. *Savage Inequalities*. New York: Crown Publishers, Inc., 1991.

Kridel, C. (Ed). *Writing Educational Biography: Adventures in Qualitative Research*. New York: Garland Publishing, Inc., 1998.

Kuhn, T. S. *The Structure of Scientific Revolutions*. Chicago: University of Chicago Press, 1962.

Kyvig, D., & Marty, M. *Nearby Histories*. Nashville: The American Association for State and Local History, 1986.

Lacey, C. *The Socialization of Teachers*. London: Methuen, 1977.

Lakoff, G., & Johnson, M. *Metaphors We Live By*. Chicago: The University of Chicago Press, 1980.

Lasser, C. *Men and Women Together: Coeducation in a Changing World*. Urbana: University of Illinois Press, 1987.

Lewin, K. *Resolving Social Conflict: Selected Papers on Group Dynamics*. G. W. Lewin (Ed.). New York: Harper and Brothers, 1948.

Lortie, D. *School-Teacher: A Sociological Study*. Chicago: University of Chicago Press, 1975.

Loveless, T. *The Tracking Wars: State Reform Meets School Policy*. Washington, D.C.: Brookings Institution Press, 1999.

Mager, R. R. *Preparing Instruction Objectives*. Palo Alto, Cal.: Feron Publishers, 1962.

Mills, C. W. *The Sociological Imagination*. New York: Oxford University Press, 1959.

Nash, G. B., Crabtree, C., & Dunn, R. E. *History on Trial: Culture Wars and the Teaching of the Past*. New York: Alfred A. Knopf, 1998.

Nias, J. *Primary Teachers Talking: A Study of Teaching as Work*. London: Routledge, 1989.

Noddings, N. *The Challenge to Care in Schools*. New York: Teachers College Press, 1992.

Norton, C. S. *Life Metaphors: Stories of Ordinary Survival*. Carbondale and Edwardsville, Ill.: Southern Illinois Press, 1989.

Oakes, J. *Keeping Track: How Schools Structure Inequality*. New Haven, Conn.: Yale University Press, 1985.

Olney, J. *Metaphors of Self: The Meaning of Autobiography*. Princeton, N. J.: Princeton University Press, 1972.

Orfield, G. *Dismantling Desegregation: The Quiet Reversal of Brown v. Board of Education*. New York: New Press, 1996.

Palmer, P. J. *The Courage to Teach: Exploring the Inner Landscape of a Teacher's Life*. San Francisco: Jossey-Bass Publishers, 1998.

Pateman, C. *Participation and Democratic Theory*. Cambridge: Cambridge University Press, 1970.

Patterson, R. S., Michelli, N. M., & Pacheco, A. *Centers of Pedagogy: New Structures for Educational Renewal*. San Francisco: Jossey-Bass Publishers, 1999.

Perrone, V. (1989). *Working Papers, Reflections on Teachers, Schools, and Communities.* New York: Teachers College Press.

Pinar, W. *Curriculum Theorizing: The Reconceptualists.* Berkeley: McCutchan, 1975.

Plato. *Plato's Republic.* Cambridge: Cambridge University Press, 1966. Pullias, E., & Young, J. *A Teacher is Many Things.* Bloomington and London: Indiana University Press, 1968.

Pullias, E., & Young, J. D. *A Teacher is Many Things.* Bloomington: Indiana University Press, 1968.

Rainey, H. P. *How Fare American Youth?* New York: D. Appleton-Century Company, 1937.

Sarason, S. B. *The Predictable Failure of Educational Reform.* San Francisco: Jossey-Bass Publishers, 1990.

Sarason, S. B. *Revisiting "The Culture of the School and the Problem of Change."* New York: Teachers College Press, 1996.

Sarason, S. B. *Teaching as Performing Art.* New York: Teachers College Press, 1999.

Schon, D. A. *Educating the Reflective Practitioner: Toward a New Design* for Teaching and Learning in the Professions.* San Francisco: Jossey-Bass, 1987.

Shor, I. *Critical Teaching and Everyday Life.* Chicago: University of Chicago, 1987.

Sikes, P. J., Measor, L., & Woods, P. *Teacher Careers: Crises and Continuities.* London: Falmer Press, 1985.

Smyth, J. *Teachers as Collaborative Learners.* Milton Keyes U.K.: Open University Press, 1991.

Spradley, J. P., *Participant Observation.* New York: Holt, Rinehart and Winston, 1980.

Spradley, J. P., & McCurdy, D. W. *The Cultural Experience: Ethnography in Complex Society.* Chicago: SRA Associates, 1972.

Stenhouse, L. *Research as a Basis for Teaching: Readings on the Work of Lawrence Stenhouse.* J. Rudduck & D. Hopkins (Eds.). London: Heinemann Educational Books, 1985.

Tyack, D., & Hansot, E. *Learning Together: A History of Coeducation in American Schools.* New Haven, Conn.: Yale University Press, 1990.

Willis, P. *Learning to Labour: How Working Class Kids Get Working Class Jobs.* Farnborough: Saxon House, 1977.

Yin, R. K. *Case Study Research: Design and Methods.* Beverly Hills, Calif.: Sage Publications, 1984.

# Index

✦